The Confederates and Federals at War

D1531126

The Confederates and Federals at War

COLONEL H.C.B. ROGERS OBE

COMBINED PUBLISHING
Pennsylvania

PUBLISHER'S NOTE

The headquarters of Combined Publishing are located midway between Valley Forge and the Germantown battlefield, on the outskirts of Philadelphia. From its beginnings, our company has been steeped in the oldest traditions of American history and publishing. Our historic surroundings help maintain our focus on history and our books strive to uphold the standards of style, quality and durability first established by the earliest bookmakers of Germantown and Philadelphia so many years ago. Our famous monk-and-console logo reflects our commitment to the modern and yet historic enterprise of publishing.

We call ourselves Combined Publishing because we have always felt that our goals could only be achieved through a "combined" effort by authors, publishers and readers. We have always tried to maintain maximum communication between these three key players in the reading experience.

We are always interested in hearing from prospective authors about new books in our field. We also like to hear from our readers and invite you to contact us at our offices in Pennsylvania with any questions, comments or suggestions, or if you have difficulty finding our books at a local bookseller.

For information, address:
Combined Publishing
P.O. Box 307
Conshohocken, PA 19428
E-mail: combined@combinedpublishing.com
Web: www.combinedpublishing.com
Orders: 1-800-418-6065

Combined Publishing edition, 2000

Originally published in 1973 by Ian Allan Publishing, London
and 1975 by Hippocrene Books, New York.
This edition published by arrangement with the estate of H.C.B. Rogers.

ISBN 1-58097-031-1

Printed in the United States of America.

To my Wife
Who at intervals throughout her married life
has heard the Rappahannock
trace its silver thread
between Grey and Blue.

Contents

Acknowledgements

I MUST THANK MY SISTER, Miss Cecilia Rogers, for the trouble she took in finding for me the sources in the United States which I should approach for Civil War photographs. I am indebted to Mr James W. Moore, of the National Archives in Washington, for his kindness in undertaking research on my behalf and for the excellent range of photographs which he provided. I am most grateful to Miss Eleanor Brockenbrough, Assistant Director of the Museum of the Confederacy, Richmond, Virginia, for her invaluable help in providing me with copies of rare photographs; and it was she, too, who brought to my notice the work of Frank Vizetelly in the Confederate States. Mrs Stuart B. Gibson, Librarian of the Valentine Museum in Richmond, Virginia, was most kind in the speed with which she came to my assistance, with the resulting provision of two valuable photographs. Very few photographs of the Confederate Army in the field were ever taken and, owing to the above persons, I believe that this book contains most of those that still exist.

Finally I must express the gratitude I owe to Mr R. H. Smith of the *Illustrated London News*; for it is due to his enthusiasm that such a good selection of Frank Vizetelly's illustrations appear in these pages. Vizetelly was such a remarkable character that some account of the way in which he acquired the material for his sketches is well worth while; and Mr R. H. Smith has kindly allowed me to include in this book a short biography of him.

As always, I owe much to the London Library for the references used in the writing of the book.

CHAPTER ONE

The American Civil War in Outline

THIS BOOK IS NOT A HISTORY of the American Civil War: it is a description of the armies of both sides; giving their equipment, their organisation, and their method of fighting, illustrated by examples from battles and campaigns. But for the benefit of those who are unacquainted with the main course of events or who may like their memory to be refreshed, it has been thought proper to start with a brief narrative of the principal operations.

In his *The Decisive Battles of the Western World*, Major-General J. F. C. Fuller states that, 'the two outstanding military inventions of the first half of the nineteenth century were the percussion cap and the cylindro-conoidal bullet'. Between them they caused a revolution in infantry tactics, because with the former the musket could be used in all weathers and the latter made the rifled musket the most deadly weapon the world had yet known. Apart from these two purely military devices, the age had ushered in a new 'way of life based on coal, steam, and machinery', and these three, when combined to form the steam-operated railway, conferred on armies a mobility that they had never previously enjoyed. It is true that in the two major conflicts preceding the American Civil War (ie, the Crimean War of 1854 and the Franco–Austrian War of 1859) railways and percussion cap rifles had been used, but the former war was in a too-limited sphere and the latter too short for their full impact on strategy and tactics to be appreciated. The war between the States in America, on the other hand, was waged for four years and over immense distances. At the start the tactics were those of the Napoleonic era; at the end they foreshadowed the methods of the First World War.

In population the United States of 1861 was a very much smaller country than it is to-day and the inhabitants were of predominantly Anglo-Saxon descent. In the 22 states which remained in the Union at the outbreak of hostilities there were 22 million people, practically all white. In the 11

9

seceding states there were 5½ million whites and 3½ million negro slaves. But a much higher percentage of the white population in the South was available for active service than in the North because the bulk of the necessary civilian labour was provided by the negro slaves. As a result the Northern superiority in mobilisable white men was in the ratio of about five to two.

The American regular army was so small as to be practically non-existent; it consisted by law of two regiments of dragoons, two regiments of cavalry, one regiment of mounted rifles, four regiments of artillery, and ten regiments of infantry, with a total establishment of 13,024 officers and men. This small body was not concentrated but was dispersed in small detachments along the western territories as a frontier force to control the Red Indians and in garrisons of the coastal forts. The only other armed forces were the state militias, which had been founded under the British colonial regime. Under British rule the State Governors could be ordered to provide the militia for general service when required and Lord Amherst made considerable use of them in the conquest of Canada. But after American Independence they were purely State troops who could only be called up by Presidential decree for a maximum of three months in a calendar year; both sides, therefore, raised national armies, firstly from volunteers and latterly by conscription.

There was little appreciation at first of the effort that would be needed. The abysmal ignorance of war in Northern political circles is shown, particularly, by President Lincoln's call on 15th April 1861 only for 75,000 militia for three months' service; and few appear to have realised firstly that the number was quite inadequate and secondly that by the time the men were trained their term of service would have expired. Nor did Lincoln make proper use of the available regular officers. Of the 1,066 then serving, 286 resigned their commissions and joined the seceding states; but of the remainder, those on the strength of regular units were left there instead of being used to train the militia. There was a rather greater appreciation of the problem in the South, where the President called for 100,000 volunteers to serve for one year and where the services of the officers who had held commissions in the United States Army were used as far as possible. However, in May Lincoln called for 42,000 volunteers to serve for three years.

The Opening of Hostilities

During the early summer of 1861 untrained militia and volunteers of both sides met in minor clashes, mostly in West Virginia and Missouri. But the first major battle occurred in the eastern theatre of war between the Union army, which had been gathering in and about Washington, and the

Confederate forces massing in Northern Virginia. On 19th July General Irvin McDowell moved out of Washington eastwards against the Confederates known to be about Centreville, some 30 miles from the capital. The Confederate army, under General Joseph E. Johnston, had taken up a position east of a stream called Bull Run and was still completing its concentration. Both generals had about 30,000 men and all, except a few regulars on the Union side, were practically untrained. On 21st July McDowell attacked Johnston's position. In a battle between raw troops, those on the defensive have a considerable advantage, and the Federal army was driven from the field, some of its regiments dissolving in panic.

The disaster of Bull Run demonstrated forcibly to the Northern politicians that there was no cheap and easy road to victory. Congress voted that 500,000 volunteers should be enlisted for the duration of the war and a new commander, General George B. McClellan, was given the task of training the force that was eventually to achieve fame as the Army of the Potomac.

In the western theatre of war the Confederate line of defence ran for about 350 miles from the Mississippi River to the pass through the Cumberland Mountains known as the Cumberland Gap. There were two opposing Union, or Federal, commands; that of General Henry W. Halleck in the west and of General Don Carlos Buell in eastern and central Kentucky.

The Opening Situation in 1862

In January 1862 McClellan (who had been made Federal Commander-in-Chief on the previous 1st November) had an army of about 180,000 men in and around Washington. He was still faced by J. E. Johnston who was at Manassas, with an army which McClellan's intelligence service reckoned at 100,000 men, but which was actually about half that number. To avoid trying to force the Confederate position, McClellan decided to use Northern supremacy at sea to ship his army down Chesapeake Bay and land it at Urbana, some 45 miles from Richmond. Learning of this plan to turn his position, Johnston promptly retired southwards behind the Rappahannock River. McClellan still felt, however, that an amphibious operation was the best method of operating against Richmond, and he conceived the more ambitious plan of landing at Fortress Monroe (which had remained in Federal hands) at the tip of the peninsula between the York and James Rivers. This was some 80 miles from Richmond and, because he would be posing a threat to Richmond and also to its communications with the south, he believed that this would force the Confederates to evacuate all North Virginia.

In eastern Kentucky a Confederate force under General Zollicoffer had advanced from the Cumberland Gap to Somerset on the Cumberland River. On 19th January General George H. Thomas, of Buell's command, defeated Zollicoffer at the Battle of Mill Springs. In February General Ulysses S. Grant, operating under Halleck's command, moved up the Tennessee River from Cairo in an amphibious attempt against Forts Henry and Donelson. The Confederate commander facing Halleck and Buell was Henry Albert Sydney Johnston. These two forts on the Tennessee and Cumberland Rivers respectively had been constructed by him to cover the railway which connected the main body of his army under his direct command at Bowling Green with a strong detachment under General Polk at Columbus on the Mississippi. Fort Henry was reduced on 5th February, largely by Grant's escorting gunboats under naval command, and Grant then moved across country to the stronger Fort Donelson, which surrendered on 16th February. This outstanding success disrupted the whole of Johnston's defence line; Columbus had been evacuated on the fall of Fort Henry and Johnston had fallen back to Nashville, and the capture of Fort Donelson was followed by the evacuation of Nashville.

A minor success in this theatre was the defeat of the Confederate forces in Arkansas under General Earl Van Dorn by the Union General Samuel Curtis on 7th March at the Battle of Pea Ridge. On the Atlantic coast there was a further exercise of Federal sea power with the landing of Union troops under General Ambrose Burnside on Roanoke Island, North Carolina, in February. The year 1862 opened, therefore, with the Union armies everywhere in the ascendant.

The Battle of Shiloh

After his withdrawal from Nashville, A. S. Johnston concentrated his forces at Corinth on the important Memphis and Charleston Railroad. Federal forces moved south along the Tennessee River and in early March they started concentrating at Pittsburg Landing, some 20 miles north of Corinth and close to the hamlet of Shiloh. Johnston advanced from Corinth and on 6th April delivered a surprise attack on the Federal positions. After initial success, during which Johnston was killed, Grant counter-attacked on 7th April and drove the Confederates from the field. General P. G. T. Beauregard, who had taken over command of the Confederate army, retreated to Corinth.

Grant had been joined by Buell on the night 6th/7th April, and on 11th April Halleck, who on 11th March had handed over his command to Grant on being appointed to supreme command in the West, arrived at Pittsburg Landing, and on 30th April started a cautious advance towards Corinth which took him a month to complete.

Meanwhile during February and March General John Pope, on Halleck's instructions, had advanced from Cairo down the Mississippi, supported by gunboats, against New Madrid and the defended Island No 10 and captured both in April. At the other end of the Mississippi Commodore David Farragut started moving up the mouth of the Mississippi from the Gulf in March. On 24th April he broke through past the Confederate forts and on 25th April captured New Orleans.

McClellan and the 'Seven Days'

On 22nd March McClellan began to move the Army of the Potomac, now 130,000 strong, to the neighbourhood of Fortress Monroe, leaving some 50,000 men covering the approaches to Washington. The transports, assembled at Alexandria, could only carry 10,000 men in one lift, so that about fifteen voyages were needed. On 23rd March General T. J. ('Stonewall') Jackson, commanding a Confederate force in the Shenandoah Valley, attacked the Federals under General James Shields at Kernstown near Winchester. Though Jackson was repulsed, his vigorous attack made Lincoln so nervous for the safety of Washington that he held back McDowell's corps of 30,000 men just as it was about to embark for the Peninsula between the York and James Rivers, and so considerably weakened the army at McClellan's disposal.

On 4th April McClellan's troops were in contact with the Confederate lines on the Peninsula manned by a division under the command of General J. B. ('Prince John') Magruder. By 20th April the main body of the Confederates in Virginia, under Johnston's command, was confronting McClellan in the Peninsula. On 3rd May, the day before McClellan's massive siege train could be brought into action against the Confederate lines, Johnston retired with his whole army towards Richmond and took up a position near it on 20th April.

McClellan's plan for the capture of Richmond included the advance of McDowell's corps from Fredericksburg to join his right flank. General R. E. Lee, who was then military adviser to the Confederate President, Jefferson Davis, recommended that Jackson in the Shenandoah Valley should be reinforced so that he could make a demonstration to try and divert Union forces from reinforcing McClellan. Jackson, on 1st May, was threatened by General N. P. Banks advancing up the Valley and by General John C. Frémont approaching from West Virginia. Leaving a force to contain Banks, he advanced rapidly against Frémont, defeated his advanced elements, on 8th May, and then returned to deal with Banks. Marching north along the Valley, he defeated Banks on 23rd May at Front Royal, pursued him to Winchester and defeated him again there, and then drove him across the Potomac. This had the desired effect, for

13

on 26th May Lincoln halted McDowell's movement to join the Federal army in the Peninsula and diverted McDowell's troops to the defence of the capital.

Jackson retreated up the Valley, slipping between Union forces converging to cut him off, and on 5th June was at Harrisonburg. On 8th June he defeated Frémont at Cross Keys and then turned to deal with Shields at Port Republic on 9th June.

Meanwhile on 31st May Johnston had attacked McClellan's isolated right wing, which was feeling towards the expected advance by McDowell, but was repulsed at the Battle of Seven Pines. Johnston himself was badly wounded and Lee took over command of the army. On 1st June Lee's new command was entitled the Army of Northern Virginia.

From 25th June to 1st July there took place the succession of Confederate assaults by which Lee drove McClellan's army from the Peninsula and which have been called the Seven Days Battles. Before the start Lee had brought Jackson from the Valley in a rapid move which was undetected by the Federals. Leaving Magruder with a comparatively small force to contain the bulk of the Union army, Lee attacked the right wing of 30,000 men under General Fitz John Porter at the Battle of Mechanicsville. Owing to faulty staff work results were indecisive and Porter retired on Gaines's Mill. There Lee attacked him again on 27th, but once more without a decisive result and Porter fell back in good order. That night McClellan ordered a general withdrawal to the James River. Lee followed up the withdrawal, but his attacks were repulsed in a series of delaying actions, while the Union supply trains and other transport moved back across the White Oak Swamp. On 1st July Confederate attacks were beaten off in a successful rearguard battle by Porter at Malvern Hill. McClellan's army then retreated to Harrison's Landing on the James River, covered by heavy rain followed by a dense fog. On 3rd August Lincoln ordered the Army of the Potomac back to Washington.

Events in the West

In the face of Halleck's advance, the Confederates evacuated Corinth on 29th May and retreated to Tupelo. Halleck now divided his forces, sending Buell eastward into Tennessee and directing Grant to operate defensively in the Mississippi Valley.

On 26th June Lincoln, dissatisfied with McClellan's conduct of affairs, appointed Pope, on the strength of his Mississippi success, to the command of a new Army of Virginia, made up of the commands of McDowell, Frémont, and Banks.

On 11th July Lincoln took a further step in the demotion of McClellan by appointing Halleck General-in-Chief. Before leaving for Washington,

Halleck appointed Grant and Buell to the separate commands, respectively, of the Armies of Tennessee and Ohio.

On 27th June General Braxton Bragg relieved Beauregard in command of the Confederate Army of the Mississippi.

The Destruction of Pope

As soon as Lee was satisfied that McClellan presented no further immediate threat, he despatched Jackson to watch Pope, who was now in central Virginia. Later he followed with the main body, leaving a force of about 20,000 men about Richmond.

Before Lee arrived Pope had started to advance, and on 9th August his leading corps under Banks attacked Jackson, who was covering the crossings of the Rappahannock. Jackson defeated Banks at the Battle of Cedar Mountain, drove him back on Culpeper, and then withdrew behind the Rapidan.

After joining Jackson, Lee on 24th August issued orders designed to beat Pope's army before it could be joined by McClellan's troops from the Peninsula. Jackson was to march north and then turn east across Pope's line of communications whilst Lee, with the remainder of the army, held Pope. Lee would then follow, join Jackson, and destroy Pope's army in the neighbourhood of Manassas Junction.

Jackson moved on 25th August, marched 54 miles in two days, wrecked Pope's supply depot at Manassas Junction on 27th August, and fell back to a defensive position west of the old battlefield of Bull Run.

On 29th August Pope moved rapidly north to deal with Jackson, who promptly attacked his advancing columns to distract attention from the approach of Lee with General James Longstreet's corps. On 30th Longstreet delivered a surprise attack on Pope's left flank. Pope was so decisively defeated in this Second Battle of Bull Run that he withdrew his shattered army into the defences of Washington.

Antietam

On 4th September Lee's army, screened by the Confederate cavalry under General J. E. B. Stuart, crossed the Potomac near Leesburg into Union territory and concentrated at Frederick. This move, after the recent Confederate victory, was at least partly political, in that it was hoped that Great Britain and France might be induced to recognise the Confederacy.

On 9th September Lee detached Jackson's corps to recross the Potomac to capture Harper's Ferry and secure a line of communication up the Shenandoah Valley.

McClellan was now in the field with his own Army of the Potomac and troops from the Army of Virginia which had been broken up, and was following up Lee. His advanced guard reached Frederick on 12th September. The Confederates had moved towards Hagerstown, but a copy of Lee's operation order of 9th September was found by the Federal troops in the town and came into McClellan's hands. McClellan advanced slowly from Frederick towards South Mountain, taking two days to cover the ten miles. At South Mountain on 14th September he became engaged with Confederate forces covering the concentration of Lee's army about Sharpsburg. On 15th September the garrison at Harper's Ferry surrendered and Jackson, leaving the division of General A. P. Hill to secure prisoners and stores, hurried to rejoin Lee.

The Confederate army held a position along the Antietam Creek, some two miles west of Sharpsburg, whilst at an average distance of two miles west of the town the Potomac ran in great loops on a north-south course. Jackson's corps was on the left and Longstreet's on the right. On 17th September McClellan, who had considerable superiority in numbers, attacked; first against Jackson's section of the front and then against Longstreet's. The battle ended when A. P. Hill's division, arriving from Harper's Ferry, attacked the Federal left flank and drove it back across the Antietam Creek. Lee offered battle again the next day, but McClellan was awaiting reinforcements and declined to take action until they arrived. On 18th Lee withdrew during the night across the Potomac.

On 5th October McClellan crossed the Potomac and advanced slowly southwards to Warrenton, where he was between Longstreet at Culpeper and Jackson who was in the Shenandoah Valley. On 7th November McClellan was relieved in command of the Army of the Potomac by General Ambrose E. Burnside.

From Corinth towards Vicksburg

On 21st July General Bragg moved towards Chattanooga with the main body of the Confederate Army of the Mississippi. But he left General Price with about 15,000 men in Tennessee to keep a watch on Grant and General Van Dorn with another 15,000 to hold the line of the Mississippi. On 30th July Price's force was distributed from Holly Springs forward to Grand Junction. Grant had about 64,000 men and accordingly wired Halleck for approval for an attack against Price. This Halleck gave, but warned Grant that he might have to send some troops to Buell north of Chattanooga. In fact Grant soon had to supply Buell with three divisions, which reduced his strength to some 46,000, located at Corinth, Memphis, Jackson Tennessee, Brownsville and other places, with a reserve at Columbus.

On 11th August Bragg ordered Van Dorn to move north and join Price. On 11th September Price, learning that General Rosecrans with

10,000 men was at Iuka, decided to attack him, but Grant withdrew Rosecrans to Corinth and on 18th ordered a movement against Price to surround him before Van Dorn could join him. Price was attacked at Iuka on 19th but slipped away on 28th and joined Van Dorn, who now took command of the combined force. Van Dorn now decided to attack Rosecrans at Corinth and on 2nd October encountered Rosecrans who withdrew into the entrenchments of the town. Grant concentrated his forces and defeated Van Dorn on 4th October, who retreated to Holly Springs. Grant now began to assemble a striking force at Grand Junction with a view to advancing on Vicksburg.

Early in August Bragg occupied Chattanooga and, with the Cavalry Generals Forrest and Morgan raiding his communications, Buell retired to Louisville. After being reinforced, he advanced and engaged the Confederates in a drawn battle at Perryville on 8th October. Bragg then withdrew through the Cumberland Gap into Tennessee. On 23rd October Rosecrans relieved Buell in command and moved forward to occupy Nashville on 6th November.

On 13th November Grant started an advance towards Vicksburg. He was opposed by General John C. Pemberton who was in command of Confederate forces at Jackson. Pemberton advanced to meet him, but, his communications threatened, fell back and Grant occupied Holly Springs, 60 miles south of Grand Junction, on 29th November. He now decided to hold Pemberton at Grenada, whilst sending General W. T. Sherman down the Mississippi, supported by Admiral David T. Porter commanding naval units at Memphis, in an amphibious operation against Vicksburg. The expedition started on 20th December.

In the meantime General Joseph E. Johnston had on 24th November been appointed to command all Confederate forces between the Blue Ridge and the Mississippi River. Johnston went to Chattanooga, where Bragg now was, and ordered him to mount a cavalry attack on Grant's communications. On 11th December Bedford Forrest and Van Dorn were both sent off on this errand by Bragg, and the latter captured the garrison at Holly Springs and destroyed all the stores assembled for Grant's advance on Vicksburg. On 20th December Grant withdrew northwards. Sherman's expedition arrived at Milliken's Bend on Christmas Day. He despatched a small detachment to destroy the railway between Vicksburg and Shreveport and disembarked the remainder of his army at the mouth of the Yazoo River. From here he launched an unsuccessful assault on the Chickasaw Bluff, north of Vicksburg, and then retired to the river.

On 26th December Rosecrans advanced from Nashville to Murfrees-boro, where Bragg had concentrated his army. On 31st there was a drawn battle at this place with heavy casualties. On 3rd January 1863 Bragg withdrew to Tullahoma.

Fredericksburg & Chancellorsville

On 13th December General Burnside with 100,000 men attacked the positions about Fredericksburg held by Lee with some 60,000. His assaults against the strong Confederate positions were beaten off with the loss of about 10,000 men. On 26th January 1863 Burnside was replaced in command of the Army of the Potomac by General Joseph E. Hooker. Hooker's defeat by Lee at the battle of Chancellorsville in May 1863 is described in Chapter Eleven.

Vicksburg

On 11th January Grant assumed direct command of the forces on the Mississippi. During the winter he initiated various works and projects for the opening of waterways to enable the Vicksburg batteries to be by-passed. But these were mainly to keep the troops employed and the politicians happy. On 29th April Grant left Sherman's corps above Vicksburg to create a diversion and moved with the remainder of the army overland to Hard Times, some 25 miles below Vicksburg and facing Grand Gulf on the opposite bank of the Mississippi. Here he established a base. Grand Gulf proving too hard to take by direct attack, Grant on 30th April moved his army across the river by disembarking at Bruinsburg, 10 miles below Grand Gulf. On 1st May he drove off the Confederate garrison of Grand Gulf and Sherman then moved south to join him.

Worried by Grant's success, Johnston hurriedly concentrated a force of 9,000 men at Jackson, Missouri, 45 miles east of Vicksburg, to attack the Union commander's rear, if he should move directly to the attack of the fortress. Grant had all his wagons loaded and then, cutting loose from his communications so that there would be none to attack, he marched against Johnston and on 14th May drove him out of Jackson. He then left Sherman to block any move by Johnston towards Vicksburg and to destroy the railways, and turned towards Pemberton, who had moved east from Vicksburg and taken up a strong position east of the Big Black River. On 16th May Grant attacked Pemberton and defeated him at the Battle of Champion's Hill, and on 19th May the Confederate commander retreated into the Vicksburg defences. Grant now laid siege to the fortress which surrendered on 4th July. This great victory gave the Federals control of the Mississippi throughout the whole of its length, and the Confederacy was cut in two.

Gettysburg

In Virginia, Lee, screened by Stuart's cavalry, moved on 3rd June 1863 into the Shenandoah Valley. On 9th June there took place the biggest cavalry action of the war when Stuart, with over 9,000 troopers, was surprised by General Alfred Pleasanton with two divisions of the Army of the Potomac's Cavalry Corps. For the first time the Federal cavalry showed that they were at last equal to the Confederates, but Pleasanton was eventually repulsed when a Confederate infantry division came to Stuart's assistance. On 13th to 14th June, in the Second Battle of Winchester, General R. S. Ewell's Corps of Lee's army defeated a Federal division under General Robert H. Milroy.

On 23rd June Lee started to cross the Potomac and his army advanced into Pennsylvania, Ewell being directed on Carlisle and Longstreet and Hill on Chambersburg, which they reached on 26th. Stuart had been instructed to watch the Federal army and report. Stuart unfortunately interpreted his instructions wrongly with the result that Lee was deprived of his cavalry.

Hooker with the Federal army was also moving north and reached Frederick on 27th June. There his plans were rejected by Halleck and he promptly resigned. The following day General George G. Meade took over command of the Army of the Potomac. By 30th the armies of both Meade and Lee were marching towards Gettysburg.

The Battle of Gettysburg, the most famous engagement of the Civil War, was basically an encounter battle in which Lee attacked Meade in a strong position and was repulsed. Battle was first joined on 1st July; by 3rd July Lee had been defeated; and on 4th July, the day that Vicksburg surrendered, he retreated. But Meade had been too hard hit to pursue. Lee withdrew slowly into Virginia and took up a position behind the Rapidan.

Chattanooga

On 23rd June 1863 Rosecrans began a slow advance against Bragg at Tullahoma and forced him to retire to Chattanooga. On 16th August Rosecrans's Army of the Cumberland advanced from Tullahoma, and at the same time Burnside with the Army of the Ohio moved forward from Lexington, Kentucky, towards Knoxville on the important Tennessee Railroad. Rosecrans, crossing the Tennessee River near Bridgeport, Alabama, threatened Bragg's communications with Alabama, and the latter fell back, evacuating Chattanooga. In the face of this new threat in the West, Longstreet's Corps was hastily despatched by rail from Virginia to reinforce Bragg. Thus augmented, Bragg turned to the offensive. On 19th September he attacked Rosecrans across the Chickamauga Creek,

19

and the following day Longstreet's Corps penetrated the Federal line, the centre and right of which fell back in disorder. Rosecrans retreated to Chattanooga, Bragg did not pursue him, but he invested Chattanooga, and cut his communications with both Burnside at Knoxville and with Hooker's Corps, which was 30 miles away at Bridgeport, having been sent by rail from the Army of the Potomac to reinforce him.

On 17th October Grant was appointed to command all Union forces between the Alleghanies and the Mississippi. He left immediately for Chattanooga, sending a telegram ahead which relieved Rosecrans from command and appointed General George H. Thomas to succeed him.

Grant arrived at Chattanooga on 23rd October and within five days had the road opened to Bridgeport through which Hooker and much needed supplies reached the Army of the Cumberland. On the Confederate side, Longstreet, who had quarrelled with Bragg, was directed to destroy Burnside's Army of the Ohio at Knoxville, 100 miles away, and thus reopen the Tennessee Railroad. Grant had ordered Sherman to march from Memphis to Chattanooga with his Army of the Tennessee.

On 24th to 25th November Grant defeated the Confederates under Bragg at the Battle of Chattanooga. On 27th he despatched Sherman to relieve Burnside at Knoxville. He arrived there on 6th December to find that Longstreet had raised the siege on 4th and withdrawn.

Grant now decided that Sherman should go to Vicksburg, and from there move to Meridian, where he was to destroy the railways around that important junction to prevent the Confederates from drawing supplies from that area and thus clear it of all large bodies of their troops. At the same time General Sooy Smith with a cavalry force was to advance from Memphis and join Sherman at Meridian. Sherman carried out his task successfully, leaving Vicksburg on 3rd February; but Sooy Smith started late and failed to reach Meridian, for he was stopped by Forrest with less than half his strength, pursued, and defeated at the Battle of Okolona on 22nd February.

Grant against Lee

On 9th March 1864 Grant was made General-in-Chief of the Union armies. He decided to exercise direct control over Meade's Army of the Potomac and to place Sherman in overall command of the armies in the western theatre. The Army of the Potomac was then about 150,000 strong and faced Lee's Army of Northern Virginia of about 61,000. The manoeuvres of these two great commanders during May and June 1864 are some of the most fascinating of the war.

Grant opened his offensive on 4th May and on the following two days was fought the Battle of the Wilderness, an area some fourteen miles long and ten miles wide covered with a dense mass of second growth saplings. All Grant's attacks were defeated with heavy casualties. Breaking off the battle, Grant on 7th May moved southward round Lee's right flank; but Lee had already anticipated such a move and had blocked it by marching a covering force to Spotsylvania Court House. This was followed by the Battle of Spotsylvania which continued until 18th May; Grant continually seeking for flanks or openings with each attempt being frustrated by Lee's movement of reserves. Losses in the fierce fighting were heavy. During the course of this battle the Cavalry Corps of the Army of the Potomac under General Philip H. Sheridan rode south towards Richmond and encountered the Confederate cavalry under Stuart at Yellow Tavern close to the City defences. In the ensuing engagement Stuart was killed.

On 29th May Grant again broke off the battle and made a flank march round Lee's right, but Lee, moving quickly, took up a position on the North Anna River and blocked Grant again. From 23rd to 31st May Grant probed this new line but found it too strong to attack. He marched again to his right only to find Lee facing him once more near Mechanics-ville, south of the Totopotomy Creek. After further edging towards the Confederate right, Grant delivered a heavy frontal assault at the Battle of Cold Harbor on 3rd June which was defeated with heavy loss to the Federals. The fighting continued till 12th June without further result.

Meanwhile during May Butler, with the Union Army of the James of 30,000 men, was advancing from Fortress Monroe by river towards Richmond. He landed at Bermuda Hundred but his further progress was defeated by General Beauregard at the Battle of Drewry's Bluff.

In the Shenandoah Valley General Franz Sigel advanced south with a force from the Department of West Virginia, but on 15th May he was attacked at New Market by General John Breckenridge with a Con-federate force and driven back.

After his defeat at Cold Harbor, Grant decided to shift his army to the south bank of the James River and to attack Petersburg, which was the key to Richmond's communications with the south. To divert Lee's attention he sent Sheridan with the Cavalry Corps towards Charlottesville to meet General David Hunter, who had replaced Sigel, and was advanc-ing up the Valley to Staunton. Lee reacted to this by despatching General Wade Hampton with two cavalry divisions against Sheridan, and General Jubal Early's Corps to stop Hunter. Wade Hampton drove Sheridan back at an engagement at Trevillian Station on the Virginia Central Railroad on 11th June, and Hunter, encountering Early near Lynchburg withdrew westwards across the Alleghanies.

Grant, having achieved his main object, withdrew the Army of the

Potomac from contact and by a masterly piece of organisation and staff work transferred it south of the James, during the period 13th to 18th June. During this move he ordered Butler to seize Petersburg if practicable; however the Union attack was badly managed and was repulsed by Beauregard. Before the Army of the Potomac could be thrown into the battle, Lee was once more facing Grant with his main army. Grant now settled down to the siege of Petersburg.

Atlanta

In the West, before Grant started his offensive, things had not been going too well for Union arms. General N. P. Banks had gone off on a useless and politically inspired campaign up the Red River into Texas, supported reluctantly by Admiral Porter. On 8th April 1864 Banks was attacked and decisively defeated at the Battle of Sabine Cross Roads by Generals Richard Taylor and Edmund Kirby Smith and driven into headlong retreat. This ruined Grant's project of using Banks for diversionary operations to assist Sherman's advance.

On 5th May 1864, however, Sherman started from Chattanooga in his brilliant Atlanta campaign. General J. E. Johnston, a master of defensive operations, confronted Sherman in a strong position at Dalton. Sherman drove him out of it on 9th May by an outflanking movement. He manoeuvred him again out of subsequent positions at Resaca on 15th May and Cassville on 19th May, and then by-passed Johnston's next position at Allatoona on 4th June. On 10th June Sherman encountered Johnston's new position on Kenesaw Mountain, Pine Mountain, and Lost Mountain. On 27th June he attacked Kenesaw Mountain and was repulsed. On 2nd July he turned Johnston's left flank and the Confederate commander retired to a position on the Chattahoochie River. Sherman turned this on 9th July and crossed the river; Johnston falling back to Peachtree Creek, just north of Atlanta. On 17th July he was relieved of command and replaced by General John B. Hood.

On 20th July Hood attacked Sherman at the Battle of Peachtree Creek but he was repulsed, and forced the next day to withdraw inside the Atlanta defences. On 22nd July Hood attacked again, in the Battle of Atlanta, and was once more defeated. Sherman now decided to move round the west of Atlanta and to operate against its railway communications. On 27th July he sent most of his cavalry on distant raids and started the movement of the main body on 28th. An attack by Hood on this day was beaten at Ezra Church. The cavalry raids were not very successful and General George Stoneman with 2,000 troopers was surrounded and captured. Between 25th and 31st August Sherman swung his army right round to the south of Atlanta, cutting Hood's railway communications and defeating a Confederate attempt to stop him. On 31st August Hood evacuated Atlanta and the following day Sherman's army marched in.

Far away in Sherman's rear the Federals had been unable to stop Confederate cavalry depredations. In March Forrest had ridden into Kentucky as far as Paducah and on return from this raid had captured Fort Pillow on the Mississippi on 12th April. In June General Samuel D. Sturgis, who had been ordered by Sherman to find and defeat Forrest, moved out of Memphis with some 3,400 cavalry and 2,000 infantry. Forrest, who had about 3,000 men, held up this force with a line of skirmishers, enveloped both flanks, and routed it at the Battle of Brice's Cross Roads on 10th June, inflicting a loss of 2,240 men in killed, wounded, and captured. The following month General A. J. Smith advanced against Forrest with a force of 14,000 men consisting of eight cavalry regiments, thirty infantry battalions, and nine batteries. Forrest, reinforced to 10,000 men, attacked Smith at Tupelo, but was repulsed. Smith, however, withdrew. On 21st August Forrest raided Memphis, penetrated the defences, and captured the Union headquarters before withdrawing.

Shenandoah Valley

Early, after Hunter's retreat, advanced down the Shenandoah Valley and on 2nd July, crossing the Potomac, invaded Maryland. On 9th July, approaching Washington, Early encountered and defeated General Lew Wallace, commanding the VIII Corps of the Middle Department (a rather scratch formation) at the Monocacy River. Grant, seeing the danger, had on 5th July ordered the VI Corps to Washington and this arrived just in time to prevent Early entering the city. Early withdrew and recrossed the Potomac on 14th. Advancing again, he defeated General George Crook at Kernstown, and marched north to Chambersburg.

On 7th August Grant placed Sheridan in command of all Washington's defence forces, concentrated a force of 48,000 men at Harper's Ferry, and gave Sheridan instructions to destroy Early's Corps. On 19th September Sheridan defeated Early at Opequon Creek and on 22nd September at Fisher's Hill. On 19th October Early counter-attacked, engaging the Union army at the Battle of Cedar Creek, 20 miles south of Winchester. Sheridan being absent, Early almost won, but Sheridan returned in the middle of the battle, rallied the Union forces and defeated Early, driving his troops back to New Market.

Sherman's March to the Sea

After the capture of Atlanta, Hood took his whole army first west and then north to cut Sherman's communications and so compel him to withdraw from Atlanta. Sherman followed for a short time in pursuit, and then sent Thomas with the Army of the Cumberland to Chattanooga and Nashville to deal with Hood whilst he returned to Atlanta. Sherman now prepared to cut loose from his line of communications and march through Georgia to the sea. On 15th November he left Atlanta on his great march with a large train of supply wagons. As he marched he destroyed all the railway communications and drew supplies for his army from a wide belt of the countryside. On 9th December he arrived before Savannah, which was held by General William Hardee with about 15,000 men. On 13th December Sherman stormed Fort McAlister and, having established communications with the Federal naval forces, began to invest the city. On 21st December Hardee evacuated Savannah and Sherman took possession.

Nashville

West of the Mississippi the Confederate General Stirling Price invaded Missouri on 1st September and advanced towards St. Louis. Finding it reinforced, he turned westwards along the south bank of the Missouri and defeated General James G. Blunt, commanding District Upper Kansas, at Lexington on 19th October and again at Independence on 22nd October. However, on 23rd October at Westport a Union cavalry force under Pleasanton, now commanding District Central Missouri, attacked Price in rear whilst he was engaged with Blunt in front and the Confederate commander was driven back into Arkansas.

On 14th November Hood, reinforced by Forrest, crossed the Tennessee River and marched towards Nashville with about 54,000 men. General J. M. Schofield, commanding the XXIII Corps was instructed by Thomas to delay Hood whilst he completed the concentration of the Army of the Cumberland. Schofield held Hood up about Columbia, Tennessee, from 24th to 27th November, and fought a delaying action at Spring Hill, Tennessee, on 29th November. He then fell back to Franklin, 15 miles south of Nashville. Here Hood attacked him on the 30th but was driven back with heavy casualties. Schofield then withdrew to Nashville. On December 15th Thomas attacked Hood in the Battle of Nashville, and by the following day Hood's army was broken and in disorderly flight.

The Last Campaigns

Grant had been carrying on trench warfare operations against the Confederate defences of Petersburg. He had managed to cut the Weldon Railroad, running from Petersburg to the south between 18th and 21st August, but an attempt on 27th and 28th October to sever the one remaining link to the south, the Southside Railroad, was repulsed.

On 1st February 1865 Sherman's march northward from Savannah was starting. His objective was the railway centre of Goldsboro', 425 miles away. His army was about 60,000 strong and he estimated that a Confederate army of some 40,000 might be assembled to bar his passage. Sherman's remarkable technique was to threaten two important points, so that the enemy were forced to divide their forces, and then either to go for one of them or else pass between the two without attacking either. On 17th February he occupied Columbia practically unopposed. Hardee in Charleston had assumed that that town was the objective, whilst Confederates at Augusta had been certain that Sherman aimed to seize it first. As it was, the capture of Columbia forced Hardee to abandon Charleston without a struggle. On 22nd February Schofield, with his XXIII Corps landed at Fort Fisher and drove the Confederate troops under Bragg from Wilmington, the port to and from which the bulk of the Confederate trade with Europe had been conducted. Schofield then marched towards the centre of North Carolina to join Sherman.

In February the Confederate Congress took the belated and long overdue step of appointing Lee Commander-in-Chief of the Army. Lee's first action was to place J. E. Johnston in command of all Confederate forces in the Carolinas to oppose Sherman's advance. On March 19th and 20th Sherman's troops encountered Johnston's at Bentonville. In the subsequent battle Johnston was beaten and withdrew. On 23rd Sherman reached Goldsboro', where he met Schofield.

On 25th March Lee attacked the Union right at Fort Steadman. The attack was repulsed. On 29th March Grant attacked Lee's right and sent Sheridan with the cavalry wide to the left to encircle that flank. Lee countered this by sending General G. E. Pickett with cavalry and two infantry divisions to attack Sheridan's left at Dinwiddie Court House, while A. P. Hill attacked the left flank of the advancing Union infantry. The whole Union advance was checked by this counter stroke, but Pickett came under increasing pressure from Sheridan and retired to Five Forks, where he entrenched. On 1st April, in much greater strength, Sheridan attacked the Confederate position at Five Forks and Pickett's defences collapsed. On 2nd April Grant launched a general assault, and on 3rd April Lee began the evacuation of the Richmond and Petersburg defences. On 6th and 7th April Anderson's and Ewell's Corps, covering the withdrawal, were overwhelmed at Sailor's Creek. On 9th April Lee ordered an attack on Sheridan's cavalry which had cut his line of withdrawal at Appomattox. But Sheridan had now been reinforced with infantry and the attack was beaten off. On the same day Lee surrendered the Army of Northern Virginia to Grant at Appomattox Court House. On 26th April Johnston surrendered his army to Sherman at Bennett's House. The war was over.

CHAPTER TWO

Infantry

Afters THE EARLY STAGES of the war, when untrained regiments on both sides were liable to panic, the infantry in both the Federal and Confederate Armies was extremely good. The great majority of the men were of Anglo-Saxon stock, and it is thus interesting to note the differences that had developed in the fighting characteristics and behaviour, due to the varying environment and living conditions in the wide expanses of North America. General Winfield Scott, the erstwhile conqueror of Mexico and at the age of 75 the first General-in-Chief of the Federal Army, commented in February 1862 that the Southern soldiers, 'have élan, courage, woodcraft, consummate horsemanship, endurance of pain equal to the Indians, but they will not submit to discipline. They will not take care of things or husband their resources. Where they are, there is waste and destruction. If it could be done by one wild desperate dash they would do it, but they cannot stand waiting . . . Men of the North on the other hand can wait; they can bear discipline; they can endure for ever. Losses in battle are nothing to them. They will fight to the bitter end.'[1] It must be remembered, of course, that this assessment was made by a Northern general, and during the fairly early stages of the war before regiments of either side had become trained and battle-hardened. As the war developed fine fighting infantry appeared on both sides, and it would be difficult to choose between the best Federal and best Confederate regiments. The infantry with which Sherman captured Atlanta and swept to the sea was superb; but it did not excel the magnificent body of fighting men in the army of General Lee. Indeed, it was William Swinton, the war correspondent of the *New York Times* with the Army of the Potomac, who wrote of Lee's soldiers: 'Nor can there fail to arise the image of that other Army that was the adversary of the Army of the Potomac—and which, who can ever forget that once looked upon it?—that array of "tattered uniforms and bright muskets"—that body of incomparable infantry, the Army of Northern Virginia—which for four years carried the Revolt on its bayonets, opposing a constant front to the mighty concentration of power brought against it; which, receiving terrible blows, did not fail to give the like; and which, vital in all its parts, died only with its annihilation.'[2]

Opinions of different elements of their own side and of their opponents varied amongst soldiers of the two armies. Colonel Lyman, on the staff of General Meade, was surprised how poorly the Germans performed out of their own country: 'They will plunder and they won't fight. Really, as soldiers, they are miserable. Actually a Yankee regiment would drive a brigade of them.' He thought the Irish were good 'if well officered'. 'The Pats will do: not so good as pure Yanks, but they will rush in and fight.'[3] Lieutenant-Colonel A. J. L. Fremantle (later General Sir Arthur Fremantle), Coldstream Guards, who visited the Confederate Army in 1863, said that the Southern troops appeared to estimate highest the north-western Federal troops who came from Ohio, Iowa, Indiana, etc.; the Irish Federals were also respected for their fighting qualities, whilst the genuine Yankees and Germans were not much esteemed.[4]

Lieutenant-Colonel Garnet (later Field-Marshal Lord) Wolseley visited Lee's headquarters in 1862 after the Battle of Sharpsburg, and wrote an account of his visit in Blackwood's Magazine.[5] Of the officers he commented: 'As is usual in impromptu armies, the chief deficiency lies with the officers, who, though possessed of zeal and high courage, seldom know more of their duty than the men under their command. The system of election from the first has worked badly; they unfortunately instituted this, and I never spoke with an officer on the subject who did not condemn it. It still holds good as regards the first appointment of officers to be second lieutenants, but all the vacancies of superior grade are filled up according to seniority. When such a system has been established it is difficult to abolish it suddenly, especially when the army is in the field.'

Lyman thought the supply of Federal officers poor. 'We have no military or social caste to make officers from. Regiments that have been officered by gentlemen of education have invariably done well, like the 2nd, 20th, and 24th Massachusetts, and the 1st Massachusetts Cavalry. Even the 44th and 45th, nine-monthers, behave with credit; though there was this drawback in them, that the privates were too familiar with the officers, having known them before.' Of the Confederate officers he says: 'I am free to confess that the bearing of the few Rebel officers I have met is superior to our own. They have a slight reserve and an absence of all flippancy, on the whole an earnestness of manner, which is very becoming to them.'[6]

Swinton has an interesting comparison between the Federal and Con-

27

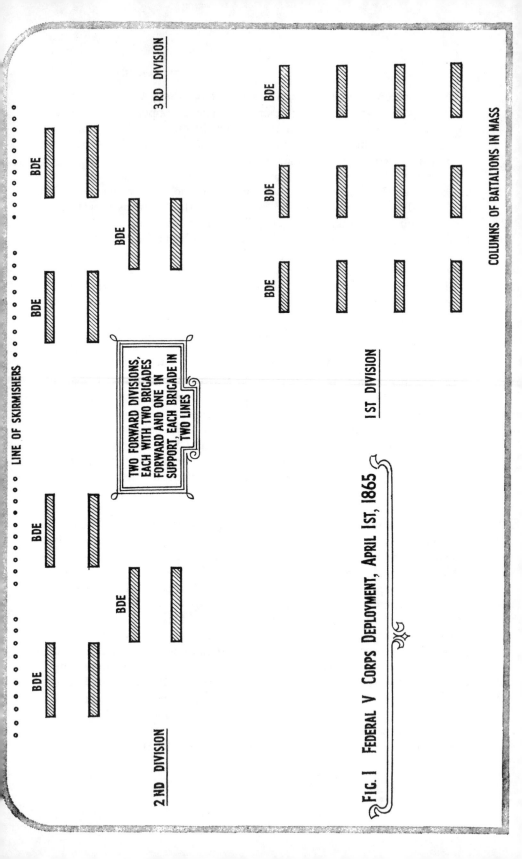

LINE OF SKIRMISHERS

3 RD DIVISION

BDE

BDE

BDE

BDE

BDE

BDE

BDE

BDE

1 ST DIVISION

COLUMNS OF BATTALIONS IN MASS

2 ND DIVISION

TWO FORWARD DIVISIONS, EACH WITH TWO BRIGADES FORWARD AND ONE IN SUPPORT, EACH BRIGADE IN TWO LINES

FIG. I FEDERAL V CORPS DEPLOYMENT, APRIL 1ST, 1865

federate Armies.[7] He writes: ' "Had there been no McClellan," I have often heard General Meade say, "there would have been no Grant; for the army made no essential improvement under any of his successors." It was common throughout the war to ascribe a high degree of discipline to the Confederate army—even higher than that of the Army of the Potomac. But in fact the discipline of the Army of Northern Virginia was never equal to that of the Army of the Potomac, though in fire and *elan* it was superior. "I could always rely on my army," said General Lee, at the time he surrendered its remnant at Appomattox Court House—"I could always rely on my army for *fighting*; but its discipline was poor". At the time of the Maryland invasion, Lee lost above twenty-five thousand men from his effective strength by straggling, and he exclaimed with tears, *"My army is ruined by straggling!"* Nothing could better illustrate the high state of discipline of the Army of the Potomac, than its conduct in such retreats as that on the Peninsula and in the Pope campaign, and in such incessant fighting as the Rapidan campaign of 1846.'

Meade was fiercely proud of the reputation of the Army of the Potomac. Lyman tells of the receipt of a despatch from Sherman for Grant which was tactlessly read aloud in Meade's presence. 'Sherman,' says Lyman, 'therein told Grant that the Army of the West, having fought, could now afford to manoeuvre, and that, if his (Grant's) inspiration could make the Army of the Potomac do its share, success would crown our efforts. The eyes of Major-General George Meade stood out about one inch as he said in a voice like cutting an iron bar with a handsaw: "Sir! I consider that despatch an insult to the army I command and to me personally. The Army of the Potomac does not require General Grant's inspiration or anybody else's inspiration to make it fight!" He did not get over it all day, and, at dinner, spoke of the western army as "an armed rabble".' In support of his chief, Lyman adds: 'Colonel Comstock and others, who have fought with both armies, say distinctly that our troops are fifty per cent better than the western, and that the good Rebel soldiers have always been kept near Richmond except when Longstreet went temporarily to the West'.[8]

Organisation

As might be expected, with regular officers of the United States Army filling senior positions on each side, the organisation of the new regiments raised by both the Union and the Confederacy reflected the pre-war organisation of the regular infantry. A regiment consisted, therefore, of ten companies, of which two were designated flank companies and were supposed to be trained as light infantry and armed with rifles. This was an organisation inherited from the days of the Napoleonic Wars, when the

29

close-formed ranks of the battalion companies were covered by a line of light infantry skirmishers. The flank companies were supposed to cover the front of a battalion until close contact, when they fell back to each flank.

A Union regiment was commanded by a colonel with a lieutenant-colonel as second-in-command. Also on the regimental headquarters there were a major, a lieutenant-and-adjutant, a lieutenant-and-quarter-master, a surgeon, an assistant surgeon, a sergeant-major, a regimental quartermaster-sergeant, a regimental commissary sergeant, a hospital steward, two principal musicians, and 24 bandsmen. In each of the ten companies there were a captain, a lieutenant, a second-lieutenant, a first sergeant, four sergeants, eight corporals, two musicians, a waggoner, and 82 privates.[9] This, at any rate, was the theoretical establishment, but the normal strength was about half this.[10] On 4th May 1861 Lincoln authorised the raising of ten new regular regiments of infantry. But these, rather surprisingly, were on a completely new organisation, having three eight-company battalions. However, only one of them was ever completed to its full establishment.[11]

The raising and maintaining of regiments was done better in the Confederacy. In the Union much was left to the individual States and there were many practices which led to inefficiency and which irritated military commanders. In Kentucky, for instance, the organisation of regiments was under the control of a military board of citizens;[12] and most States preferred to raise new regiments, rather than to complete existing units from the bottom and allow vacancies for promotion amongst officers and N.C.O.s to be filled by war-experienced men; with the result that old battalions dwindled away to skeletons. As early as September 1863 Lyman noted that many of the regiments in the III Corps of the Army of the Potomac, had no more than 200 men.[13] A noteworthy exception was Wisconsin, which kept its old regiments filled with recruits. 'The result was,' said General Sherman, 'that we estimated a Wisconsin regiment equal to an ordinary brigade.[14] In the Confederacy it was the general practice to maintain existing regiments, but, contrary to the Union, insufficient use was made of available State machinery for raising troops.

In both armies regiments were formed into infantry brigades. In the Confederate Army brigades were generally formed of regiments from the same State and, as regiments were rarely moved from one brigade to another, *esprit de corps* was of the brigade rather than of the regiment; in fact, the brigade could more properly be regarded as the regiment, and the regiments in it as its battalions. Brigades were almost always referred to by names of their commanders; even in official returns numbers were rarely used, and in the inspection reports of 1864 they were not even mentioned. Thus, in the I Corps, Pickett's Division consisted of the four Virginian Brigades of Steuart, Corse, Hunton, and Terry. Each had five regiments, though the number could vary between three and six.

In the Federal Army, on the other hand, regiments were changed between brigades frequently; and brigades were often moved from one division, and even corps, to another and acquired new numbers in the process. For brigades and divisions were numbered only according to the formation to which they belonged; thus a division would be the 1st, 2nd, or 3rd, of a particular corps, whilst a brigade was the 1st, 2nd, or 3rd of its division.

McClellan originally organised the Army of the Potomac into divisions of three brigades, each of four regiments. (The corps organisation was introduced by President Lincoln into the Army of the Potomac as it was moving to the Peninsula in 1862. The Confederate Army adopted it after the end of the campaign in the Peninsula).[15]

The Federal brigade organisation was seriously affected by the practice in many States of letting regiments run down in strength and raising new ones, and also of raising regiments for limited periods of nine months, two years, or three years, instead of for the duration of the war. To show the effect of this at the end of the war, it will suffice to take, as a typical example, V Corps of the Army of the Potomac as it was on 1st April 1865.

Each of the three infantry divisions of the V Corps had three infantry brigades, but of vastly different strengths and composition. In the 1st Division its 1st Brigade had only two regiments, the 185th New York and the 198th Pennsylvania, both of which had been formed in September 1864, probably with inexperienced officers, and sent to join the Army of the Potomac before Petersburg a month later; being young regiments they were undoubtedly pretty well up to strength. The 2nd Brigade had three similar regiments, the 187th, 188th, and 189th New York, all raised in October 1864, and coming rather uncommonly from the same State. The 3rd Brigade was a very different body, consisting of no less than eight regiments, of which seven were the following old Army of the Potomac units raised between September 1861 and September 1862, and all probably of very low strength: the 83rd, 118th, and 155th Pennsylvania; the 1st and 16th Michigan; the 32nd Massachusetts; and the 20th Maine. Of these the 1st Michigan was a three-year regiment and in 1864 it had been graded by the State as 'reserve' and continued with re-enlisted personnel. The last unit was the 1st Maine Sharpshooter (ie Rifle) Battalion, formed at the end of 1864, probably by transferring good shots from other regiments.

In the 1st Brigade of the 2nd Division there were six regiments: the

31

140th and 146th New York, formed in September and October 1862; the
5th New York Veteran Regiment, which consisted of recruits and re-
enlisted veterans of the two-year 5th New York and other similar regiments mustered out in May 1863; the 15th New York Heavy Artillery,
which, as it was no longer required in the Washington forts and as heavy
artillery were also trained as infantry, was posted to the Army of the
Potomac in 1864; the 114th Pennsylvania, formed in August 1862; and
the 61st Massachusetts, which was only raised in October 1864. The 2nd
Brigade of this division was composed entirely of Maryland regiments
(another of the uncommon one-State brigades) raised in 1861 and 1862.
These were the 1st, 4th, 7th, and 8th; of which the 1st was a three-year
regiment, and those men who re-enlisted were sent off on 'veteran furlough' in April–May 1864. There were six regiments in the 3rd Brigade,
2nd Division: the 3rd, 4th, and 8th Delaware; the 190th and 191st
Pennsylvania, both formed from veterans and recruits in 1864 from time
expired regiments of the Pennsylvania 'Reserve Corps' (see Chapter
Three); and the 210th Pennsylvania, a new unit raised in September 1864.

The 1st Brigade, 3rd Division, had seven regiments: the 91st, 143rd,
149th, and 150th Pennsylvania, all dating from 1861-2; the 91st New
York of September 1861, and the 6th and 7th Wisconsin of September 1861.
In the 2nd Brigade there were only four regiments: the 97th and 104th
New York of 1861-2, the 16th Maine of 1862; and the 39th Massachusetts
of 1862. But the 3rd Brigade had no less than ten regiments: the 76th,
94th, 95th, and 147th New York, all raised between November 1861 and
September 1862; and the 11th, 56th, 88th, 107th, 121st, and 142nd
Pennsylvania, of which the 11th was a three-year regiment composed of
veterans re-enlisted and given six weeks furlough. The 11th was raised
in August 1861 and the remainder up to September 1862.[16]

Weapons

At the start of the war there was a very considerable variety in the firearms
with which the infantry on both sides were equipped; and right up to the
end of the war several different types of rifles were carried by Federal and
Confederate infantry. Initially, owing to the rapid expansion, many
infantry regiments in both armies were armed with flintlock muskets, and
even in November 1861 most of the Virginian militia regiments were so
armed.[17] The reason for this was that manufacture of flintlocks had only
stopped in the early 1840s, so that there were large stocks in the various
arsenals—mostly the US Model 1822. The smoothbore percussion musket
was introduced in 1841, with the US Model of that year. In the same year
a muzzle-loading rifle was produced, which later became known as the
'Mississippi' because the Mississippi Volunteers were armed with it

during the Mexican War of 1845–6. It fired a round ball and was extensively used during the early part of the Civil War. In the early 1850s the Minié rifle was adopted in the US Army and many of the Model 1841 percussion muskets were rifled to take the Minié bullet.

In the Confederate Army the limited supplies of Minié and other rifles in the State arsenals were soon exhausted and percussion muskets converted from flintlocks then became the general issue. General Josiah Gorgas, Confederate Chief of Ordnance, said that when he assumed his appointment he found that within the Confederacy the arsenal contained only 15,000 rifles and 120,000 inferior smoothbore muskets, together with some old flintlocks at Richmond, and Hall's rifles and carbines at Baton Rouge. There was no powder except for small quantities at Baton Rouge and at Mount Vernon, Alabama, which were leftovers from the Mexican War.[18] As late as the Battle of Gettysburg in 1863 some of the Confederate infantry were still armed with the smoothbore percussion muskets.[19]

The Federals were not much better off than the Confederates when the war started. The 13th New York Regiment was equipped with rifles at the Battle of Bull Run in 1861, but later in the year General Anderson, commanding in Kentucky, who had been promised 40,000 of the new Springfield rifles, received instead 12,000 Belgian smoothbore muskets which were so poor that the Governors of Pennsylvania and Ohio had already refused to take them.[20]

From 1855 all new United States weapons were rifled, and the most common rifles during the Civil War were the US 'Springfields' of which the first models were produced in 1861. But the next most numerous were the British Enfields, of which over 800,000 were bought by both the Union and the Confederacy.[21] In May 1861 Major Huse of the Confederate Army was sent to England to buy the first batch of 10,000 Enfields,[22] and in 1862 General Alexander Lawton's Brigade, for instance, was armed throughout with Enfield rifles.[23] The Enfield was a particularly good weapon; there was both a long-barrelled and short-barrelled model, and for the Confederate Army there was a specially made officer's rifle, known as a 'Jeff Davis' Enfield. Many copies of the Enfield rifle were made in the armouries of the Confederacy; notably at Arkadelphia in Arkansas, Tyler in Texas, and by Cook & Brothers of New Orleans. When New Orleans was threatened by the advance of the Union forces the factory was moved to Athens in Georgia. The head of the firm, F. W. C. Cook, subsequently raised an infantry regiment and was killed in action in 1864.[24]

All these rifles were muzzle-loaders, and indeed only a small proportion of the small arms carried in the Civil War were breech-loaders. The breech-loading rifle should more properly, perhaps, be dealt with in the chapter on cavalry, because it was primarily a cavalry weapon; but it will

33

be more convenient to discuss it here. A cavalryman preferred a breech-loader, of course, because it was much easier to load when mounted, and, because they were for cavalry use, most breech-loaders were made as carbines. The Federal cavalry began to receive them in the second year of the war. The most popular in early days was the Sharps, with a breech-block which was dropped by pulling the trigger guard forward. In 1863 this was replaced by the remarkable Spencer, a magazine rifle, which was issued to most of the Federal cavalry as a carbine and to some of the infantry as a musket.

The most accurate of all rifles was the British muzzle-loading Whitworth. This was a great favourite in the Confederate Army as a sniper's rifle for sharpshooter units and a number were purchased from the Whitworth Rifle Company of Manchester. The Whitworth had a hexagonal bore, instead of the usual grooves, and its main disadvantage was the amount of fouling that accumulated in this type of bore.

General Sherman was most impressed with the Spencer rifle as an infantry weapon. On 22nd November 1864 one of his brigades, under General Walcutt, was attacked by the Confederate General G. W. Smith's Division from the town of Macon. Some of Walcutt's regiments were armed with Spencer rifles, and they produced such a rapid fire that the Confederates retreated with heavy casualties, and Smith later insisted that his attack had been repulsed by at least a division.[25]

In December 1863 the 7th Connecticut Regiment was issued with Spencers in place of its muzzle-loading Enfields. One of the soldiers in the regiment subsequently wrote home: 'The Rebs made three charges on us but we stood up to the rack with our seven shooters . . . and piled the Rebs in front of us . . . The Rebs hate our guns they call them the Yanks 7 Devils they say the Yankeys stand up there with their G.D. coffy mills wind em up in the morning, run all day shoot a thousand times. . . . they are a good rifel'.[26]

Explosive bullets were used to a small extent by both armies. Colonel Theodore Lyman wrote in May 1864: 'The Rebels were firing a great many explosive bullets, which I never saw before. When they strike they explode, like a fire-cracker and make a bad wound, but I do not suppose, after all, that they are worse than the others'.[27]

Bayonets were carried by all infantry but the casualties inflicted by them seem to have been few. This was due, as always, partly to the moral effect of the bayonet; for a line of troops charging with gleaming, vicious looking, steel could shake the nerves more than a hail of bullets. But when troops did come into close contact they generally preferred to knock their opponents out with the musket butt rather than to use the bayonet; for unless a man has been properly trained in bayonet fighting he is apt to find it a clumsy weapon. Sherman says that his troops, generally fighting in wooded country rarely came into actual contact with the enemy; but when, as at Peachtree Creek and Atlanta, the lines did become inter-mingled, the men fought individually in every possible style, more frequently with the musket clubbed than with the bayonet.[28] There is, however, evidence that bayonets were used. General George A. McCall, commanding a division in the Union Army, says of the action at Frayser's Farm in the Peninsula: 'I had ridden into the regiment to endeavour to check them, but with only partial success. It was my fortune to witness one of the fiercest bayonet charges that ever occurred on this continent. Bayonet wounds, mortal and slight were given and received.'[29] At Sharpsburg Colonel Clarke of the 27th North Carolina Regiment reported that his ammunition was exhausted. He was ordered to hold on with the bayonet and replied that he would 'hold till ice forms in regions where it was never known!'[30] At Gaines's Mill in the Peninsula Hood's Texan Brigade fixed their bayonets in the pause before their assult. And then Porter's tired Federal troops felt 'there was something irresistible about the line of bayonets coming at them through the smoky brush'.[31] At the Battle of Spotsylvania, during the savage fighting at the 'Bloody Angle', the opposing lines were so close that they tossed rifles with bayonets fixed over the parapets as javelins.[32] On the other hand, Fremantle says of Liddell's Arkansas Brigade that many 'had lost or thrown away their bayonets which they don't appear to value properly, as they assert that they have never met any Yankees who would wait for that weapon':[33] a contention which certainly testifies to the moral effect of the bayonet, but hardly provides a reason for dispensing with it!

The favourite and most generally used hand weapon was the Colt revolver, which existed in several models and in various calibres. The Remington was also used by the Federals, and the British Deane and Adams was purchased by both North and South.

Machine guns were little used during the war. The most notable was the 1862 model of the Gatling gun of which an improved and much more successful version was produced in 1865. General B. F. Butler, com-manding the Army of the James, bought twelve of these early Gatlings which were used, without much damage to the Confederates, at the siege of Petersburg. The gun had six barrels which were revolved by a crank handle on the right hand side of the breech. Rounds were fed by gravity from a hopper magazine thrust on to the top of the breech.[34]

Dress, Equipment, and Appearance
The dress and equipment with which the infantry were officially provided were very unlike that which they actually wore. Because of the far greater

manufacturing resources of the Union, the dress work throughout the war by the Confederate soldier was often, apart from its generally grey colour, hardly recognisable as uniform at all.

The dress and equipment of the Union infantryman included a blue jacket; trousers; short gaiters; a knapsack on the back with rolled blanket above; haversack, bayonet, and water bottle on the left side; and cartridge and cap boxes on the right. The headdress was a képi. Officers were dressed in blue frock coat and broad brimmed black felt hat; but the junior infantry officer, at any rate, were soon wearing a short jacket, or 'blouse', and képi, presumably because in the more official dress they were too conspicuously different from their men.

The Confederate infantryman's official dress also included a képi, which was light blue; and he wore a double breasted jacket of a grey or 'butternut' colour with light blue facings, and light blue trousers: a sartorial splendour which, from those who ever wore it, soon disappeared.

Gaiters did not last long in the Union infantry and the soldiers in the Western armies, at any rate, got rid of their knapsacks fairly quickly. Sherman, who cared as little as Wellington what soldiers on active service looked like, considered that an infantryman should carry his musket, equipment with 40 to 60 rounds of ammunition, shelter tent, blanket or overcoat, and extra pairs of trousers, socks and drawers. He believed that, instead of carrying a knapsack, the blanket, tent, and spare clothing should be rolled into the form of a scarf and worn from the left shoulder to the right hip; whilst the haversack, worn on the left side, should hold bread, cooked meat, salt, and coffee. He thought that a soldier could carry about 50lbs without impairing his health or activity.[35]

In October 1863, according to Lyman, the infantry soldier in the Army of the Potomac was still carrying a knapsack, well stuffed, and surmounted by a rolled grey blanket. Three days rations were carried in the haversack and Lyman noted one man with a large tin coffeepot and another with a small frying pan.[36]

In the early part of the war some of the Confederate infantry were immaculately turned out; notably the regiments of General R. Taylor's Louisianian Brigade. Taylor, one of the best types of regimental officer, paid particular attention to the marching ability and comfort of his men. He insisted on proper-fitting boots and frequent halts on the march; at the same time making the men feel that to fall out on the march was a disgrace. In 1862 the Brigade came under the command of 'Stonewall' Jackson, and in his *Destruction and Reconstruction* Taylor describes the arrival of his Louisianians as follows: 'A mounted officer was despatched to report our approach and select a camp, which proved to be beyond Jackson's forces, then lying in the fields on both sides of the Valley pike.

Over 3000 strong, neat in fresh clothing of grey with white gaiters, bands playing at the head of their regiments—not a straggler, but every man in his place, stepping jauntily as if on parade, though it had marched twenty miles or more—in open column, with the rays of the declining sun flaming on polished bayonets, the brigade moved down the hard smooth pike and wheeled on to the camping-ground. Jackson's men, by thousands, had gathered on either side of the road to see us pass.'[37]

Jackson's infantry of 1862 marched light, carrying only their rifles, ammunition, haversacks with several days rations, and blankets. Some men still had knapsacks, but if long distances had to be covered they were ordered to leave them behind. Many of the soldiers of Lee's army, by September of that year and after months of hard marching and fighting, had torn hats without brims, strands of ropes for belts, and rawhide moccasins which they had made themselves.[38]

Wolseley said of the Confederate infantry: 'The infantry accoutrements are the same as those used in the Federal army; indeed I saw very few that had not been taken from the Northeners. Their cartridge-boxes resemble those which our sergeants used to wear, being nearly square, very thin, and only holding forty rounds. The interior arrangement of these boxes is far from convenient; for, having expended the twenty rounds in the upper division of the tin case, which fits closely inside, it has to be withdrawn altogether, and turned with the other side uppermost, to admit of your getting at the twenty rounds in the second compartment. To be obliged to do this in action would be troublesome.

'Almost every regiment has a small band of brass instruments. I cannot say much for the music, but it was at least enlivening.

'The officers marched in front of their companies after the French fashion, the covering sergeant marching upon the pivot flank and being responsible for distance and direction. Several regiments were to a man clothed in the national uniform of grey cloth, whilst others presented a harlequin appearance, being dressed in every conceivable variety of coat, both as regards colour and cut. Grey wideawake hats, looped up at one side, and having a small black feather, are the most general head-dress; but many wear the Yankee black hat or casquette of cloth. That which is most unmilitary in their general appearance is the long hair worn alike by officers and men. They not only allow their locks to hang down the backs of their coats, but many pass them behind their ears as women do. Some, doubtless, are ambitious of imitating the cavaliers of Charles I's time in dress and appearance, as I noticed many, particularly of the mounted officers, copy their style, as portrayed in Vandyke's pictures, in every particular, the colour of their clothing alone excepted. As the regiments marched past me, I remarked that, however slovenly the dress

37

of the men of any particular company might be, their rifles were invariably in good serviceable order. They marched, too, with an elastic tread, the pace being somewhat slower than that of our troops, and not only seemed vigorous and healthy, but each man had that unmistakable look of conscious strength and manly self-reliance, which those who are accustomed to review troops like to see.'[39]

The following year, 1863, Lieutenant-Colonel A. J. L. Fremantle, Coldstream Guards, spent some time with the Confederate Army, touring from Texas to Virginia and finishing up at the Battle of Gettysburg. In the western armies he noted that most of the officers were dressed in a blue-grey frock coat, and that the infantry had blue facings, the artillery red, the cavalry yellow, the staff white, and the doctors black. The infantrymen he says were well clothed but without any uniformity in colour or cut, but nearly all wore grey or brown coats and felt hats. Fremantle was told that even if a regiment were clothed in proper uniform by the Government, it would be parti-coloured in a week because the soldiers preferred the coarse homespun jackets and trousers made by their families.

In Virginia Fremantle visited Pender's Division of Lee's Army of Northern Virginia, which consisted of two North Carolina brigades, one South Carolina, and one Georgia. He writes: 'The soldiers of this division are a remarkably fine body of men. . . . Their clothing is serviceable, so also are their boots, but there is the usual utter absence of uniformity as to colour and shape of their garments and hats: grey of all shades, and brown clothing, with felt hats predominate.'

When Fremantle left the Confederate Army to return home after Gettysburg, he had to cross the lines between the opposing armies. He thus had his first sight of Federal troops, and was not impressed. 'I did not think much of the Northern troops,' he writes. 'They are certainly dressed in proper uniform, but their clothes are badly fitted, and they are often round-shouldered, dirty, and slovenly in appearance; in fact, bad imitations of soldiers. Now, the Confederate has no ambition to imitate the regular soldier at all. He looks the genuine Rebel; but in spite of his bare feet, his ragged clothes, his old rug, and toothbrush stuck like a rose in his buttonhole, he has a sort of devil-may-care reckless self-confident look, which is decidedly taking.'[40]

However, according to Lyman,[41] however dirty and slovenly the Federal soldiers looked, their muskets always shone like silver.

One of Lee's constant worries was the lack of shoes for the army. On 3rd September 1862 he wrote to President Davis. 'The army is not properly equipped for an invasion of an enemy's territory. It lacks much of the material of war, is feeble in transportation, the animals being much reduced, and the men are poorly provided with clothes, and in thousands of instances are destitute of shoes.'[42] And again, in his report of the operations in Maryland in 1862 he wrote: 'The arduous service in which our troops had been engaged, their great privations of rest and food, and the long marches without shoes over mountain roads, had greatly reduced our ranks before the action began.'[43] On 19th October 1863 he wrote to the Secretary of War: 'Nothing prevented me continuing on his front (ie General Meade's at Gettysburg) but the destitute condition of the men, thousands of whom are barefooted, a greater number partially shod, and nearly all without overcoats, blankets, or warm clothing.'[44]

Regimental Colours were carried into action by both sides, though there was some difference in design and practice. In the Union Army each regiment had two Colours—the National, which was the national flag with the name of the State and number of the regiment on the centre red stripe; and the Regimental, which was blue, charged in centre with either the American eagle surmounted by 13 stars or the State arms, and having the number and State of the regiment on a scroll below. Any battle honours were also borne on this Colour. Both Colours were 6ft 6in in the fly and 6ft in the hoist. (Lyman noted on 9th September 1863 that the flags of many of the regiments were so tattered that the battle honours, such as 'Fair Oaks' and 'Williamsburg' could hardly be read.) This system followed, of course, the British tradition in the Colours of a regiment and had probably been inherited from the militia Colours carried in the days of the British colonial administration. The Colours were carried in action by sergeants.

The story of the flags of the Confederacy is a little complicated. The first national flag of the Secession was turkey red with a white star in the centre and a crescent in the upper corner next to the hoist. This extraordinary flag, which would seem more appropriate to the Ottoman Empire, was sewn together (and perhaps designed) by some Charleston ladies when the State seceded in 1860. It had a brief life on the flagpole of the Charleston Custom House. As more States seceded, a blue flag was adopted which retained the white star but omitted the crescent. This flag was plugged by a singer called Harry McCarty, who toured the deep South with his song 'The Bonny Blue Flag'. In the West the Confederate regiments adopted this design with a white border as a battle flag, which was carried by each regiment and inscribed with their battle honours. This flag was noted by Fremantle when he visited the western theatre of operations in 1863.[45]

The next Confederate flag was the 'Stars and Bars', which was of similar design to the flag of the United States, except that there were only eleven stars and three stripes (two red and one white). This flag was carried by regiments at the Battle of Bull Run in 1861, but it was found that it was sufficiently like the 'Stars and Stripes' to lead to confusion. A new flag was therefore designed by Colonel William Porcher Miles, who was Chairman of the House Military Committee C.S.A. and something of a heraldic enthusiast. In a letter to General G. T. Beauregard in August 1861 he gave the following description of the proposed flag: 'In the form I proposed the cross was more heraldic than ecclesiastical, it being the saltire of heraldry . . . The stars ought always to be white, or argent . . . Stars, too, show better on an azure field than any other. Blue stars on a white field would not be handsome or appropriate. The white edge to the blue is partly a necessity to prevent what is called false blazoning, or a solecism in heraldry, viz. blazoning colour on colour or metal on metal. It would not do to put a blue cross, therefore, on a red field. Hence the white, being metal argent, is put on the red, and the blue on the white. The introduction of the white between the blue and the red adds also much to the brilliancy of the colours and brings them out in strong relief. But I am boring you with my pet hobby.'[46]

And so was born the famous battle flag, carried particularly by the regiments of the Army of Northern Virginia. Its heraldic description is, 'Gules, on a saltire azure, fimbriated argent, thirteen stars of the last'; or, for the uninitiated, red with a blue St Andrew's cross, edged white, and bearing on it thirteen white stars. Fremantle saw it in Pender's Division of Lee's Army, and wrote: 'The colours of the regiments differ from the blue battle flags I saw with Bragg's army. They are generally red with a blue St Andrew's cross showing the stars . . . Most of the colours in this division bear the names Fredericksburg, Seven Pines, Harpers Ferry, Chancellorsville, &c.'[47]

This design was so attractive that the Confederacy adopted it as part of a new national flag which was white with the above device occupying the upper quarter next to the hoist. Fremantle saw it at Charleston, flying from most of the forts and thought it bore a strong resemblance to the British White Ensign. However, if there was no wind, or only a breeze, it could be mistaken for a white flag, so a little time later the white field was given a broad red edging.

Drill and Tactics

Sherman presents an attractive picture of a Brigadier-General Strong, one of the many politically appointed officers. Strong had been a merchant and told Sherman that he never professed to be a soldier and had expected to be a quartermaster or commissary-general. Sherman says that, 'He was a good kind-hearted gentleman, boiling over with patriotism and zeal. I advised him what to read and study, was considerably amused at his receiving instruction from a young lieutenant who knew the company and battalion drill, and could hear him practise in his room the words of command, and tone of voice, "Break from the right, to march to the left! Battalion, halt! Forward into line!" etc.'[48]

Before the outbreak of the war the drill and tactics manual of the United States Army was *Hardee's Tactics* by W. J. Hardee, later a General and corps commander in the Confederate Army. It was very suitable for the instruction of volunteers because the movements laid down were few and simple. In the standard battle formation for a regiment, eight companies were drawn up in two ranks, either in line or column (ie each company in line, one behind the other), and the remaining two companies were deployed as a line of skirmishers covering the regimental front. Other formations could be adopted to suit tactical circumstances, for instance six companies in line behind the skirmishers and two in reserve. On approach to close contact the skirmishers normally fell back to take post in line on each flank.[49]

On a higher level, a brigade might attack with all its regiments in line, or with two regiments in front and two behind in support, or in column with one regiment in line in front, perhaps two behind, and one deployed as skirmishers. An attack might then be delivered in successive waves. As will be apparent there were many possible ways of deploying a brigade.

Tactics, of course, are based primarily on weapons, and though these were sound they were based on the smoothbore musket and differed little from those used by Wellington in the Peninsular War. As the war developed and the influence of the rifle made itself felt, two things happened: firstly, the skirmish line was so strengthened that it often became the first wave of the attack, whilst the troops in close order behind became supports to strengthen the attack or exploit success; and secondly, to protect themselves against the rifles of the attackers and to use with maximum effect the deadly fire of their own rifles, defending troops made more and more use of such field fortifications as trenches, breastworks, abattis, and wire entanglements.

A method of deploying infantry, which should obviously have been avoided, was used by the Confederate General A. S. Johnston at the Battle of Shiloh (in which he was killed) in April 1862. His army advanced in three lines, each about 10,000 strong, followed by a reserve of some 7,000. Each line was preceded by a strong swarm of skirmishers and there was about 500 yards distance between them. But instead of dividing the front into corps and divisional sectors, he put Hardee's Corps and one brigade of Bragg's in the first line, Bragg's Corps less the one brigade in the second line, and Polk's Corps together with Breckenridge's Division in the third line. Inevitably the lines closed up as the army approached the enemy's position, till they were all on top of each other and hopelessly mixed up. As the only way of restoring some sort of control, the three corps commanders agreed to divide the tangled mass between them, Hardee taking the left, Polk the centre, and Bragg the right.[50]

A typical simple infantry advance (though it had an unfortunate ending) is quoted by Sherman in his report of the pursuit after the Battle of Shiloh, in which he was commanding a division. 'I ordered the two advance companies of the Ohio Seventy-Seventh, Colonel Hildebrand, to deploy forward as skirmishers and the regiment itself forward into line with an interval of one hundred yards. In this order we advanced cautiously until the skirmishers were engaged. . . . The enemy's cavalry came down boldly at a charge, led by General Forrest in person, breaking through our line of skirmishers, when the regiment of infantry, without cause, broke, threw away their muskets and fled.'[51] The formidable Bedford Forrest was a bit too much for green troops!

The Confederate infantry under Jackson's command soon realised the value of cover in the attack, and by 1862 they were advancing by rushes from one cover to another, and it became the general practice to build up the firing line to within effective range of the enemy by infantry detachments working their way forward in skirmishing order.[52] In due course, the normal method of attack in all the Confederate armies was by small columns moving forward in short rushes behind clouds of skirmishers and in successive lines.[53] The Federals in the Army of the Potomac still tended to attack in heavy columns. At the Battle of Fredericksburg in December 1862, for instance, Couch's 2nd Corps attacked with French's Division leading followed by Hancock's Division in support; both divisions advanced on a one-brigade front with a distance of 200 paces between brigades. The two divisions came under terrific fire and were repulsed with a loss of nearly half their strength; though the attack was pressed with the utmost gallantry.[54]

Sherman's army, on the other hand, suited their tactics, he says, to the wooded country in which most of their fighting was done. They moved forward in strong skirmishing lines, taking advantage of the shape of the ground and every bit of cover. Even so, they had to compete with very cleverly sited enemy defences, with cleared fields of fire and various types of entanglement.[55]

On 19th August 1864 a Confederate force carried out a manoeuvre which seems more suitable to a body of troops marching on to a cere-monial parade than to one carrying out an attack in the field. Warren's Corps of the Army of the Potomac was operating south of Petersburg on the Weldon Railroad and trying to set up a line of skirmishers between the right of the corps and the left of the main body of the army. Before this had been established a Confederate force broke through the picket line 'with', says Swinton, 'heavy fire in column of fours, left in front'. That is, the Confederates had, from line, moved to the left in fours, so that a right turn into line would bring the original front line to the front; and this is what happened. As the force penetrated to the rear of Warren's right flank, so in succession (probably by regiments) the troops turned right into line and swept in column across the rear of the whole of the Federal corps capturing 2,500 prisoners, including one brigade commander.[56]

Warren's Corps, in the organisation given earlier in this chapter, went into action on 1st April 1865 in a deployment that was probably typical of the period. The 2nd Division (Ayres) was on the left, the 3rd Division (Crawford) on the right, and the 1st Division (Griffin) in reserve behind the right. Each of the two forward divisions had two brigades in front and one in support, and each brigade was in two lines of battle with skirmishers ahead; whilst the 1st Division was in column of battalions in mass.[57] It seems likely that composite battalions were formed from weak regiments.

The construction of breastworks and trenches owed its effective origin to General R. E. Lee, when he took over the command of the army in the Peninsula in 1862. He allocated between the various divisions the task of fortifying a defensive line in front of Richmond, each divisional commander being responsible for the defence of his own front. Very soon there was a continuous line of breastworks, and the defences increased daily.[58] General Armistead Long, Military Secretary to Lee at the time, accompanied him as he rode round the lines. The opening entry of a journal which Long kept thenceforward through the war, reads: 'June 3rd—The day has been a very busy one. The General went to the lines early in the morning and did not return till afternoon. The work was in rapid progress all along the line. . . . When he arrived in General Toombs's part of the line he found that general had been true to his word; he had "no picks nor spades" but he was having logs piled up for defence. General Lee laughed at this freak of Toombs's and remarked, "Colonel Long, when General Toombs gains a little more experience he will be convinced that *earth* is a better protection than logs".'[59]

Once field fortifications had arrived, General Fuller says that it has been calculated that less than one in every eight assaults succeeded. Attacking infantry were under the additional disadvantage, with the muzzle-loading single-shot rifle, of having to fire standing and halt to reload after each volley.[60]

The Confederate infantry of Lee's Army of Northern Virginia soon became particularly skilled. Lyman writes: 'hastily forming a line of battle, they then collect rails from fences, stones, logs and all other materials, and pile them along the line; bayonets with a few picks and shovels, in the hands of men who work for their lives, soon suffice to cover this frame with earth and sods; and within one hour, there is a shelter against bullets, high enough to cover a man kneeling, and extending often for a mile or two. When our line advances, there is the line of the enemy, nothing showing but the bayonets, and the battle-flags stuck on the top of the work. It is a rule that when the Rebels halt, the first day gives them a good rifle-pit; the second, a regular infantry parapet with artillery in position; and the third a parapet with an abattis in front and entrenched batteries behind. Sometimes they put this three days work into the first twenty-four hours. Our men can, and do, do the same; but remember our object is offense—to advance. You would be amazed to see how this country is intersected with field-works extending for miles and miles in different directions and marking the different strategic lines taken up by the two armies, as they warily move about each other.'[61]

The Federals made a particularly effective use of the skirmish line in defence—really an outpost line in front of the main position. At Chancellorsville the skirmish line in front of Hancock's Corps was commanded by Colonel N. A. Miles. It was composed of the 57th, 64th, and 66th New York, with detachments of the 52nd New York, 2nd Delaware, and 148th Pennsylvania, occupying an advanced line of rifle pits. In his report Hancock said: 'During the sharp contest of that day, the enemy were never able to reach my line of battle, so strongly and successfully did Colonel Miles contest the ground.' (But General E. P. Alexander says that the Confederate attack in this sector was only a feint).[62]

At the Battle of Spotsylvania in May 1864 the Federals tried out an entirely new method of attack on a fortified position. Wright's VI Corps was detailed for the operation and twelve of its regiments were placed under the command of Colonel Emery Upton, one of the brigade commanders, who had formulated a new theory of attack. He decided that the answer to a heavily defended line was to form a massive column and assault on a narrow front without firing. The first line of the assault was to capture the enemy trench line immediately in front of it and then push on; the next two lines were to follow the first and then fan out right and left respectively to clear trenches to the flanks of the breach; and the fourth line was to reinforce where needed. Upton reckoned on his breakthrough being exploited and widened by supporting troops. The attack was launched at 6 pm on 10th May and achieved surprise and success, but the supporting troops failed to arrive and the Confederates, counterattacking, had restored the line by dark.[63] It was all rather like the tank attack at Cambrai in 1917.

On 12th May at 4.30 am, as a faint dawn was struggling through the fog, Hancock's Corps advanced to repeat Upton's tactics on a larger scale. The attack was led by Barlow's Division, forming on open ground which extended up to the enemy's trenches. The division advanced in column for several hundred yards without firing a shot and pushing through the Confederate pickets. Half way to their objective the men gave a cheer and broke into double time. They swarmed into the hostile trenches and, after a desperate but brief struggle, carried the enemy line. Birney's Division, advancing through the woods on Barlow's right, reached the objective at about the same time. Nearly 4,000 prisoners were taken, including nearly the whole of Johnson's Division of Ewell's Corps. But the two Federal divisions, disorganised in pursuit, came up against a fresh line of breastworks half a mile further on, and as there had again been no adequate provision to exploit success, they were repulsed and followed up by the Confederates in a counter-attack.[64]

The last Federal attempt at an assault with masses of troops was at the Battle of Cold Harbor on 3rd June 1864. Long, who was there, writes of it: 'The battle that succeeded was one of the most desperately contested and murderous engagements of the war. Along the whole Federal line a simultaneous assault was made on the Confederate works, and at every point with the same disastrous result. Rank after rank was swept away until the column of assault was almost annihilated. Attack after attack was made, and men fell in myriads before the murderous fire from the Confederate line. . . . In the brief space of one hour the bloody battle of the 3rd of June was over, and 13,000 dead and wounded Federals lay in front of the lines behind which little more than 1,000 of the Confederate force had fallen.

'A few hours afterwards orders were sent to the corps commanders to renew the assault. . . . Though the orders to advance were given, not a man stirred. The troops stood silent, but immovable, presenting in this unmistakable protest the verdict of the rank and file against the murderous work decided on by their commanders.'[65]

Swinton, who was also there but as a correspondent, writes: 'The manner of the attack ordered was of the kind so often made in the course of this campaign—a general assault along the whole front of six miles, to be made at half-past four in the morning.

'Next morning, with the first grey light of dawn struggling through the clouds, the preparations began: from behind the rude parapets there was an upstarting, a springing to arms, the muffled commands of officers forming the line. The attack was ordered for half-past four, and it may have been five minutes after that, or it may have been ten minutes, but it was certainly not later than forty-five minutes past four, when the whole line was in motion, and the dark hollows between the armies were lit up with the fires of death.

'It took hardly more than ten minutes of the figment men call time to decide the battle. There was along the whole line a rush—the spectacle of impregnable works—a bloody loss—then a sullen falling back, and the action was *decided*.'[66]

Swinton gives the same story as Long about the men refusing to attack again, and approximately the same estimate of casualties.

On 15th June 1864 General 'Baldy' Smith advanced with his Corps to the attack of Petersburg. In view of the strength of the Confederate defences he considered that to assault the works in column would entail too many casualties, and he decided therefore to try a heavy line of skirmishers. Towards 7 pm, therefore, a cloud of skirmishers advanced from his three divisions, whilst the remaining troops waited in line of battle to exploit success. The skirmishers, faced by only an inconsiderable body of defenders, carried the lines, but it was by then dark and Smith decided not to try and exploit. By the next morning it was too late, for the Confederates had reinforced, and Cold Harbor had taught a bitter lesson.

Miles, who had done so well with Hancock's skirmish line at Chancellorsville was now a Brigadier-General. On 26th July 1864 he used the skirmish line of his brigade alone to capture four guns. The distribution between skirmish line and main body is interesting. At this time the brigade consisted of the 61st New York, 2nd New York Heavy Artillery, 81st, 140th, and 183rd Pennsylvania, 26th Michigan, 28th Massachusetts, and 5th New Haven. Of these eight regiments, three were under the command of Colonel J. C. Lynch to form the skirmish line: 183rd Pennsylvania, 28th Massachusetts, and 26th Michigan.[67] The regiments were probably of various strengths, but the 183rd Pennsylvania was a new regiment, only completed in March 1864, so that probably half the brigade strength was in the skirmish line. As an attack formation, the column was probably about dead in the Army of the Potomac.

Notes

1   Quoted by Major-General J. F. C. Fuller, *The Generalship of Ulysses S. Grant, 1929*
2   William Swinton, *Campaigns of the Army of the Potomac, 1866*
3   Colonel Theodore Lyman, *Meade's Headquarters 1863–1865*; Letters, Massachusetts Historical Society, 1922
4   Lieutenant-Colonel A. J. L. Fremantle, *The Fremantle Diary*; ed. Walter Lord, 1956
5   Lieutenant-Colonel Garnet Wolseley, *A Month's Visit to the Confederate Headquarters*, Blackwood's Magazine, Jan. 1863

6   Lyman, op. cit.
7   Swinton, op. cit.
8   Lyman, op. cit.
9   Jack Coggins, *Arms and Equipment of the Civil War,* 1962. J. R. Sypher, *History of the Pennsylvania Reserve Corps,* 1865.
10 B. H. Liddell Hart, *Sherman*
11 General William T. Sherman, *Memoirs,* 1875
12 ibid.
13 Lyman, op. cit.
14 Sherman, op. cit.
15 Swinton, op. cit., A. L. Long, *Memoirs of Robert E. Lee,* 1887
16 Frederick H. Dyer, *A Compendium of the War of the Rebellion,* 1908
17 Colonel G. F. R. Henderson, *Stonewall Jackson,* 1898
18 Long, op. cit.
19 Major-General J. F. C. Fuller, *The Generalship of Ulysses S. Grant,* 1929
20 Sherman, op. cit.
21 Coggins, op. cit.
22 Fuller, op. cit.
23 Clifford Dowdey, *Lee,* 1970
24 Colonel H. C. B. Rogers, *Weapons of the British Soldier,* 1960.
25 Sherman, op. cit.
26 Bell Irvin Wiley, Introduction to *A Compendium of the War of the Rebellion,* 1959 edition
27 Lyman, op. cit.
28 Sherman, op. cit.
29 James Longstreet, *From Manassas to Appomattox,* 1896
    Swinton, op. cit.
30 Longstreet, op. cit.
30 Longstreet, op. cit.
31 Dowdey, op. cit.
32 ibid.
33 Fremantle, op. cit.
34 Coggins, op. cit.
35 Sherman, op. cit.
36 Lyman, op. cit.
37 Quoted by Henderson, op. cit.
38 Henderson, op. cit.
39 Wolseley, op. cit.
40 Fremantle, op. cit.
41 Lyman, op. cit.
42 Long, op. cit.
43 ibid.
44 ibid.
45 Fremantle, op. cit.
46 Colonel H. C. B. Rogers, *The Pageant of Heraldry,* 1955
47 Fremantle, op. cit.
48 Sherman, op. cit.
49 Fuller, op. cit.
50 ibid.
51 Sherman, op. cit.

52 Henderson, op. cit.
53 Fuller, op. cit.
54 Swinton, op. cit.
55 Sherman, op. cit.
56 Swinton, op. cit.
57 ibid.
58 Long, op. cit.
59 ibid.
60 Fuller, op. cit.
61 Lyman, op. cit.
62 Swinton, op. cit.
    General E. P. Alexander, *Military Memoirs of a Confederate*, 1907.
63 Bruce Catton, *Grant Takes Command*, 1968
64 Swinton, op. cit.
65 Long, op. cit.
66 Swinton, op. cit.
67 ibid.
    Dyer, op. cit.

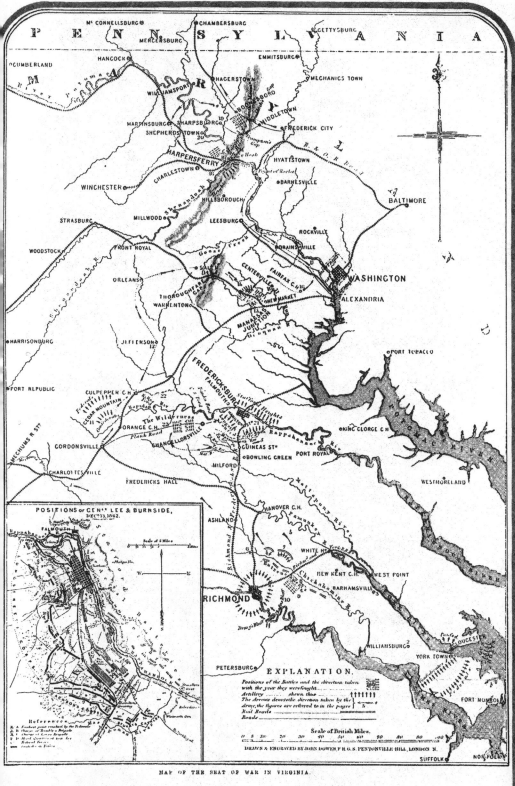

MAP OF THE SEAT OF WAR IN VIRGINIA.

Map showing the battles fought in Virginia and Maryland up to and including Chancellorsville. [Illustrated London News]

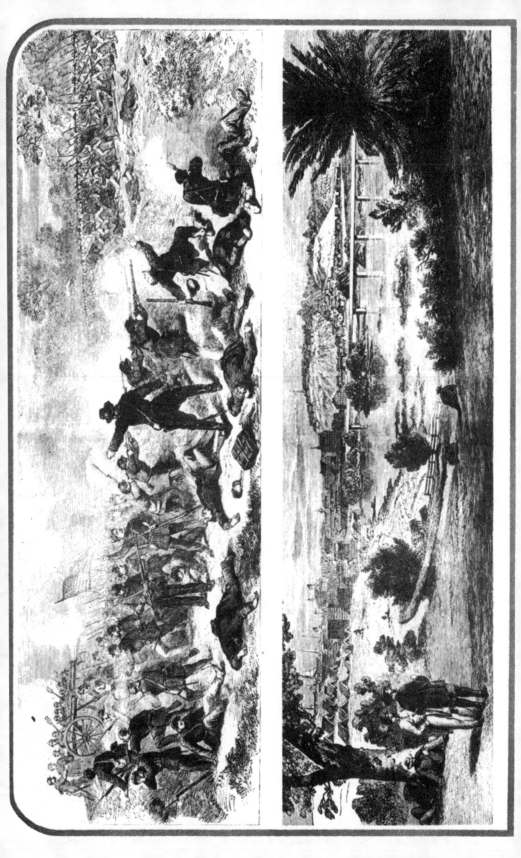

OPPOSITE PAGE:

TOP: *The Second Battle of Manassas, by Frank Vizetelly.* [Illustrated London News] The description given by the Illustrated London News of the episode depicted is as follows: *"The Last Stand made by the Federals at Manassas"* . . . refers to the last disastrous days of the command of the vainglorious Pope, when the Federals were driven back from the Rapidan upon Arlington Heights opposite Washington. Our artist writes hereupon:—

"The Yankee army, towards the close of the day, sought refuge in a gully near the Alexandria and Orange Railroad. For some hours they fought against the Confederates, who used stones and rocks, their ammunition being exhausted. The Confederates kept the Federals off, and eventually remained masters of the field. The engraving shows the division of General Longstreet charging with the bayonet against the masses assembled to stay the triumphant progress of the Southern arms". BOTTOM: *View of Richmond, Virginia, by Frank Vizetelly.* [Illustrated London News] The Illustrated London News says of this drawing, 'The *"View of Richmond from the West"* . . . shows the picturesque site of this city, climbing as it does the hills which skirt the north bank of the James River. The railroad bridge given in the Engraving connects the city with its chief suburb, Manchester.'

LEFT: *An enlarged section of the Plate at the top of the page opposite. It shows one soldier ramming down the charge in his muzzle-loading rifle and another inserting the percussion cap.* [Illustrated London News]

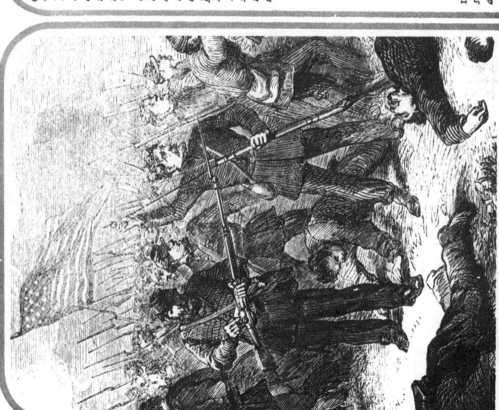

Federal soldiers in conversation. Note the types of uniform worn and the piled percussion rifles with triangular bayonets. The rifles appear to be the U.S. 'Springfield'. [U.S. Signal Corps photo No. III-B-157 (Brady Collection) in the National Archives.

Officers of the 164th and 170th New York Infantry. Both regiments were closely associated throughout their service. They both served in a brigade commanded by General M. Corcoran, and later in his division whence the first acquired the title of 'Corcoran Guard' and the second that of the '4th Corcoran legion'. Both were posted to the 4th Brigade, 2nd Division, II Corps, of the Army of the Potomac in May 1864 and took part in the campaign under Grant. The different types of uniforms and headresses, and also the swords and methods of wearing them are of interest. No two officers appear to be dressed alike! [U.S. Signal Corps photo No. III-B-253 (Brady Collection) in the National Archives]

Company B, 9th Mississippi Infantry, C.S.A., at Pensacola, Florida, in 1861. Note the peculiar mixture of dress, and the cross and waist belts and long sword bayonets which two of the men are wearing. [The Museum of the Confederacy, Richmond, Virginia]

A Confederate regiment in camp near Mobile. [The Museum of the Confederacy Richmond, Virginia]

The Federal advance on Centreville, by Frank Vizetelly. The occasion was the evacuation of Centreville by the Confederate army under General J. E. Johnston, on 8th March 1862. William Swinton (Campaigns of the Army of the Potomac) says that, 'so skilfully was the enterprise managed, that the first intimation thereof gained by the Union forces was the smoke of the burning huts, fired by the Confederates on their retirment.' Note the march formation of the Federal infantry. [Illustrated London News]

Confederate cavalrymen taken prisoner by the Federals at the cavalry battle of Brandy Station on 9th June 1863, and shown here at Fairfax Court House, some 15 miles west of Alexandria. The soldiers on the extreme right and left are the Federal guards. [U.S. War Dept General Staff photo No. 165-SB-34 in the National Archives]

Captain E. A. Flint of the 1st Massachusetts Cavalry in November 1864. Horse and rider took part in a charge at Gettysburg against the Confederate cavalry. The regiment was in the 1st Brigade, 2nd Division, Cavalry Corps, of the Army of the Potomac. Note the standard McClellan pattern saddle. [U.S. Signal Corps photo No. 111-BA-1964 (Brady Collection) in the National Archives]

THE CIVIL WAR IN AMERICA: RECONNAISSANCE MADE BY GENERAL STONEMAN, ACCOMPANIED BY THE COMTE DE PARIS AND THE DUC DE CHARTRES, TO CEDAR RUN.—FROM A SKETCH BY OUR SPECIAL ARTIST.—SEE NEXT PAGE.

COMTE DE PARIS.   GENERAL STONEMAN.
DUC DE CHARTRES.

A Federal reconnaissance force, illustrated by Frank Vizetelly. [Illustrated London News]. The Illustrated London News has the following comment on this sketch: 'On the 14th inst. (i.e. 14th March 1862), immediately after the occupation of Manassas Junction by the Federalists, a strong reconnaissance of cavalry and infantry, under the command of General Stoneman, accompanied by the two Orleanist Princes, started on the track of the retreating Secessionists. They pushed on as far as Cedar Run, about twenty-seven miles from the junction, driving in the enemy's pickets which they fell in with in the neighbourhood. The subject chosen for illustration . . . is the halt of the party and examination of escaped contrabands (slaves) from Gordonsville, the present head-quarters of the Confederate army of the Potomac.' (Johnston's army was at that time so-called.)

THE CIVIL WAR IN AMERICA: ADVANCED POST OF GENERAL BLENKER'S DIVISION SURPRISED AT ANANDALE, VIRGINIA, BY CONFEDERATE CAVALRY.—FROM A SKETCH BY OUR SPECIAL ARTIST

An attack by Confederate cavalry, by Frank Vizetelly. [Illustrated London News]. The Illustrated London News describes this incident as follows: 'Our Special Artist (i.e. Vizetelly) in the Federal camp, visiting the advanced posts on 12th ult. (i.e. 12th December 1861), came upon General Blenker's pickets at Anandale, about ten miles from Washington. Whilst he was in the neighbourhood a dash was made at them by a squadron of Confederate cavalry—fine, rough-looking fellows, dressed in nondescript uniforms, red shirts, grey tunics; some with boots and some without; armed with sabres and revolvers. Many of them were very powerfully built, and as they rushed in among the men of the 45th New York they clutched at them and dragged thirteen off at a gallop. Three or four were killed on each side. An Engraving of this dashing attack, from a sketch by our Special Artist, is given...'. (Brigadier-General Louis Blenker was commanding a division in which the 45th New York ('5th German Rifles') was one of the infantry regiments.)

General J. E. B. Stuart with his headquarters detachment, illustrated by Frank Vizetelly. [Illustrated London News] The Illustrated London News description of this illustration reads: 'Our Special Artist in America has sent to us an Illustration . . . showing the Confederate scouting party under General Stuart, skirmishing with a portion of General Pope's army in the neighbourhood of Culpeper Courthouse. General Stuart's fame reached England after his marvellous raid round the extreme right of M'Clellan's army, whilst the latter was threatening Richmond. It is unnecessary to remind our readers of this gallant dash, which will take its place in the history of cavalry tactics. Probably many will be surprised at the rough and worn appearance of the men, especially when they are told that many of the privates are worth from 50,000 to 100,000 dollars each. The rudeness of their equipments, consisting mainly of old rusty sabres and shot-guns, is in a great degree owing to the blockade, which shuts them out of the market of good carbines and fine-tempered blades. As it is, they are the finest irregular body of horse in the world.' (Note the Confederate standard carried by the orderly and the ornate headdress of the trumpeter.)

CHAPTER THREE

Cavalry

BOTH SIDES WERE AGREED that during the first part of the war the Confederate cavalry was far better than that of the Union Army. General W. T. Sherman gave an opinion of the former in an appreciation of the post-war problems of reconstruction which he wrote on 17th September 1863. In an analysis of the various classes of people in the Confederate States he included, 'The young bloods of the South: sons of planters, lawyers about towns, good billiard-players and sportsmen, men who never did work and never will. War suits them, and the rascals are brave, fine riders, bold to rashness, and dangerous subjects in every sense. They care not a sou for negroes, land, or anything. They hate Yankees *per se*, and don't bother their brains about the past, present, or future. As long as they have good horses, plenty of forage, and an open country, they are happy. This is a larger class then most men suppose, and they are the most dangerous set of men that this war has turned loose upon the world. They are splendid riders, first-rate shots, and utterly reckless. Stewart, John Morgan, Forrest, and Jackson, are the types and leaders of this class. These men must all be killed or employed before we can hope for peace. They have no property or future, and therefore cannot be influenced by anything, except personal considerations. I have two brigades of these fellows in my front, commanded by Cosby, of the old army, and Whitfield, of Texas. Stephen D. Lee is in command of the whole. I have frequent interviews with their officers, a good understanding with them, and am inclined to think, when the resources of their country are exhausted, we must employ them. They are the best cavalry in the world, but it will tax Mr Chase's genius for finance to supply them with horses. At present horses cost them nothing; for they take where they find, and don't bother their brains as to who is to pay for them; the same may be said of the cornfields, which have, as they believe, been cultivated by a good-natured people for their special benefit.'[1]

49

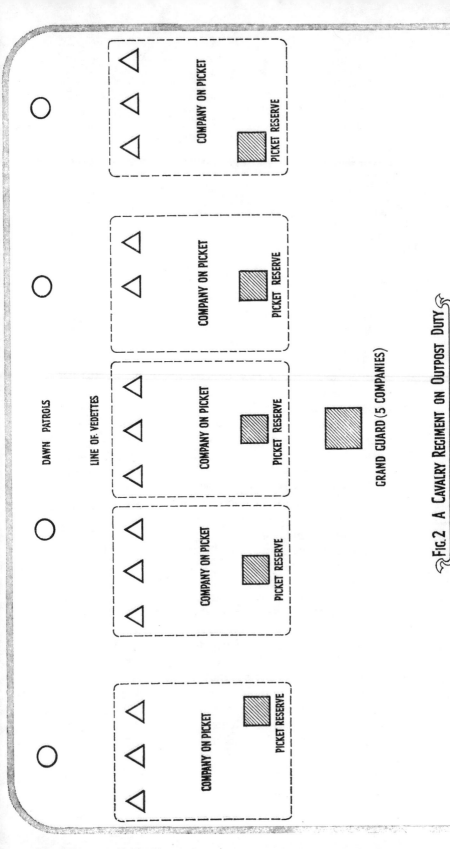

Fig. 2 A Cavalry Regiment on Outpost Duty

Sherman's views on the relative value of Confederate and Federal cavalry had not changed a year later. On 29th September 1864 he telegraphed from Atlanta to Halleck, Army Chief of Staff, 'I take it for granted that Forrest will cut our road. . . . His cavalry will travel a hundred miles where ours will ten. . . . Hood now rests twenty-four miles south. . . . I can whip his infantry, but his cavalry is to be feared.' And on 9th October he telegraphed Grant, 'It will be a physical impossibility to protect the roads, now that Hood, Forrest, Wheeler, and the whole batch of devils, are turned loose without home or habitation.[2]

Later Sherman commented: 'On the 31st of October (1864) Forrest made his appearance on the Tennessee River opposite Johnsonville (whence a new railroad led to Nashville), and with his cavalry and fieldpieces actually crippled and captured two gunboats with five of our transports, a feat of arms which, I confess, excited my admiration.'[3]

Wolesley, in his account of his visit to the Confederate Army, gave his opinion of the cavalry on both sides; but as Wolesley notoriously exaggerated the defects of anything of which he disapproved, his comments on the Federal horsemen must be treated with some reserve. He wrote: 'Of the cavalry I saw but little, as General Steuart had left for his raid into Pennsylvania the day I reached headquarters, and only returned a couple of days before I commenced my homeward journey. I did remark, however, that all the men rode well, in which particular they present a striking contrast to the Northern cavalry, who can scarcely sit their horses even when trotting. Indeed, I have no doubt but that all who have seen the Northern troopers on duty in Washington, will agree with me in thinking them the greatest scarecrows under the name of cavalry that they ever saw. Apropos of them: a Southern lady told me that on one occasion, when jesting with a Northern officer about the inability of his troopers to contend with the Southern "chivalry", although the latter were not half so numerous, he said, "What can we do? we can never catch them; for whilst we are opening the gates they are all over the fences." Every white man in the South rides from childhood and consequently is at home in the saddle; whereas to be on horseback is a most disagreeable position for a Yankee, and one in which he rarely trusts himself. In the North thousands keep horses, but only to drive them. "What is the use of having good roads if you don't drive on them," they say. To have a horse that can trot a mile in two minutes forty seconds, is the pride of the New Englander; but a good fencer would be as useless to him as an elephant. The troopers in the Southern cavalry have their own horses; and upon the breaking out of the war they provided themselves with arms as well. Sabres have since been issued to them by the Government, and they have mostly armed themselves with carbines and revolvers taken from their discomforted brethren of the North. Their knowledge of drill is limited, and altogether their constitution resembles much that of our irregular Indian cavalry.'[4]

However, by the latter stages of the war the best of the Federal cavalry were very good indeed.

Organisation

In the pre-War United States Army there were five regiments of cavalry, the 1st and 2nd Dragoons, the 1st Mounted Rifles, and the 1st and 2nd Cavalry. The last two of these regiments were raised in 1855, to protect the great acquisition of territory after the Mexican War. In these two regiments were officers who were destined to achieve fame in the Civil War. Colonel E. V. Sumner, commanding the 1st Cavalry, was later commander of the II Corps in the Army of the Potomac; and the second-in-command of the regiment was Brevet-Colonel J. E. Johnston, who became, next to Lee, probably the most able of the Confederate generals. The 2nd Cavalry were commanded by Colonel A. S. Johnston who was killed whilst commanding the Confederate forces at the Battle of Shiloh. His second-in-command was Brevet-Colonel R. E. Lee, later the brilliant Commander of the Confederate Army of Northern Virginia. The 2nd Cavalry could probably boast of having more officers who were to distinguish themselves in the Civil War than any other unit. Besides A. S. Johnston and Lee, there were Hardee (Confederate corps commander), Thomas (commander of the Federal Army of the Cumberland and victor of the Battle of Nashville), Hood (the Confederate commander whom Thomas defeated at Nashville), Van Dorn (Confederate general in the West), Fitz Lee (Confederate cavalry general), Stoneman (commander of the Cavalry Corps in the Federal Army of the Potomac), and Kirby Smith (wounded while commanding a Confederate brigade at the Battle of Bull Run).[5] On 4th May 1861 a sixth cavalry regiment, the 3rd Cavalry was formed. In spite of their titles these cavalry regiments were all organised and trained in the same way, and they were therefore renamed, in the above order, 1st to 6th Cavalry.

A United States cavalry regiment was originally organised into five squadrons of two companies each. On the formation of the 3rd Cavalry in 1861 another squadron of two more companies was added. The twelve-company organisation was thereafter adopted for the volunteer regiments of the Federal Army, but the squadron was dropped and, instead, battalions of, usually, four companies were formed when a regiment was required to find detachments. The company and battalion nomenclature was logical because the cavalry usually fought as dragoons, or mounted infantry.

A Federal cavalry regiment was commanded by a colonel with a lieutenant-colonel as second-in-command and there were three majors who were available to command battalions if these were required. On the regimental headquarters there were three officers, usually lieutenants, to fill the appointments of adjutant, quartermaster, and comissary, and there were also a surgeon and his assistant. The regimental headquarters also included a sergeant-major, quartermaster-sergeant, commissary sergeant, saddler sergeant, chief farrier or blacksmith, and two hospital stewards. A company consisted of a captain, 1st lieutenant, 2nd lieutenant, 1st sergeant, quartermaster-sergeant, commissary sergeant, 5 sergeants, 8 corporals, 2 teamsters, 2 farriers, 1 saddler, 1 waggoner, 2 musicians, and about 70 privates.[6]

The organisation of a Confederate cavalry regiment was very similar, but there were only ten companies and only one major. A company had an additional 2nd lieutenant, 5 sergeants, only 4 corporals, 1 farrier, and 1 blacksmith.[7]

In both the Confederate and Federal Armies cavalry regiments were grouped in brigades and, when required, in cavalry divisions and corps. In the Federal Army the cavalry brigades, like the infantry brigades, were not permanent and regiments were often moved from one brigade to another.[8] In the Confederate Army regiments were not generally moved between brigades (though this did happen more often than in the infantry) and the brigades, composed mostly of regiments from the same State, were fairly permanent bodies. The most usual strength of a Confederate cavalry brigade was five regiments, but there could be six or as few as two.[9] Federal cavalry brigades varied between six and three regiments.[10] There were, in addition, some interesting mixed formations. For instance, on 28th April 1862 a so-called 'Flying Brigade' was formed in McCall's Division of McDowell's Corps. It was composed of the 1st Pennsylvania Cavalry, the 1st New Jersey Cavalry, and four companies of the 13th Pennsylvania Infantry (1st Rifles)—a regiment which had been raised and trained as 'rifle skirmishers'. The brigade was intended for outpost and reconnaissance duties, but it was such a useful formation that it was detached to join in the pursuit of 'Stonewall' Jackson up the Shenandoah Valley after his defeat of Banks at Front Royal and Winchester.[11] This combination of cavalry and rifles is an interesting precursor of the British armoured brigade with its cavalry regiments and rifle battalion.

In the Gettysburg campaign the Confederate General J. E. B. Stuart's famous Cavalry Division of the Army of Northern Virginia was organised into six brigades: Wade Hampton's (1st North Carolina, 1st South Carolina, 2nd South Carolina, Cobb's Georgian Legion, Jeff Davis's Legion, and Phillips's Georgian Legion), Robertson's (4th North

Carolina, and 5th North Carolina), Fitz Lee's (1st Maryland Battalion, 1st Virginia, 2nd Virginia, 3rd Virginia, 4th Virginia, and 5th Virginia), Jenkin's (14th Virginia, 16th Virginia, 17th Virginia, 34th Virginia Battalion, and 36th Virginia Battalion), Jones's (6th Virginia, 7th Virginia, 11th Virginia, 12th Virginia, and 35th Virginia Battalion), and W. H. F. Lee's (2nd North Carolina, 9th Virginia, 10th Virginia, 13th Virginia, and 15th Virginia).[12] The units designated 'battalion' and 'legion' were on a lower establishment than the others, which were all 'regiments'.

At the same period the Cavalry Corps of the Army of the Potomac, commanded by General A. Pleasanton was organised into three divisions each of three brigades. The 2nd Brigade of the 1st Division was a very small one, consisting only of the 6th New York Cavalry, 17th Pennsylvania Cavalry, and Companies A and C of the 3rd West Virginia Cavalry. The third brigade of the 1st Division was designated a 'Reserve' Brigade and was only attached; it was obviously something of an élite force because it consisted, except for the 6th Pennsylvania Cavalry, of Regular regiments: the 1st, 2nd, 5th, and 6th US Cavalry.[13]

Some indication of the number of peacetime horsemen in the Northern States is perhaps given by the relative numbers of cavalry and infantry regiments raised. Examples are: Indiana, 13 cavalry and 152 infantry; Illinois, 17 cavalry and 156 infantry; Iowa, 9 cavalry and 51 infantry; Kentucky, 17 cavalry and 55 infantry; Massachusetts, 5 cavalry and 71 infantry; Michigan, 11 cavalry and 35 infantry; Missouri, 32 cavalry and 266 infantry; New York, 32 cavalry and 254 infantry; Ohio, 13 cavalry and 227 infantry; Pennsylvania, 28 cavalry and 258 infantry; Tennessee, 20 cavalry and 23 infantry.[14]

In the Western Federal armies regiments of mounted infantry were frequently included with cavalry regiments in cavalry brigades. The following are examples: the 4th Kentucky Infantry Regiment, reorganised as mounted infantry in spring 1864, after veteran furlough; the 17th Indiana Infantry Regiment, mounted in February 1863 and armed with Spencer carbines, and then dismounted again in November 1864; the 72nd Indiana Infantry Regiment, mounted in March 1863 and dismounted in November 1864; the 9th Illinois Infantry Regiment, mounted March 1863; the 92nd Illinois Infantry Regiment, mounted March 1863; the 98th Illinois Infantry Regiment, mounted March 1863 and armed with Spencer carbines; and the 123rd Illinois Infantry Regiment, mounted in March 1863, armed with Spencer carbines, and dismounted again in November 1864.[15] It will be observed that Illinois and Indiana were particularly favoured for mounted infantry, which suggests that maximum use had not been made in those States of men who could ride.

Brief mention was made in Chapter Two of the Pennsylvania Reserve

Corps, and this quite unique body of the Union Army included units of all three fighting arms. When Lincoln issued his first call for 75,000 men for three months service the quota of regiments allotted to Pennsylvania was 14, but the State voluntarily raised this number to 25. Indeed the far-sighted Governor Curtin of Pennsylvania foresaw that the army planned by the President would prove quite inadequate. On 20th April 1861 he convened the State legislature and recommended that as Pennsylvania's long borders with disaffected States needed a well-organised military force to protect them, they should raise immediately at least fifteen regiments of cavalry and infantry, exclusive of the units they had provided for the United States.

As a result of the Governor's recommendation a Bill was passed by the State Legislature authorising the organisation of 'the Reserve Corps of the Commonwealth, and to be composed of thirteen regiments of infantry, one regiment of cavalry, and one regiment of light artillery. The said regiments shall . . . be enlisted in the service of the State for a period not exceeding three years or for the war . . . and further to be liable to be mustered into the service of the United States at such times as requisitions may be made by the President of the United States.'

These regiments were eventually accepted into the service of the Union just before the Battle of Bull Run, but not in time to take part in it. They were soon organised into a division of three brigades, and unlike the great majority of Federal infantry brigades these remained together and the units of the Pennsylvania Reserve had a very strong corporate *esprit de corps*. The cavalry regiment was the 1st Pennsylvania, already mentioned in connection with the 'Flying Brigade', and the 13th Pennsylvania Infantry which supplied four companies for that brigade also belonged to the Reserve Corps.[16] The foundation of the Corps furnishes a very interesting example of the powers of State Governors in raising troops— though the troops so raised were not supposed to serve outside the State borders unless mustered into the service of the United States.

Weapons

The weapons carried by the cavalry of both sides were very similar, and consisted generally of one or more of the following: rifle or carbine (or initially even a shot gun), revolver, and sabre. The 1st Pennsylvania Cavalry, for instance, started off with a sabre and pistol for each man and ten carbines to each company; eventually every man had a carbine.[17] Several Confederate regiments were armed with the lance in the early stages of the war because of the shortage of sabres. Lances were manu-factured by local artisans.[18] One Federal regiment, the 6th Pennsylvania Cavalry (Rush's Lancers) was also armed with lances until May 1863[19] and

Company C of this regiment charged a Confederate picket line near Hanover Court House with this weapon on 24th May 1862. Units organised by Bedford Forrest in 1862 for the Confederate Army in the West had all too few arms, and at least half the men were equipped with shot guns and squirrel rifles.[20]

In the Western theatre of war, Fremantle noted that the Confederate 51st Alabama Cavalry were all armed uniformly with long rifles and revolvers but did not carry sabres. He does not specify the type of rifle, but the British Enfield was a great favourite with the Southern Cavalry. Fremantle says that in the Army of Northern Virginia the cavalry did carry sabres, but that they had little idea how to use them and much preferred their carbines and revolvers. He adds that they habitually rode with their swords between the left leg and the saddle.[21]

The Enfield, of course, was a muzzle-loader; but most of the Federal carbines were breech-loaders. Initially the majority were single shot weapons, but in the later stages of the war the Federal cavalry were armed throughout with the Spencer magazine carbine. With their short barrels, carbines were handier than rifles for use on horseback, but they were far less accurate; and for this reason the Confederate cavalry in the West, who normally fought as mounted infantry, preferred rifles. Butler's South Carolina Cavalry Brigade, which joined Lee's army in May 1864, was armed with rifles and the men were very expert in their use. As part of a composite cavalry division under Fitz Lee, one and a half regiments of the South Carolinians gave the Federals such a nasty shock at the action of Haw's Shop on 28th May 1864 that the Federal cavalry commander estimated them as 4,000 mounted infantry.[22]

Towards the end of the war there was a great shortage of arms for the Confederate cavalry and General R. E. Lee wrote in a circular letter on 25th January 1865 that, 'To arm and equip an additional force of cavalry there is a need of carbines, revolvers, pistols, saddles, and other accoutrements of mounted men. Arms and equipment of the kind desired are believed to be held by citizens in sufficient numbers to supply our wants. . . . They are needed to enable our cavalry to cope with the well-armed and equipped cavalry of the enemy. . . . I therefore urge all persons not in the service to deliver promptly to some of the officers designated below such arms and equipments (especially those suitable for cavalry) as they may have. . . .'

Dress, Equipment, and Horses

The comments made on the respective dress of the infantry of the opposing armies are applicable in general to the cavalry. At the same time, the Confederate horsemen were usually better clad than the foot soldiers because their clothing was not subject to the same hard usage and their long riding boots did not often wear out. Cavalry officers in the Confederate Army, particularly the younger ones, often affected a somewhat dandified dress, with western type hats adorned with long feathers or plumes, and with the front of their jackets bedecked with much yellow braid. The official uniform of officers and men was faced with yellow—yellow collar and cuffs and a yellow stripe down the trouser leg. The képi was an official headdress for both sides; as worn by Confederate cavalry it had a yellow top, but in the later stages of the war it had been almost universally replaced by some sort of broad-brimmed hat.

The standard saddle in the Federal cavalry was the McClellan pattern which had been adopted by the US cavalry in 1858. It was designed by George B. McClellan, first commander of the Army of the Potomac. The saddle tree was made of wood (either beech or poplar), with a leather seat over a black rawhide cover and with iron gullet and cantle plates. (The former is a curved metal plate reinforcing the wooden pommel, whilst the latter is at the curved arch at the back of the saddle tree.) The stirrups were of wood with leather hoods. The girth was peculiar to British eyes. It was known as a 'cinch', and at each end of it was a ring which was connected by straps to the pommel and cantle of the saddle. Under the saddle there was blanket. A deep carbine boot hung diagonally on the offside. The trooper had to sit very upright and probably could not exert as much grip as with contemporary British saddles.[23] Saddle bags were standard, and blanket roll, poncho, etc were attached by straps to the saddle.[24] Lyman says that the Federal cavalrymen were almost obscured by the bags of oats and the blankets and coats piled on pommel and crupper; whilst their carbines hung on one side and their sabres on the other.

McClellan wrote a letter from Europe in 1856 which shows the origin of the saddle. He said that he had decided on a saddle 'adapted from the Prussian Hungarian Saddle'.[25] The McClellan saddle (also known as the 'American saddle') was, with slight variations, used up till the time that horses disappeared from the US Cavalry.[26] According to Lyman it was almost impossible to rise at the trot in one of these saddles, and he records British officers, visiting the Army of the Potomac, and trying to do so.[27] The Confederates also used this type of saddle but a large proportion of their saddles were imported, including many of the flat or English pattern. The McClellan saddle was purchased in large numbers by the British Army during the Boer War, but it was never very popular with the British soldier on account of the unfamiliar cinch fastenings which it had.[28]

At the start of the war horsemastership in most Federal cavalry regiments, not perhaps surprisingly, was poor, and sore backs and other troubles became all too prevalent. The trouble was that in many cavalry regiments a large proportion of the officers were as ignorant as the men. However, by being made to walk and lead their horses when backs were sore and other measures, green troopers learned to look after their mounts and to the proper fitting of their saddlery.[29]

The horses used by the cavalry of both sides fall roughly into two groups. The first was the Eastern horse, which was bred from parents brought up in Virginia or Kentucky, or imported from Europe. The second has been variously described as the Texan, Mustang, or Bronco, and was bred on the Western plains. It was also sometimes called the Indian Pony. It was descended from horses brought from Spain to what is now Mexico; they bred rapidly and, running wild, spread northwards. It is an ugly horse, standing about 14.2 hands, but it is very active and has great endurance.[30]

Henderson says of the Virginian cavalrymen that: 'Their horses were their own, scions of good Virginian stock, with the blood of many a well-known sire . . . in their veins. . . .' He comments that: 'Every great plantation had its pack of hounds, and fox-hunting, an heirloom from the English colonists, still flourished. His stud was the pride of every Southern gentleman, and the love of horse-flesh was inherent in the whole population. No man walked when he could ride, and hundreds of fine horsemen, mounted on steeds of famous lineage, recruited the Confederate squadrons.'[31]

The Virginian cavalry, and doubtless all other cavalry recruited from at least the eastern side of the Confederacy, were therefore mounted on horses of the hunter type. It is probable that the regiments raised in the more western areas had the Texan horse, a breed which had been widely used already in the US cavalry. Federal regiments, as regards their horses, were probably similarly divided, though obtaining sufficient saddle horses of any type presented considerable difficulties in the North. The 1st Pennsylvania Cavalry, one of the regiments of the crack Reserve Corps, was, as might be expected, exceptionally well mounted. J. R. Sypher says: 'Nearly all the original horses were selected with great care and purchased by some of the officers of the regiment in the State of Pennsylvania; the remainder were selected by Colonel Bayard from the Government horses at Washington. These horses, under good care and training during the succeeding winter, became, notably the best horses in the United States service; some of them were accounted the best in the regiment, after five new lots had been worn out in its campaigns. The original team horses, performed all the labour of the regiment for more than two years, and still were the most hardy regimental teams in the cavalry service in the army of the Potomac.' These horses were ridden too by competent men, for, continues Sypher, 'This regiment was composed of the choicest materials in the State of Pennsylvania; the Governor refused all applications for the formation of cavalry companies from large towns and cities. The companies were recruited wholly from the rural districts of a large State, at a time when infantry was the favourite arm of the service. The men, therefore, who joined the regiment, chose the cavalry service, for the love of it, and because they were practical horsemen. They were mostly country labourers and farmers accustomed to the use and care of horses, and at least good, if not properly trained riders.'[32]

The shortage of horses in the North is shown by a statement by William O. Studdard, a member of the White House Secretariat when Grant was appointed General-in-Chief. Abraham Lincoln told him: 'When Grant took hold I was waiting to see what his pet impossibility would be, and I reckoned it would be cavalry as a matter of course, for we hadn't horses enough to mount even what men we had. There were fifteen thousand or thereabouts up near Harper's Ferry and no horses to put them on. Well, the other day, just as I expected, Grant sent to me about those very men; but what he wanted to know was whether he should disband them or turn 'em into infantry.'[33] There was great difficulty in the latter part of the war in keeping the cavalry in the field mounted. During the fighting at Spotsylvania in 1864 General Sheridan was ordered to operate against Lee's communications, but, says Swinton, 'the dismounted men of the Army of the Potomac and those with worn and jaded animals' were ordered to remain and guard the Army's baggage and supply trains. They amounted to nearly one half of the Army's cavalry.[34] The Confederate cavalry in Virginia, towards the end of the war, suffered more from lack of proper forage than from shortage of horses. A Confederate cavalry officer wrote from the Shenandoah Valley in August 1864, 'Our horses had been fed on nothing but hay for some time and were quite weak.'[35]

The Standards carried by the cavalry were smaller than the infantry Colours. Those of the Confederates, for instance, were 30 inches square as compared with the 48 inches of the 'battle flags' of the infantry. Cavalry Standards were also emblazoned with battle honours. After the action at Falmouth, near Fredericksburg in April 1862 the Governor of Pennsylvania ordered that 'Falmouth, 18th April, 1862' should be inscribed on the Standard of the 1st Pennsylvania Cavalry as a reward for its gallant conduct. This Standard, of the same design as the infantry Colours of the Pennsylvania Reserve Corps, was of blue silk, fringed with yellow, with in the centre the arms of the State surrounded by thirteen golden stars, and below it the number of the Regiment.[36]

Tactics and Tactical Employment

The most important duties of cavalry in the Civil War were undoubtedly reconnaissance and protection, and it was as outposts that cavalry were most valuable. A regiment forming an outpost would retain a reserve (called a 'grand guard') of anything up to half its strength, depending on the country and the length of front, whilst the remainder were disposed as a chain of pickets. Each picket retained a reserve and posted well out in front a sufficient number of vedettes (single sentries) to cover the sector allotted to it. Patrols were constantly on the move between various parts of the outpost system, and these were sent out before dawn, well in advance of the vedettes, to detect any early movement of the enemy.[37]

Long considered General J. E. B. Stuart, commanding the Confederate cavalry of the Army of Northern Virginia, to be unequalled as an outpost officer. 'Throughout a line of fifty miles his eye and hand were everywhere present; his pickets and scouts never slept; the movements of the enemy were immediately discovered and promptly reported to the commander-in-chief.'[38]

Jackson's cavalry in the Shenandoah Valley, under that remarkable young leader Colonel Turner Ashby, were very effectively employed from the start and established an early ascendancy over their Federal opponents. Of Ashby Henderson says: 'In command of a few hundred mounted riflemen and a section of horse artillery he was unsurpassed'.[39] Jackson established his cavalry outposts so far forward that they were virtually picketing the enemy troops, rather than his own. He expected them to provide such information about the enemy strength and dispositions as would enable him to deduce what the hostile commander intended to do. The secondary function and effect of this advanced screen was to prevent the enemy cavalry from obtaining any information about the Confederate dispositions and intentions.

Good as they were, however, Ashby's cavalry had no conception of military discipline, and their commander had no idea how to exert it. If worthwhile pillage came their way, the troopers might depart with their loot to deposit it in their homes, perhaps even one or two days distant, without ever thinking that their absence might harm their army or was in any way reprehensible.[40]

Lyman gives an interesting account of the cavalry of the Army of the Potomac in action in September 1863. He rode up to a little knoll where there was a picket reserve, with its horses tied to trees, and in front were the mounted vedettes, part of the chain which covered the whole front of the cavalry force. When the order was given to advance, columns of skirmishers rode through the picket line, deployed, and went forward at a brisk trot or canter, making, he says, a connected line as far as the eye could reach. Behind them came the supports in close order, followed by the field batteries.

Away in front he could see the Confederate vedettes. They, 'stared a few minutes, apparently without much curiosity, then turned tail and moved off, first at a walk, then at a trot, and finally disappeared over the ridge at a gallop.'

As the Federal cavalry approached, the Confederates opened fire with guns and later with rifles, to which the Federals, when they got near enough, replied with carbines. The Federal cavalry's advance brought them into wooded country where the Confederates stood on the defensive. The leading Federal regiments dismounted and moved forward into the woods; and here Lyman heard for the first time the celebrated Confederate yell, coming from troops holding the far side of a high bank covered with bushes. However this was only a rearguard position and the Federals drove their enemy out of the woods into the open country beyond.[41]

Fremantle says that in the Western theatre the Confederate cavalry normally fought dismounted, leaving one man in charge of each four horses whilst the remainder deployed as infantry skirmishers. On outpost, Confederate vedettes were posted at about 300 to 400 yards from each other. He gives the following admirable description of Confederate cavalry of General Polk's Corps in a typical dismounted action:

'We found General Martin giving orders for the withdrawal of the cavalry horses in the front and for the retreat of the skirmishers. It was very curious to see three hundred horses suddenly emerge from the wood just in front of us, where they had been hidden—one man to every four horses, riding one and leading the other three, which were tied together by their heads. In this order I saw them cross a cotton field at a smart trot, and take up a more secure position. Two or three men cantered about in the rear, flanking up the leading horses. They were shortly afterwards followed by the men of the regiments, retreating in skirmishing order under Colonel Webb, and they lined a fence parallel to us. The same thing went on on our right. . . . The way in which the horses were managed was very pretty. . . . They were never far from the men, who could mount and be off to another part of the field with rapidity, or retire to take up another position, or act as cavalry as the case may require.'[42]

Of the cavalry in the Army of Northern Virginia, Fremantle formed a rather different opinion; but it was an opinion largely based on the comments by Confederate officers of other arms, who thought that the cavalry waged a comparatively comfortable war. When the army was on the march towards Gettysburg, Fremantle suggested that it would be a good thing to have some cavalry present to follow up broken infantry.

(Lee at this time was without cavalry due to Stuart's unfortunate raid, which is mentioned below.) But Confederate officers told him that they did not think their cavalry capable of doing this. They regarded them as excellent at raiding and cutting communications, but said that they had no idea of charging infantry under any circumstances. Fremantle felt that the infantry and artillery of the Army of Northern Virginia did not respect the cavalry very much and he says that they often jeered at them. After the Battle of Gettysburg, during the withdrawal, Fremantle was critical of both Confederate and Federal cavalry. He writes: 'Cavalry skirmishing went on until quite dark, a determined attack having been made by the enemy, who did his best to prevent the trains from crossing the Potomac at Williamsport. It resulted in the success of the Confederates; but every impartial man confesses that these cavalry fights are miserable affairs. Neither party has any idea of serious charging with the sabre. They approach one another with considerable boldness, until they get within about forty yards, and then, at the very moment when a dash is necessary, and the sword alone should be used, they hesitate, halt, and commence a desultory fire with carbines and revolvers.'[43]

The absence of Lee's cavalry during the movements before Gettysburg probably cost him the battle. General Long, who was on Lee's staff at the time, gives an account of the occurrence which shows what Lee expected of his cavalry.

'Previous to the passage of the Potomac, General Stuart was instructed to make the movements of the cavalry correspond with those of the Federal army, so that he might be in position to observe and report all important information. In the performance of this duty Stuart had never failed and probably his great confidence in him made Lee less specific in his instructions than he would otherwise have been. But on this occasion, either from the misapprehension of instructions or the love of the éclat of a bold raid, Stuart, instead of maintaining his appropriate position between the armies, placed himself on the right flank of the enemy, where his communications with Lee were effectually severed. This greatly embarrassed the movements of General Lee, and eventually forced him to an engagement under disadvantageous circumstances. . . . On reaching Chambersburg, General Lee, not having heard from Stuart, was under the impression that the Federal army had not yet crossed the Potomac. It was not until the night of the 28th that he learned that the enemy had reached Frederick. This important information was brought by a scout from Hood's Texas brigade. On receiving this news Lee immediately ordered the advance of Robertson's and W. E. Jones's divisions of cavalry, which Stuart had left to guard the passes of the Blue Ridge. This cavalry, however, did not arrive in time to be of any service in the movements preceding the battle. . . . When Lee and his staff were ascending South Mountain firing was heard from the direction of Gettysburg. This caused Lee some little uneasiness. The unfortunate absence of the cavalry prevented him from knowing the position and movements of the enemy, and it was impossible to estimate the true condition of affairs in his front. . . . General Lee now exhibited a degree of anxiety and impatience, and expressed regret at the absence of the cavalry. He said that he had been kept in the dark ever since crossing the Potomac, and intimated that Stuart's disappearance had materially hampered the movements and disorganized the plans of the campaign. . . . General Lee had previously considered the possibility of engaging the enemy in the vicinity of Gettysburg, but the time and position were to have been of his own selection. This could have been easily effected had not the cavalry been severed from its proper place with the army. . . . Later . . . the General, as if he had been thinking over his plans and orders, turned to me with the remark, "Colonel Long, do you think we had better attack without the cavalry? If we do so, we will not, if successful, be able to reap the fruits of victory".[44]

Lee agreed with Long's opinion that it would be better to attack before the enemy could be strengthened. It is interesting that Lee echoed Fremantle's views on the need of cavalry to exploit a victory. However, instead of victory there was defeat, and it must be rare that the absence of cavalry has had such an influence on the course of history. If Lee had had his cavalry he would almost certainly have won at Gettysburg (or wherever the battle had been fought). Victory would have led to the fall of Washington and the probable recognition of the Confederacy by foreign Powers. It is more than conceivable that the moral effect on the war-weary north would have led to the end of the war and the independence of the Confederate States of America.

A year after Gettysburg a notable little victory was gained in the Western theatre of war by Confederate cavalry alone. The action took place on 10th June 1864 at Brice's Cross Roads, Mississippi, a densely wooded area with heavy scrub undergrowth and a field of fire limited everywhere to only a few yards; though round the cross roads themselves there was one of the few cleared spaces. A Federal force in the general area commanded by General S. D. Sturgis consisted of a cavalry division under General Grierson and an infantry division (of two white and one coloured brigades) under the command of General McMillen. Grierson, leading the Federal march, arrived at Brice's Cross Roads (a road centre of some importance) and drew up his two brigades in a crescent formation north-east of it.

General Bedford Forrest, in command of a Confederate cavalry division of four brigades, learned of the Federal movement and sent forward his advanced guard brigade, commanded by General Lyon, to locate the enemy. Lyon, finding the Federal cavalry in position, informed Forrest, dismounted his brigade and deployed across the road running north from Brice's. He then pushed forward, driving back the Federal skirmishers, and consolidated his position by building a breastwork. General Rucker, arriving with the second Confederate brigade, dismounted two regiments to take post on Lyon's left, and kept the third as a mounted reserve. The third brigade under General Johnson formed on Lyon's right. Regiments attacked individually on their own sectors but were unable to make much headway. Forrest now gave the signal for a general assault and the Confederates, attacking dismounted, drove the enemy cavalry from their positions, just as Federal infantry reached the field and deployed behind the cavalry. The Federal cavalry now fell back through their infantry to reorganise. At this juncture General Bell arrived with Forrest's remaining brigade and his artillery and formed on Rucker's left.

As soon as Bell was in position Forrest ordered a general advance, and the dismounted troopers worked their way through the trees and undergrowth. Heavy enemy fire brought the advance to a stop. Forrest then galloped to his guns and ordered the battery commander to move them to case shot range as soon as his bugles sounded the charge in ten minutes time. This attack broke the Federal infantry and the Confederates, mounting, pursued the whole Federal force. In this brilliant action, which had been won through Forrest's drive and leadership, the Confederates had been heavily outnumbered.[45]

Notes

1 General William T. Sherman, *Memoirs*, 1875
2 ibid.
3 ibid.
4 Lieutenant-Colonel Garnet Wolseley, *A Month's Visit to the Confederate Headquarters*, Blackwood's Magazine, January 1863
5 A. L. Long, *Memoirs of Robert E. Lee*, 1887
   Frederick H. Dyer, *A Compendium of the War of the Rebellion*, 1908
6 Jack Coggins, *Arms and Equipment of the Civil War*, 1962
7 ibid.
8 Dyer, op. cit.
9 Long, op. cit.
10 Dyer, op. cit.
   Sherman, op. cit.
11 J. R. Sypher, *History of the Pennsylvania Reserve Corps*, 1865

12 Long, op. cit.
13 Dyer, op. cit.
14 ibid.
15 ibid.
16 Sypher, op. cit.
17 ibid.
18 Long, op. cit.
19 Coggins, op. cit.
20 Captain E. W. Sheppard, *Bedford Forrest*, 1930
21 Lieutenant-Colonel A. J. L. Fremantle, *The Fremantle Diary*; ed. Walter Lord, 1956
22 Clifford Dowdey, *Lee*, 1970
23 Major G. Tylden, *Horses and Saddlery*, 1965
24 Coggins, op. cit.
25 Tylden, op. cit.
26 ibid.
27 Colonel Theodore Lyman, *Meade's Headquarters 1863–1865*; Letters, Massachusetts Historical Society, 1922
28 Tylden, op. cit.
29 Coggins, op. cit.
30 Tylden, op. cit.
31 Colonel G. F. R. Henderson, *Stonewall Jackson*, 1898
32 Sypher, op. cit.
33 Bruce Catton, *Grant Takes Command*, 1968
34 William Swinton, *Campaigns of the Army of the Potomac*, 1866
35 ibid.
36 Sypher, op. cit.
36 Sypher, op. cit.
37 Coggins, op. cit.
38 Long, op. cit.
39 Henderson, op. cit.
40 ibid.
41 Lyman, op. cit.
42 Fremantle, op. cit.
43 ibid.
44 Long, op. cit.
45 Sheppard, op. cit.

CHAPTER FOUR

Artillery

Equipment

ONTRARY, PERHAPS TO THE popular estimate of the Civil War armies, contemporary opinion on both sides seems to have regarded the artillery as the best arm of the service. Wolseley, writing of his visit to the Army of Northern Virginia, said: 'The artillery has been the favourite branch of the service and consequently is entirely composed of good men. It was much better drilled than the infantry, and indeed, for all practical purposes, its manoeuvres were executed in the most satisfactory manner.'[1] On the Federal side, Lyman said that the artillery was the best looking arm in the Army of the Potomac.[2] Certainly the problems facing the Confederates and Federals needed good artillery officers, for rarely, if ever, can armies have taken the field with such a wide variety of artillery equipments. They were all muzzle-loaders, but they were variously made of wrought iron, cast iron, and brass and they included both smooth-bore and rifled pieces.

The smooth-bore equipments of the field artillery varied in range from about 1,000 yards to 1,700 yards, whilst the rifled equipments had ranges of from 4,000 to 6,000 yards. The pieces most commonly used were: smooth-bore—6-pr. gun, 12-pr gun, 12-pr. Napoleon gun/howitzer, and 24-pr. howitzer; rifled—3-in. 'Ordnance' gun, 10-pr. Parrott gun, and 20-pr. Parrott gun. In addition the Confederate Army had a few British Whitworth and Blakeley rifled guns,[3] and both sides used 30-pr. Parrotts as a medium artillery equipment. The Napoleon piece owed its origin to a French decision that the 12-pr. should be the only calibre in their field artillery; but as their existing equipment of this type was very heavy, the Emperor Napoleon III designed in 1853 a 12-pr. gun/howitzer to fire common shell, and this was the standard French field equipment in the Crimean War. This piece was introduced into the United States in 1857 and adopted as the standard equipment for the Field artillery. It became the most popular field gun of the Civil War.[4]

66

After the First Battle of Bull Run, it was decided in the Federal Army that rifled pieces were to constitute one-third of the field equipments and smoothbore pieces two-thirds; and that rifled pieces were to be of US Ordnance or Parrott manufacture, whilst the only smoothbore field equipment should be the light 12-pr. Napoleon.[5]

The Parrott rifled muzzle-loaders were accurate long-range weapons, but they had an unenviable reputation for bursting. They were made of cast iron, strengthened by wrought iron superimposed rings, which proved a most unsuitable method of manufacture. The Report on Ordnance of 25th February 1869, presented to the United States Senate, stated that, 'in the attack on Fort Fisher all the Parrott guns in the fleet burst. By the bursting of five of these guns at the first bombardment, 45 persons were killed and wounded, while only 11 were killed or wounded by projectiles from the enemy's guns during the attack.'[6] At the Battle of Fredericksburg the Confederate 30-pr. Parrotts were particularly effective, but one of them, in a two-gun battery, suddenly burst. Standing close to it at the time were General Lee and his staff, officers of First Corps Headquarters, and the officers and gunners of the battery; but no one was hurt. A little later the second big Parrott burst, but again without hurting anybody. (One of the guns exploded at its 39th round and the other at its 54th.)[7]

Whatever hopes there may have been of standardising equipment had soon to be given up, because of the rapid expansion of the armies and the loss or destruction of equipment. In the Confederate Army particularly the field artillery embraced a wide range of rifled and smoothbore pieces. Of the Army of Northern Virginia, Wolseley said: 'Its harness and entire equipment had been taken from the Yankees. The guns used are Parrotts, Napoleons, 12-pounders, howitzers, and 3-inch rifled guns, all muzzle-loaders, the last being the only gun made in the Confederate States. There are a few batteries of Blakeley's guns made in England, of which the officers entertain a high opinion.'[8] Fremantle, a year later, said much the same: 'The artillery is of all kinds—Parrotts, Napoleons, rifled and smooth bores, all shapes and sizes. Most of them bear the letters US, showing that they have changed masters.'[9]

After the Battle of Gettysburg, Fremantle had a long talk with General Pendleton, the parson who was Chief of Lee's Artillery. Pendleton told him that the 12-pr. Napoleons were universally regarded as the best and simplest ordnance for field purposes. They were made of brass with chambers, were very light, and had a long range. Pendleton said that a large number were cast in Augusta and elsewhere in the Confederacy, so that Wolseley was either wrong in his statement that the 3-in. rifled gun was the only one made in the Confederate States, or else manufacture of the Napoleons started after his visit. (General W. N. Pendleton, D.D., was Captain of the Rockbridge Artillery at the First Battle of Bull Run. There he was heard to call to his battery, 'Fire! And may God have mercy on their guilty souls!')[10]

The Cohorn mortar was a very popular light small piece. It could be carried by two or three men and fired with a small charge. It threw a 24-lb. shell over a distance of 1,000 yards, and was very effective against rifle pits because it had such a high trajectory that the shell came down almost vertically.

There was an even greater variety in the heavy ordnance. This was divided into two main classes; siege or garrison, and 'seacoast', and comprised both rifled muzzle-loaders and smoothbore. Coast defence was the primary task which faced General Lee when he arrived at Charleston in November 1861 to assume command of the department of South Carolina, Georgia, and Florida. There was a great shortage of guns suitable for coast defence. Those in use had been there for thirty years and were too light to compete with the heavy guns of the Federal Navy. Lee sited positions for new batteries of heavy guns. The Confederate ordnance department was now prepared to cast guns of the heaviest calibre, and requisitions were accordingly submitted for 8in. and 10-in. smoothbore guns to equip the batteries covering the channels which could be entered by enemy gunboats. These heavy smoothbore pieces were preferred to rifled guns because experiments had shown that the crushing effect of the solid round shot was more destructive than the small breach and deeper penetration of the 80-pr. Whitworth rifled muzzle-loader's projectile, or 'bolt' (as for some reason it was called).[11]

McClellan used some very large siege and seacoast guns in the Peninsular campaign. The former were semi-mobile and could be moved on gun carriages; but the seacoast pieces (100-pr. and 200-pr. mortars and 13-in. howitzers) had to be mounted on stationary platforms. It was to delay the forward movement of this heavy artillery that Lee designed the first railway-mounted gun ever to be used in war. The gun was mounted on a flat truck with its front covered by an armoured shield made of rails.[12]

With these many different types and calibres of ordnance ammunition supply was a complicated business. Against troops in the open solid shot was most often used—round shot from the smoothbores and conical shot, or bolts from the rifled pieces—on account of its range and accuracy. Shrapnel, or spherical case shot, was also used against troops in the open at distances of between 500 and 1,500 yards; its effect was much more widespread than solid shot, but not so accurate owing to the difficulty of cutting the fuse to the right length. (Spherical case shot was invented by Lieutenant Henry Shrapnel, R.A., and was a hollow iron sphere containing a large number of bullets, a bursting charge, and a fuse to fire the charge.) Canister was used against troops at close ranges of less than about 350 yards. Shell was fired at buildings and troops under cover. Cartridge bags were made of serge, flannel, or similar material. For the Napoleons the ammunition was 'fixed' (projectile fixed to the cartridge case) whereas separate ammunition (projectile and charge loaded separately) was used for the rifled equipments.[13]

Lyman says that if one was standing in front or behind round shot, after they had gone some distance, they could be seen distinctly. After hitting the ground they made a great hop, and then went on in decreasing bounds until they had exhausted their impetus. They were considered more dangerous than conical shot, which struck only once, vaulted into the air 'with a noise like a catherine's wheel' and then toppled over and dropped.[14]

Organisation

Before the outbreak of the war and before the adoption of either rifled pieces of Napoleon smoothbores, the scales and establishments of ordnance had been laid down by the United States Secretary at War. In normal conditions the allotment was one piece for every 1,000 infantry and 2 pieces for 1,000 cavalry. Of these, two-thirds were guns and one-third howitzers, and of the guns 12-prs. constituted one quarter and 6-pr. three quarters, whilst the howitzers were in similar respective proportions of 24-prs. and 12-prs. Percentages of ammunition carried for these various equipments were as follows: 12-pr. gun—solid shot 76, canister 12, shrapnel 12; 6-pr. gun—shot 70, canister 20, shrapnel 10; 24-pr. howitzer —shell 52, shrapnel 35, canister 13; 12-pr. howitzer—shell 48, shrapnel 40, canister 12. Light artillery was organised in either horse or field batteries, each of which had six equipments—either four 12-pr. guns and two 24-pr. howitzers, or four 6-pr. guns and two 12-pr. howitzers. The former had 12 ammunition wagons, or caissons, and the latter 6. Rather surprisingly the only equipment which was allotted six horses to draw it was the 12-pr. gun, all the others had only four.[15]

An artillery battery was divided into sections each of two equipments and one limber ammunition wagon (or caisson), all under the command of a lieutenant. In addition a battery had six more ammunition wagons with the reserve ammunition, a travelling forge, and a battery wagon carrying tents and supplies. The usual gun crew was nine men; in horse artillery they were all mounted, but in field artillery they either rode on limbers and wagons or walked beside the piece.[16]

After the Federal disaster at the First Battle of Bull Run, the task of reorganising the light artillery was given to Major (later Brigadier-General)

Barry, the Chief of Artillery. It was decided that batteries should consist of six equipments as far as possible, and never less than four; and that guns or howitzers should be of the same calibre. Batteries were to be allotted on a scale of four to each division, and of these one was to be a Regular Army battery and its captain was to be commander of the divisional artillery. In addition there was to be a light artillery reserve of 100 pieces and a siege train of 50 pieces. A reorganisation was badly needed, for when McClellan took command of the Army of the Potomac there were only nine imperfectly equipped batteries with a total of 30 pieces. But the reorganisation was pushed ahead so rapidly that before the army took the field it had 92 batteries with 520 pieces and a strength of 12,500 men.[17]

The amount and organisation of the artillery provided by the various States in the Union varied enormously. Both heavy and light artillery were raised in regiments, in battalions, in independent batteries, or even in companies. Delaware produced one Heavy Artillery Company and one Light Artillery Battery; Illinois raised a large number of independent Light Artillery Batteries; Massachusetts provided thirty companies of Heavy Artillery and seventeen batteries of Light Artillery; New York had a number of regiments and independent battalions of Heavy Artillery, two regiments each of twelve batteries of Light Artillery, and thirty-six independent batteries of Light Artillery; and Missouri raised two Light Artillery Regiments each of twelve batteries lettered A to M (excluding J). These examples are typical of a strange diversity. The tactical unit, however, was the battery; batteries did not fight as part of the regiments or battalions to which they belonged, though they might be formed temporarily into battalions in the field. There was no particular horse or field artillery; light batteries could be used in either role, but with a greater establishment of horses in the former. Battery I of the 1st Michigan Regiment of Light Artillery, for instance, was in a Horse Artillery Brigade of the Army of the Potomac in 1863, but in 1864 it was in the artillery of the 3rd Infantry Division of the XI Army Corps. No other battery of this regiment ever served as horse artillery. Most of the horse artillery, however, was supplied by batteries of the US Regular Artillery, presumably because all their men were trained to ride.[18]

In the Confederate Army there were permanent batteries of horse artillery, which were not interchangeable with those batteries classified as light artillery. After the Battle of Chancellorsville, Lee reorganised the artillery of the Army of Northern Virginia. It then consisted of sixty batteries of light artillery and six batteries of horse artillery, 'whose personnel,' says Long, 'were unsurpassed by any troops in the army, though they were imperfectly organised.' Lee grouped the light artillery into battalions of four batteries each, which produced fifteen battalions. The horse artillery batteries were grouped into another battalion. Each battalion was commanded by a lieutenant-colonel with a major as second-in-command; and two or three battalions, if grouped together, were commanded by a colonel. The whole of the light artillery was formed into three divisions, each of five battalions, and each division was commanded by a brigadier-general. One of these divisions was allotted to each of the three infantry army corps; and of these one battalion was allocated to each infantry division, the remaining two battalions, under the command of a colonel, forming the corps reserve artillery. The chief of the corps artillery reported to and received orders from the corps commander, and the chief of the artillery of the army reported direct to the commander-in-chief.[19]

In the Pennsylvania Reserve Corps of the Federal Army, its 15th Regiment became the 1st Regiment Light Artillery. Eight companies were recruited, and from these eight companies were formed eight batteries lettered A to H. They never all served together or as a constituent part of the Reserve Corps; but three batteries were assigned in October 1861 to McCall's Division (which was composed of units of the Pennsylvania Reserve Corps), together with one regular battery: these were Batteries A, B, and C of the 1st Pennsylvania Light Artillery and Battery C of the 5th US Artillery. In spite of the hopes of avoiding mixed calibres the Pennsylvania batteries had an odd assortment of equipments. One had two smoothbore 12-pr. guns and two 24-pr. howitzers; another had two James's rifled 6-pr. guns and two smoothbore 6-prs.; whilst the third had four smoothbore 6-prs. In addition General McCall acquired for his division eight Parrott rifled 10-prs. of which six were mounted and ready for service and which he proposed to distribute amongst the batteries.[20]

The Confederate batteries were usually neither numbered nor lettered but were generally known by their commander's name and their State, together with some sub-title. For instance, after Lee's reorganisation, the artillery of Rodes's Division of the Second Corps was commanded by Lieutenant-Colonel Thomas H. Carter and consisted of Carter's Virginia Battery (King William Artillery), Fry's Virginia Battery (Orange Artillery), Page's Virginia Battery (Morris Artillery), and Reese's Alabama Battery (Jefferson Davis Artillery). When the Confederate forces were assembling at the start of the war, there arrived in Richmond the Washington Artillery from New Orleans; a crack battalion, the officers and men of which considered themselves as belonging to the very best families of Louisiana. This unit was, indeed, the oldest and best drilled artillery unit in the Confederacy and it fought with distinction at the First Battle of Bull Run.[21]

71

Artillery in Action

It was McClellan's excellent artillery that probably saved his army from destruction in the 'Seven Days' Battles in the Peninsular in 1862. He had hoped for impressive results from the massive pieces of his siege train in the attack on Yorktown, and there was great disappointment among the artillery and engineer officers when the Confederates abandoned their works before they could be used, because they believed that these guns could have destroyed the Confederate defences in a few hours. Barry, the Chief of Artillery, reckoned that these 200-pr. and 100-pr. Parrott rifled guns were so accurate that, combined with cross fire from 13-in. and 10-in. seacoast mortars, they 'would have compelled the enemy to surrender or abandon his works in less than twelve hours.' Subsequent operations proved Barry wrong, for, says Swinton, 'the rude improvised earthworks of the Confederates showed an ability to sustain an indefinite pounding'.[22]

But it was his reserve artillery under General Hunt which saved McClellan from decisive defeat at the Battle of Malvern Hill. This consisted of eighteen batteries of 100 guns of, says Sypher, 'the most approved pattern, the choice in finish and equipment in the United States Army'. The guns, ammunition wagons, battery wagons, and others, numbered about 300 vehicles. General McCall was given the responsibility of looking after all these, and when his own divisional artillery and divisional vehicles were added, he had a train seven miles long. Malvern Hill was within the range of the Federal gunboats, and their heavy guns were a valuable addition to the Union defence. A Confederate officer said, 'It was terrible to see those two hundred and sixty-eight pound shells crashing through the woods, and when one exploded it was as though the globe had burst'.[23]

Artillery played a major part in the Battle of Sharpsburg, or Antietem. On the Confederate side there was the notable incident of a corps commander himself taking immediate command of two abandoned guns. Long records the occasion as follows: 'Among the cases of individual gallantry, one of the most conspicuous was that of General Longstreet, with Majors Fairfax and Sorrell and Captain Latrobe of his staff, who, on observing a large Federal force approaching an unoccupied portion of his line, served with such effect two pieces of artillery that had been left without cannoneers that the Federals were arrested in their advance and speedily forced to retire beyond the range of the guns.'[24] Longstreet says of this incident (without mentioning that it was he who was firing the guns) that two brass guns were charged and double charged with spherical case (ie, shrapnel), and that at the discharge they leaped into the air from 10 to 12 inches.[25]

72

In equipment, the Federal artillery at Sharpsburg was considerably superior to that of the Confederates. There was a duel, for instance, between four Federal batteries placed on a ridge on the east side of the Antietam and the Confederate Washington (Louisiana) Artillery of four batteries (called 'companies'), in which the former showed such a marked superiority that the Confederate General D. H. Hill called it 'the most melancholy farce in the war;' adding that the Confederate batteries 'could not cope with the Yankee guns'.[26] Longstreet said that in the Army of the Potomac 'The artillery appointments were so superior that our officers sometimes felt humiliated when posted to unequal combat with their better metal and munitions'.[27] At the same time the Confederate artillery played a major part in defeating the Federal attack. The right division of Hooker's Federal Corps was totally stopped by General 'Jeb' Stuart's horse artillery posted on commanding ground on his right and front.

After the failure of the Federal attack at Sharpsburg, Lee contemplated a counter-attack on the following morning and thought that the enemy's right might be overwhelmed, despite an adverse report by Jackson, whose corps was on the Confederate left. General Stephen D. Lee, then a Colonel commanding the artillery of Longstreet's Corps, relates what happened in a letter to the late Colonel G. F. R. Henderson: 'During the morning a courier from headquarters came to my battalion of artillery with a message that the Commander-in-Chief wished to see me. I followed the courier, and on meeting General Lee, he said, "Colonel Lee, I wish you to go with this courier to General Jackson, and say that I sent you to report to him". I replied, "General, shall I take my batteries with me?" He said, "No, just say that I told you to report to him, and he will tell you what he wants". I soon reached General Jackson. He was dismounted, with but few persons round him. He said to me, "Colonel Lee, I wish you to take a ride with me," and we rode to the left of our lines with but one courier, I think. We soon reached a considerable hill and dismounted. General Jackson then said, "Let us go up this hill, and be careful not to expose yourself, for the Federal sharpshooters are not far off." The hill bore evidence of fierce fights the day before. A battery of artillery had been on it, and there were wrecked caissons, broken wheels, dead bodies, and dead horses around. General Jackson said: "Colonel, I wish you to take your glasses and carefully examine the Federal line of battle." I did so, and saw a remarkably strong line of battle, with more troops than I knew General Lee had. After locating the different batteries, unlimbered and ready for action, and noting the strong skirmish line, in front of the dense masses of infantry, I said to him, "General, that is a very strong position, and there is a large force there". He said, "Yes. I wish you to take fifty pieces of artillery and crush that force, which is the Federal right.

Can you do it?" I can scarcely describe my feelings as I again took my glasses, and made an even more careful examination. I at once saw such an attempt must fail. More than fifty guns were unlimbered and ready for action, strongly supported by dense lines of infantry and strong skirmish lines advantageously posted. The ground was unfavourable for the location of artillery on the Confederate side, for to be effective the guns would have to move up close to the Federal lines, and that, too, under fire of both infantry and artillery. I could not bring myself to say all that I felt and knew. I said, "Yes, General; where will I get the fifty guns?" He said, "How many have you?" I replied, "About twelve out of the thirty I carried into action the day before." (My losses had been very great in men, horses, and carriages.) He said, "I can furnish you some". I replied, "Shall I go for the guns?" "No, not yet," he replied. "Colonel Lee, can you crush the Federal right with fifty guns?" I said, "General, I can try. I can do it if anyone can". He replied, "That is not what I asked you, sir. If I give you fifty guns can you crush the Federal right?" I evaded the question again and again, but he pressed it home. Finally I said, "General, you seem to be more intent upon my giving you my technical opinion as an artillery officer, than upon my going after the guns and making the attempt". "Yes, sir," he replied, "and I want your positive opinion yes or no." I felt that a great crisis was upon me, and I could not evade it. I again took my glasses and made another examination. I waited a good while, with Jackson watching me intently. I said, "General, it cannot be done with fifty guns and the troops you have here". In an instant he said, "Let us ride back Colonel".'

Stephen Lee felt that he had shown a lack of nerve and begged that he be permitted to make the attempt, saying that if the task was given to another officer he was ruined. However, Jackson said that everyone knew he was a brave officer and would fight the guns well, and he told him to report their conversation to General Lee. Stephen Lee never knew until many years later, when he saw Jackson's report of the battle, that Lee had told Jackson to take fifty guns and crush the Federal right.[28]

The Battle of Fredericksburg was the occasion of another fierce artillery duel. General Long says that this was the first time that the Confederate artillery was systematically massed for battle. General Lee gave him the task of selecting positions for the artillery, with the result that on the day of the battle two hundred pieces of artillery were in position and so arranged that at least fifty pieces could be brought to bear on any threatened point; and on Fredericksburg and Deep Run, the Federal points of attack, a hundred guns could be concentrated.[29] Confronted by a terrific fire, the Federal assaults were beaten back with tremendous casualties.

On the Federal side, Swinton stood beside Pettit's Battery of 10-pr. Parrott guns whilst it engaged a Confederate battery. He writes: 'Pettit, in fifteen minutes, by his excellent shots, caused the Confederate gunners to leave their guns; and the pieces were only dragged off by the men crawling up and attaching prolonges to them'.[30] (Prolonges were long ropes, one of which was attached to the trail of the gun and the other to the limber.)

But probably the most momentous artillery cannonade of the war took place at the Battle of Gettysburg. In the Confederate plan for the attack on the third day of the battle, Pickett's Division was to lead the assaulting column after a preliminary artillery bombardment. The Confederates placed 145 guns in position along the ridge occupied by Longstreet and Hill. On the Federal side General Hunt, Chief of Artillery, had crowned their ridge on the left and centre, where it was apparant that the attack would fall, with 80 guns. This was not as many as the Confederates had deployed but all that he could conveniently fit into the available space. As batteries expended their ammunition, however, they were replaced by batteries of the artillery reserve, sent by its chief, Colonel R. O. Taylor.

At about 12 o'clock the preparations for the attack had been completed and the massed Confederate artillery opened their concentration on Cemetery Hill. Hunt withheld his fire until the first Confederate vehemence had slackened. The Federal batteries then replied and there 'ensued,' says Long, 'one of the most tremendous artillery engagements ever witnessed on an open field: the hills shook and quivered beneath the thunder of two hundred and twenty-five guns as if they were about to be torn and rent by some powerful convulsion.'[31]

Samuel Wilkinson, a journalist, described the Confederate artillery bombardment as witnessed from the headquarters of General Meade, commanding the Army of the Potomac. He wrote:

'In the shadow cast by the tiny farm-house sixteen by twenty, which General Meade had made his headquarters, lay wearied staff officers and tired journalists. There was not wanting to the peacefulness of the scene the singing of a bird, which had a nest in a peach tree within the tiny yard of the whitewashed cottage. In the midst of its warbling, a shell screamed over the house, instantly followed by another, and another, and in a moment the air was full of the most complete artillery prelude to an infantry battle that was ever exhibited. Every size and form of shell known to British and to American gunnery shrieked, whirled, moaned, whistled and wrathfully fluttered over our ground. As many as six in a second, constantly two in a second, bursting and screaming over and around the headquarters, made a very hell of fire that amazed the oldest officers. They burst in the yard—burst next to the fence on both sides, garnished as usual with the hitched horses of aides and orderlies. The fastened animals reared and plunged with terror. Then one fell, then another—sixteen laid dead and mangled before the fire ceased. . . . Through the midst of the storm of screaming and exploding shells, an ambulance, driven by its frenzied conductor at full speed, presented to all of us the marvellous spectacle of a horse going rapidly on three legs. A hinder one had been shot off at the hock. A shell tore up the little step of the Headquarters Cottage, and ripped a bag of oats as with a knife. Another soon carried off one of its two pillars. Soon a spherical case burst opposite the open door—another ripped through the open garret. The remaining pillar went almost immediately to the howl of a fixed shot that Whitworth must have made. . . . Not an orderly—not an ambulance—not a straggler was to be seen upon the plain swept by this tempest of orchestral death thirty minutes after it commenced. . . . Shells through the two lower rooms! A shell into the chimney that fortunately did not explode. Shells in the yard. The air thicker and fuller and more deafening with the howling and whirling of these infernal missiles. The chief of staff struck— Seth Williams, loved and respected through the army. . . . An aide bored with a fragment of iron through the bone of the arm. Another cut with an exploded piece of case shot. And the time measured on the sluggish watches was one hour and forty minutes.'[32]

Hunt, finding the Federal ammunition running low and considering it unsafe to bring up ammunition wagons from the rear owing to the number that had been hit and exploded, directed that firing should be gradually stopped. The Confederate batteries had nearly exhausted their own ammunition and they too stopped.[33] This was the moment for the infantry attack, and the long lines of Pickett's Division led the advance towards the silent Federal position. Immediately those Federal batteries still in action opened a spasmodic fire. The rifled guns fired all their canister and then were either withdrawn or left inactive on the ground to await the issue of the infantry fight. The Confederate guns were unable to give their infantry support for they had no ammunition left.

The shortage of Confederate ammunition was, says Lee, in his report on the battle, unknown to him when the assault took place, and to it he ascribes the failure of the infantry attack, because, 'Owing to this fact . . . the enemy was enabled to throw a strong force of infantry against our left. . . . It finally gave way, and the right, after penetrating the enemy's lines, entering his advance works and capturing some of his artillery, was attacked simultaneously in front and on both flanks and driven back with heavy loss. . . . The severe loss sustained by the army and the reduction of its ammunition rendered another attempt to dislodge the enemy inadvisable, and it was therefore determined to withdraw.'[34]

In spite of the absence of his cavalry when most needed, Lee would probably have won the Battle of Gettysburg but for a staff failure in the supply of artillery ammunition. Seldom can such a failure have influenced so decisively the course of history.

General E. P. Alexander, commanding the artillery of Longstreet's Corps as well as his own battalion, performed a notable feat on the second day of the Battle of Gettysburg. Placing himself at the head of six batteries, he led them at a gallop behind the charge of the infantry, up to the position abandoned by the Federals—six batteries in line with 400 horses—and then brought them faultlessly into 'action front'. J. C. Wise, in *The Long Arm of Lee* (1959), says that 'perhaps no more superb feat of artillery drill on the battlefield was ever witnessed'.[35]

Recoil of the larger pieces was very tiring for the gun teams in prolonged action. At Gettysburg one battery of four 24-pr. howitzers and two 12-pr. guns was sited on a rocky slope, and the labour of running up these equipments after each recoil was so exhausting that eight volunteers were obtained from an infantry regiment to help the gunners.[36]

Indirect fire was used by the Confederates at the Battle of Chancellorsville, probably for the first time by Confederate artillery and perhaps for the first time by either side. This was due to Alexander, who put deflection marks on intervening ridges.[37]

Confederate shells were all too often defective, and were generally very inferior to those of the Federals. Many shells failed to burst or burst prematurely, and some tumbled in flight. At Gettysburg a large number of rifled guns were restricted to solid shot because their fuses were unreliable.[38]

In action ammunition chests on limbers and ammunition wagons were usually dismounted in action and placed under cover in the gun pits. During the Battle of Spotsylvania orders were given that all guns in forward positions should be withdrawn from action in preparation for a rapid and silent night move. Alexander, believing an enemy attack on existing positions would take place that night, compromised by ordering the artillery of Longstreet's Corps to remain in action but for all ammunition chests to be mounted and carriages placed on the roads ready for quick and quiet withdrawal if necessary.[39]

After the Battle of Cold Harbor, having no Coehorn mortars, Alexander improvised mortar fire with howitzers and thus prevented the construction of an enemy battery. Later he ordered some mortars to be made in Richmond and obtained them on 24th June 1864. They were only 12-prs., but they were light and manoeuvrable and were used effectively against Federal emplacements of 60 mortars ranging from 24-pr. Coehorns to 10-in. 'Sea-Coast'.[40]

77

Notes

1 Lieutenant-Colonel Garnet Wolseley, *A Month's Visit to the Confederate Headquarters*, Blackwood's Magazine, January 1863
2 Colonel Theodore Lyman, *Meade's Headquarters 1863–1865*; Letters, Massachusetts Historical Society, 1922
3 Major-General J. F. C. Fuller, *The Generalship of Ulysses S. Grant*, 1929
4 Colonel H. C. B. Rogers, *Artillery through the Ages*, 1972
5 William Swinton, *Campaigns of the Army of the Potomac*, 1866
6 Rogers, op. cit.
7 James Longstreet, *From Manassas to Appomattox*, 1896
   General E. P. Alexander, *Military Memoirs of a Confederate*, 1907
8 Wolseley, op. cit.
9 Lieutenant-Colonel A. J. L. Fremantle, *The Fremantle Diary*; ed. Walter Lord, 1956
10 ibid.
11 A. L. Long, *Memoirs of Robert E. Lee*, 1887
12 Clifford Dowdey, *Lee*, 1970
13 Rogers, op. cit.
   Jack Coggins, *Arms and Equipment of the Civil War*, 1962
14 Lyman, op. cit.
15 Major-General G. G. Lewis & Others, *Aide-Memoire to the Military Sciences*, 1853
16 Coggins, op. cit.
17 Swinton, op. cit.
18 Frederick H. Dyer, *A Compendium of the War of the Rebellion*, 1908
19 Long, op. cit.
20 J. R. Sypher, *History of The Pennsylvania Reserve Corps*, 1865
21 J. Cutler Andrews, *The South Reports the Civil War*, 1970
   Alexander, op. cit.
22 Swinton, op. cit.
23 Sypher, op. cit.
24 Long, op. cit.
25 Longstreet, op. cit.
26 Swinton, op. cit.
27 Longstreet, op. cit.
28 Colonel G. F. R. Henderson, *Stonewall Jackson*, 1898
29 Long, op. cit.
30 Swinton, op. cit.
31 Long, op. cit.
32 Sypher, op. cit.
33 Swinton, op. cit.
34 Long, op. cit.
35 Alexander, op. cit.
   T. Harry Williams, note to above, 1962
36 Alexander, op. cit.
37 J. C. Wise, *The Long Arm of Lee*, 1959, quoted by T. Harry Williams in note to above
38 Alexander, op. cit.
39 ibid.
40 ibid.

CHAPTER FIVE

Engineers and Signals

W HEN ONE CONSIDERS THE enormous area over which the war was waged, the very long distances over which command and control were exercised, the dependence on railways for movement and supply, and the obstacles presented by the great rivers, it seems surprising that engineer and signal troops were so few. Considering, too, that their organisation was built up from practically nothing to meet the needs of a new type of war, it is amazing what they accomplished.

Before the war, though engineer officers had been widely employed on both military and civil projects, there were very few engineer NCOs and men; and for communications the various military headquarters and posts had depended entirely on the private telegraph companies.

The United States engineer organisation, which was continued in the Federal Army, comprised two separate establishments, the Corps of Engineers and the Corps of Topographical Engineers. The former was responsible for planning and supervising the construction and main-tenance of works (both field and permanent), railways, roads, and bridges, and for surveying; whilst the latter prepared and provided maps—an unusually important task because there were practically no large scale maps of the country over which the war was fought. In 1863 the Federal Army recognised that the two Corps were complementary and they were amalgamated as the Corps of Engineers.[1]

In the North, Engineer troops were only raised by the States of New York, Missouri, Pennsylvania, and Kentucky; and from the US Regular Army there came the 1st Engineer Battalion. New York contributed the 1st Engineer Regiment (Serrell's Engineers), the 15th Engineer Regiment which had been converted from the 15th New York Infantry Regiment, and the 50th Engineer Regiment which was likewise converted from the 50th New York Infantry—both in October 1861. Of these, the 1st Engineer Regiment spent most of its time in South Carolina coastal operations and finally took part in the siege of Petersburg. The 1st US Engineer Battalion and the 15th and 50th New York Engineer Regiments together formed the Engineer Brigade of the Army of the Potomac. Missouri raised Bissell's Engineer Regiment, which in 1864 was amalgamated with the 25th Missouri Infantry to form the 1st Missouri Engineer Regiment. Bissell's, in its original and later amalgamated form, spent all its time in the Western theatre, and was part of Sherman's army in the march from Atlanta to the Sea. From Michigan came the 1st Michigan Engineer Regiment which also served only in the Western theatre, but was generally split up; its companies serving separately on engineer duties wherever required. These duties included bridge construction, train operating, and demolition of railway track during the march to the Sea. From Kentucky came Patterson's Engineer Company which was employed on general engineer work in the Western theatre. Pennsylvania contributed Wrigley's Engineer Company which spent most of its time in West Virginia.[2]

The Confederate Army started with engineer officers but no other ranks at all. All the engineer labour was done by the Pioneer Corps which consisted of men drafted from infantry regiments. In 1863 two Engineer Regiments were formed, the regimental establishment being fixed at ten companies, each of 100 NCOs and men.

The pioneer of signals in the pre-war United States Army was Albert J. Myer, an army surgeon. Whilst a medical student he invented a *Signal Language for Deaf Mutes*, which was a form of visual signalling. He managed to arouse army interest in his methods and, as a result, in 1860 he ceased his duties as a surgeon and became Signal Officer to the Army in the rank of Major. Two assistants were posted to him; Lieutenants E. P. Alexander and J. E. B. Stuart. Alexander later organised the Confederate Signal Corps and was subsequently probably the most eminent artillery officer in the Confederate Army, whilst Stuart was, of course, the famous Confederate cavalry commander.[3]

In the Federal Army there was no separate Signal Corps until 1864. Before that the Army signal service was only concerned with visual signalling and field cable. All line communications in rear of major headquarters came under the United States Military Telegraph Corps, which was attached to the Quartermaster General's Department and operated by civilian personnel belonging to the private telegraph companies.[4] There was considerable friction between this organisation and Army Signals. Myer, as the Chief Signal Officer and a Colonel, tried to get the Telegraph Corps transferred to his control, and the resulting quarrel led to his being relieved of his appointment.[5]

Alexander organised a signal service in the Confederate Army at the start of the war and in 1862 it became a separate Signal Corps. This might

fairly claim to be the first such corps in the world. It was commanded by
Captain William Norris for the remainder of the war and came under the
authority of the Adjutant General's Department. It was responsible for
visual signalling, field telegraph, and intelligence. As in the North,
telegraph communications in rear of the major headquarters were operated
and maintained by civilian personnel, but they continued to be managed
by the private telegraph companies, under the general control of the
Signal Corps.[6]

Field Works

The construction of trenches and breastworks is discussed in Chapter Two.
Although the engineers were responsible for the plan and layout of an
organised system of field defences, the actual construction of them was
normally undertaken by the infantry; and indeed in the latter stages of the
war no infantry soldier needed urging to provide himself with cover
from fire and from view. Of field works in the Atlanta campaign, Sherman
says: 'The enemy and ourselves used the same form of rifle-trench, varied
according to the nature of the ground, viz: the trees and bushes were cut
away for a hundred yards or more in front, serving as an abatis or
entanglement; the parapets varied from four to six feet high, the dirt taken
from a ditch outside and from a covered way inside, and this parapet was
surmounted by a "head-log", composed of the trunk of a tree from twelve
to twenty inches at the butt, lying along the interior crest of the parapet
and resting in notches cut in other trunks which extended back, forming
an inclined plane, in case the head-log should be knocked inward by a
cannon shot. The men of both armies became extremely skilful in the
construction of these works, because each man realized their value and
importance to himself, so that it required no orders for their construction.
As soon as a regiment or brigade gained a position within easy distance
for a sally, it would set to work with a will and would construct such a
parapet in a single night; but I endeavoured to spare the soldiers this
hard labor by authorizing each division commander to organize out of
the freedmen who escaped to us a pioneer corps of two hundred men . . .
These pioneer detachments became very useful to us during the rest of
the war, for they could work at night while our men slept. . . . During
this campaign hundreds if not thousands of miles of similar intrenchments
were built by both armies, and as a rule whichever party attacked one of
them got the worst of it.' Sherman said that the defences of Chattahoochee,
occupied by Johnston's Confederate army on 4th July 1864, were some
of the strongest field fortifications that he ever saw. A negro who escaped
to the Union lines told him that he was one of about 1,000 slaves who had
been at work for a month or more on these lines.[7]

Lyman has a description of trenches built by the Army of the Potomac which might have applied to the First World War: 'Our entrenchments were most extraordinary in their extent, with heavy traverses, where exposed to enfilade, and all done by the men, as it were, spontaneously.' In the Federal lines in front of Richmond he noted, 'A breastwork, behind which were dug a number of little cellars about two feet deep, and over these were pitched some small tents. And there you could see officers sitting, with only their heads above ground, writing or perhaps reading; for it was a quiet time and there were no bullets or shells.'[8]

In November 1863 General Meade moved forward with the intention of crossing the Rapidan at the lower fords and interposing between the widely separated wings of General Lee's army. His intention was balked by the very strong defences which he encountered at the Confederate position along the Mine Run. Swinton gives the following description of this formidable position: 'The Confederate line was drawn along a prominent ridge or series of heights, extending north and south for six or eight miles. This series of hills formed all the angles of a complete fortification, and comprised the essential elements of a fortress. The centre of the line presented four or five well-defined facings of unequal length, occupying a space of more than three thousand yards, with such angles of defence that the fire of the enemy was able to enfilade every avenue of approach, while his right and left flanks were not less strongly protected. Stretching immediately in the rear and on the flanks of this position was a dense forest of heavy timber, while some twelve hundred yards in front was Mine Run—a stream of no great width, but difficult for infantry to cross from the marshy ground and dense undergrowth of stunted timber with which it was frequently flanked on either side, as well as from the abrupt nature of its banks. In addition to these natural defences, the enemy quickly felled in front of a large extent of his position a thick growth of pine as an abatis, and hastily constructed trenches and breastworks for infantry. The position was, in fact, exceedingly formidable.' The Army of the Potomac came up against this position on 28th November 1863, and General Warren with the II Corps was sent to ascertain the practicability of turning the Confederate right. Warren gave a favourable report and, it having also been reported that the Confederate left was weak, General Meade decided to attack on both wings on the morning of 30th with Warren opening the attack. But the presence of Warren's troops had attracted Lee's attention to his right and at dawn on 30th Warren saw that he was now faced by artillery in position and infantry behind breastworks. As an engineer himself he saw that his task was hopeless, and took it upon himself to suspend the attack. His soldiers had come to the same conclusion and, 'were seen quietly pinning on the breast of their blouses of blue, slips of paper on which each had written his *name*!'[9]

The Confederate defences had been sited by Lee personally. Long says: 'Lee rode along the banks of the stream, and with his great engineering skill selected the points to be defended and gave the necessary orders. In a remarkably short space of time an extended line of works was erected, composed of double walls of logs filled in with earth and with a strong abatis in front.'[10]

Wire entanglements (not yet barbed) were used very effectively by the Federal General W. F. Smith in the operations before Petersburg. There was a large amount of telegraph wire in the vicinity and Smith gave orders for the whole front to be covered with this by winding it round tree stumps. The Confederates attacked in a fog, did not see the wire and, tripping over it, came under heavy and prepared fire from the Federals.[11]

Bridging

In preparation for his March to the Sea, Sherman allotted to each of the four corps into which his army was divided a detachment of engineers and a pontoon train, giving a bridging length of 900 feet. By combining two trains the length of 1,800 feet which they provided was enough for any of the rivers they would have to cross. The leading division of a corps was responsible for erecting a bridge and for providing such labour as was required by the engineers. 'But,' writes Sherman, 'habitually the leading brigade would, out of the abundant timber, improvise a bridge before the pontoon train could come up, unless in the cases of rivers of considerable magnitude. . . . The pontoons in general use were skeleton frames, made with a hinge, so as to fold back and constitute a wagon body. In this same wagon were carried the cotton canvas cover, the anchor and chains, and a due proportion of the balks, chesses, and lashings.'[12]

On a visit to England some years after the war, Sherman saw at Aldershot a pontoon train of which the boats were sheathed with wood and felt and were made very light; but he thought that they would be more liable to chafing and damage than the cheaper American pattern. Lyman has an amusing description of these pontoons. He says that they consisted of a boat-shaped frame wrapped in a great sheet of canvas and put into the water, and that :'It looks as if the Commander-in-Chief has undertaken the washing business on a large scale, and was "soaking" his soiled clothing.'[13]

Maps

Mapping was something of a problem for both sides. Swinton says of an early operation by Federal forces that the marches of two columns 'were based on the showing of an old and incorrect map,' according to which one column was three miles closer to the objective than the other, when actually it was four miles further away. The unfortunate result was that troops of the two columns fired on each other under the impression that they were engaging the enemy.[14]

Of the 'Seven Days' campaign, the Confederate General Richard Taylor wrote in *Destruction and Reconstruction*, 'From Cold Harbor to Malvern Hill inclusive, there was nothing but a series of blunders, one after another, and all huge. The Confederate commanders knew no more about the topography of the country than they did about Central Africa.' And in *The Rise and Fall of the Confederate Government* (1881), Jefferson Davis said, '. . . we had no maps of the country in which we were operating; our generals were ignorant of the roads and their guides knew little more than the way from their homes in Richmond.' Long, however, disputes the latter part of this statement. He says, 'The inhabitants of that region supplied efficient guides, and his (Lee's) staff officers had been employed in making themselves acquainted with the roads and natural features of the country over which the army was likely to operate.' He also includes in his book a reproduction of the official map used by Lee in the campaign; and this, though on a small scale, shows all the roads in the area.[15]

By 1864 map-making in the Army of the Potomac was well organised. Lyman says that before the campaign of that year opened the engineers had prepared a series of large-scale maps compiled from every source that they could find; such as state, county, and town maps, and information given by residents, refugees and other people. In spite of this (or perhaps because of it) they were often very inaccurate. Some places (eg Spotsylvania) were two or three miles out of position, 'and roads ran everywhere except where they were laid down.' Lyman supposed that there was insufficient material to make a map on as large a scale as one inch to a mile. For more detailed and accurate maps the engineers surveyed the country as an advance progressed. Topographers were sent out as far as possible in front and on either flank. Each made local maps by calculating distances and pacing distances with their horses. They brought these maps into their headquarters in the evening, and during the night the various maps were co-ordinated to produce a map of the whole area. The next day (if it was sunny) photographic copies of this master map were made and sent to major headquarters. The engineers at these headquarters added to or corrected the maps as necessary, and from these adjustments the master map was amended and a new one prepared and issued.[16]

Signals in Action

Signals played an important part in the Confederate victory at the First Battle of Bull Run. Indeed, the first visual message transmitted by flag during the war was a warning from E. P. Alexander, the Signal Officer, to General Evans, commanding the Confederate brigade on the left flank. Alexander arrived at Manassas on 2nd July 1861, bringing with him equipment for visual signal stations but no signallers. Selecting some intelligent and well-educated men, who appeared suitable for later promotion, he started a short course of instruction. He then prepared a signal plan to provide skeleton communications for the transmission of orders and information. He established a central station on a high rocky point a mile east of Manassas, with good observation over possible enemy routes of advance, and three out stations. Of these, one was a McClean's House in the centre of the Confederate position and near to the command post of Johnston and Beauregard, one was at Centreville (later withdrawn), and the third was on the left by the Stone Bridge by which the Warrenton Turnpike crossed Bull Run and close to Evans's Brigade. On the day of the battle, from his central station, Alexander had been looking out for any Union flanking movement, and seeing the brass barrel of a field gun glinting in the sunshine and then the shimmer of lines of bayonets, he signalled: 'Look out for your left; you are turned.'[17]

Myer, appreciating the contribution of signals to the Confederate success, submitted a proposed organisation to provide all communications in the field. This was approved, and it ultimately included visual signal stations, telegraph operating personnel, cable laying detachments, and signal officers to serve on the headquarters of armies, corps, and divisions. In addition, signal detachments were provided to accompany reconnaissance parties and to provide communications between artillery batteries and observation posts. The cable detachments laid lines, generally up to about eight miles in length, and these were often spurs from the permanent telegraph route to the headquarters of formations, which were built at each halting place during an advance or withdrawal. Reels of field cable were carried on wagons and, because the insulation of the wire was poor, the cable was normally secured to short poles or to trees. Mounted 'telegraphers' tapped into the lines of the main telegraph routes at the points from which these spurs were constructed.[18] Visual signalling was operated with flags by day and torch by night. In the Federal Army signal flags were white with a central red square, or red with a central white square, or black. The type of flag used depended on the background. The signal code was based on Baine's telegraph alphabet. There were only two flag indications, a dot and a dash representing respectively the figures 1 and 2; and letters were a combination of these; eg, B was 1221. It was a very simple but very slow system.[19]

Signal stations were established on the top of prominent heights for use both as relay stations on a visual chain between headquarters and as intelligence observation posts. In the latter capacity they signalled reports of any movement they saw. Service at a hill-top signal station could be hazardous as such a station was an obvious artillery target. At the Battle of Gettysburg a signal station may have been an agent that saved the Federal Army from defeat. This station was established on Little Round Top, a key hill which was otherwise devoid of troops. General Warren, the Chief Engineer, arrived just as the signal station was packing up to leave, and saw Confederate infantry approaching the hill. Telling the signal officer in command to carry on waving his flags in the hope that the Confederates would believe the hill to be strongly held, he hurried off to get troops to occupy it.[20]

Hill-top signal stations were noticed by Fremantle in the Western theatre; he wrote: 'The enemy is about fifteen miles distant, and all the tops of the intervening hills are occupied as signal stations, which communicate his movements by flags in the daytime and by beacons at night. A signal corps has been organised for this service.' (When Fremantle left Richmond to join Lee's army he was accompanied, he says, 'by a sergeant of the Signal Corps, sent by my kind friend Major Norris.')[21]

Visual signal stations were much used by both sides during Sherman's Atlanta campaign. On 10th June 1864 Sherman's army arrived in front of a strong Confederate position which included three prominent hills, known as Kenesaw Mountain, Pine Mountain, and Lost Mountain. 'On each of these hills', says Sherman, 'the enemy had signal stations.' Sherman set up his headquarters in an abandoned house, and at the back of it, on the roof of an old gin-house, was his signal station. Because both sides could read the messages sent by the signallers on the hills, they were always encyphered. Sherman's signal officer told him that by studying the Confederate transmissions he had learned the key of their cypher and could read their messages. From these he had gleaned the information that the Confederate General Polk had been killed.

For the attack on Kenesaw Mountain Sherman had a site cleared on the top of a hill for his tactical headquarters, and here he had a signal station with visual terminals and with line communications built to it. On 6th July he wrote in a despatch for transmission to General Halleck, Army Chief of Staff at Washington, 'The telegraph is finished to Vining's Station, and the field wire has just reached my bivouac, and will be ready to convey this message as soon as it is written and translated into cipher.'[22]

After the capture of Atlanta, Hood, commanding the opposing Confederate army, moved northward to try and get Sherman to withdraw from the city by attacking his communications. Sherman deduced that the Confederates would attack his post at Allatoona on the railway line between Chattanooga and Atlanta. The telegraph line had been cut between Atlanta and Allatoona. From his headquarters at Vining's Station, Sherman's signal detachment sent a message from him to General Corse at Rome, telling him to hurry to the assistance of Allatoona. The message was sent by flag 11 miles to the signal station on Kenesaw Mountain, and from there relayed by flag over the 12 miles to Allatoona. From Allatoona it went by line to Rome. Sherman then went to Kenesaw. At the time of his arrival the signal officer there had had no news from Allatoona, but whilst Sherman was with him the signal officer caught the faint glimpse of a flag and after much difficulty made out the letters C, R, S, E, H, E, R, and reconstructed the message, 'Corse is here.'[23]

Perhaps the most signal-minded of commanders on either side was Grant. Colonel James F. Rusling of the Quartermaster-General's staff, visiting Grant's headquarters at Nashville, found that the General disliked long letters and wordy reports, but noted that he had a telegraph in his office and spent much time talking by wire with all parts of his command.[24] This must be the earliest instance of the use by a commander of a method of communication, known to a much later generation of signal officers as 'key conversation'.

As the war progressed, so increased use was made of field telegraph communications. At the Battle of Spotsylvania signallers of General Hancock's Corps were groping through drenched pine thickets at night looking for the lines that had been laid the previous day to connect his headquarters with those of General Meade; and at the Battle of Cold Harbor, Meade established a command post at the headquarters of General Wright's Corps, from which he was in touch by field telegraph with all Corps commanders and with General Grant, the Commander-in-Chief. Grant, in his *Personal Memoirs* describes the telegraph organisation of his signals: 'Insulated wires . . . were wound upon reels. . . . Two men and one mule were detailed to each reel. The pack saddle on which this was carried was provided with a rack . . . so that the reel, with its wire, would revolve freely. There was a wagon, supplied with a telegraph operator, battery and telegraph instruments for each division, each corps, each army, and my headquarters. . . . The mules thus loaded were assigned to brigades, and always kept with the command they were allotted to.'[25]

Sherman considered that telegraph was by far the best means of communication for an army covering a large area. He had little faith in flags and torches, because in his experience when they were most needed the view was cut off by fog or trees. During 1864 hardly a day passed that

87

Grant was not in possession of Sherman's current situation report, though they were sometimes separated by more than 1,500 miles of telegraph route. Sherman says that, 'On the field insulated wire could be run on improvised stakes or from tree to tree for six or more miles in a couple of hours, and I have seen operators so skilful, that by cutting the wire they could receive a message with their tongues from a distant station.' The ordinary commercial wires along the railways formed the usual telegraph lines for an army, and these were easily repaired and extended as the army advanced.[26]

Balloons

On 6th June 1862 Long entered in his diary: 'General McClellan has not shown any disposition to advance. He has two balloons out to-day. Our troops are, however, so well sheltered by the timber that his balloon reconnaissances will avail him but little.'[27]

A Federal Balloon Corps was formed by the balloonist Thaddeus Lowe, and it was in the Peninsular campaign of 1862 that it was first extensively used. Reports were transmitted to the ground by means of a light telegraph wire. The Balloon Corps was first put under the Corps of Topographical Engineers; but Hooker, when he took over command of the Army of the Potomac, transferred it to the Signal Corps—a more logical organisation because Signals were charged with intelligence from observation. The results obtained hardly justified the effort, with the unwieldy equipment of the time, and the Balloon Corps was subsequently disbanded.[28]

The Confederates used a balloon during the Seven Days Battles. Alexander says that he was placed in charge of it and that it was manufactured in Savannah by Dr Edward Cheves and sent to General Lee for use in reconnoitring the enemy lines. It was made of silk of many patterns (apparently ladies' dress material), varnished with gutta-percha carsprings dissolved in naptha, and inflated at the Richmond gas works with ordinary town gas. Alexander observed the Battle of Gaines Mill from it and signalled information of reinforcements crossing the Chickahominy to reinforce Porter's Corps. When the Federals had retired to Malvern Hill, the inflated balloon was towed down the river and ascensions made from the deck of a small armed tug, the *Teaser*. On 4th July 1862 this vessel went aground below Malvern Hill on a falling tide and both tug and balloon were captured, though the crew escaped. A. J. Myer was watching and wrote with delight to his wife: 'Major Alexander was on board and had to swim ashore to escape—He had with him a balloon made of ladies silk dresses which we captured.'[29]

Notes

1 Jack Coggins, *Arms and Equipment of the Civil War*, 1962
2 Frederick H. Dyer, *A Compendium of the War of the Rebellion*, 1908
3 Major-General R. F. H. Nalder, *The Royal Corps of Signals*, 1958
4 Coggins, op. cit.
5 Nalder, op. cit.
6 Coggins, op. cit.
   T. Harry Williams, introduction to *Military Memoirs of a Confederate*
7 General W. T. Sherman, *Memoirs*, 1875
8 Colonel Theodore Lyman, *Meade's Headquarters 1863–1865*; Letters, Massachusetts Historical Society, 1922
9 William Swinton, *Campaigns of the Army of the Potomac*, 1866
10 A. L. Long, *Memoirs of Robert E. Lee*, 1887
11 Swinton, op. cit.
12 Sherman, op. cit.
13 Lyman, op. cit.
14 Swinton, op. cit.
15 Long, op. cit.
16 Lyman, op. cit.
17 General E. P. Alexander, *Military Memoirs of a Confederate*, 1907
18 Nalder, op. cit.
19 Coggins, op. cit.
20 Swinton, op. cit.
21 Lieutenant-Colonel A. J. L. Fremantle, *The Fremantle Diary*; ed. Walter Lord, 1956
22 Sherman, op. cit.
23 ibid.
24 Bruce Catton, *Grant Takes Command*, 1968
25 U. S. Grant, *Personal Memoirs*, 1886; quoted by General Sir James Marshall-Cornwall in *Grant*, 1970
26 Sherman, op. cit.
27 Long, op. cit.
28 Coggins, op. cit.
29 Alexander, op. cit.
   T. Harry Williams, notes to above, 1962

CHAPTER SIX

Railways

N EVER BEFORE OR SINCE THE American Civil War have the opposing armies depended so much on railways for movement and supply. The armies were far too large and the distances far too great for military needs to be met by horse transport. And yet, as compared with Europe, the railways in North America were most primitive affairs. Railway routes followed the natural contours of the ground as far as possible, and the track was of the flimsiest kind. Sleepers were generally laid straight on the bare earth without any stone or gravel ballast. The rails were generally of 'T' section, made of wrought iron and weighing from 35 to 68 lbs. per yard. But there were still long lengths of much earlier and weaker types. The poorest of these was the old 'strap' rail, which consisted of a thin iron strap secured to the upper surface of a 'stringer' of wood.[1] This type of rail was first used on the mineral railways of England in the days before steam locomotives, when the wear on the wooden rails was too excessive from heavy traffic. Nicholas Wood wrote in 1838:[2] 'In the United States of America, where iron is costly and timber plentiful and cheap, a greater temptation exists for railways of this description, and we accordingly find that, a great proportion of the railways in that country, consist of timber plated with iron. The abundance and cheapness of timber has, however, enabled the Americans to improve this description of railroad, far beyond what it existed originally, or what the capabilities of England afforded. The sleepers of the American railroads, are generally made of white oak, from eight to ten inches broad, and ten inches deep. . . . The bar or plate of iron, laid upon the top of the rails, is generally from two to two and a quarter inches broad, and half an inch, to five eighths of an inch thick . . . and is fastened to the rails by iron spikes, mostly about four and a half inches long, which pass through oblong holes pierced in the bars eighteen inches apart.'

Rather later types of this form of construction were the 'U' and flanged rails, which were also attached to wooden stringers. Although when the Civil War broke out most of this early track was to be found in sidings, there were still lengthy stretches on the main lines. The combined iron and wooden rail was spiked directly to the sleepers, and the rails were connected by chairs at the joints. Bridges were generally of the wooden trestle type.

Owing to the low power of the locomotives, steep gradients were avoided as far as possible, and railways were taken round hills to avoid the cuttings and tunnels which would have otherwise been necessary to keep the gradients within acceptable limits. The track was therefore frequently and sharply curved, and this necessitated locomotives with a flexible wheel base, so that engines with a leading bogie and two coupled axles (ie 4–4–0) became typical and almost universal on all American railways of the time for both passenger and freight traffic.

Because of the poor track, trains seldom exceeded a speed of 25 mph, and the power of the locomotives limited the weight of the trains to about 150 tons, or 15 loaded cars. The passenger cars had no heating or light, were braked by hand individually, and were divided into first and second classes. Freight wagons consisted of 'house' cars (box wagons), platform cars (flat trucks), cattle cars, and others.

In addition to the disadvantages of poor track and low-powered loco-motives, the Confederate States, over which most of the war was fought, had three different gauges for their railways. The railway system was made up of a very large number of small and individualistic companies with little common policy. Most of the railways in Virginia and North Carolina were of 4ft 8½in gauge, and there was another stretch of this between Montgomery in Alabama and the State border with Georgia. Practically all the other railways were built to a gauge of 5ft. But in Louisiana, on the west side of the Mississippi there two companies with lines reaching westwards from New Orleans and Vicksburg respectively which were 5ft 6in.

Only two routes connected Richmond with the western States of the Confederacy. One of these, which was 5ft gauge throughout, ran through Lynchburg, Knoxville, Chattanooga, and Corinth to Memphis, and thence south through Jackson to New Orleans. The other went south to the port of Wilmington on the 4ft 8½in gauge; thence, with a change to 5ft, through Augusta to Atlanta and on to the border with Alabama, where the gauge changed again to 4ft 8½in before continuing to Mont-gomery; and here the 5ft was resumed for the remaining link to Mobile. When the war started a 48-mile 4ft 8½in gauge line was being built from Greensboro to Danville, which would, on completion, give an alterna-tive route between Richmond and Augusta, and thus a third route to the

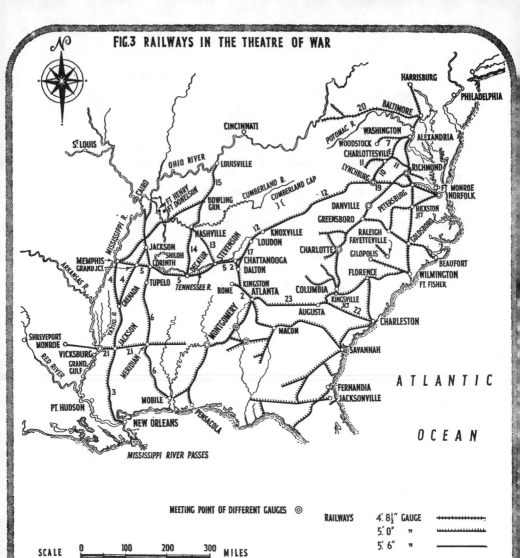

FIG.3 RAILWAYS IN THE THEATRE OF WAR

MEETING POINT OF DIFFERENT GAUGES ⊚

RAILWAYS 4' 8½" GAUGE
5' 0" "
5' 6" "

SCALE 0 100 200 300 MILES

Some of the Railroad Companies

1 Piedmont RR (Not completed till May 22nd, 1864)
2 Western & Atlantic RR
3 New Orleans, Jackson, & Great Northern RR
4 Mississippi Central RR
5 Memphis & Charleston RR
6 Mobile & Ohio RR
7 Manassas Gap RR
8 Danville RR
9 Norfolk & Petersburg RR
10 Orange & Alexandria RR

11 Virginia Central RR
12 East Tennessee & Virginia RR
13 Nashville & Chattanooga RR
14 Nashville & Decatur RR
15 Louisville & Nashville RR
16 Richmond, Fredericksburg & Potomac RR
17 East Tennessee & Georgia RR
18 Weldon RR
19 Southside RR
20 Baltimore & Ohio RR
21 Southern Mississippi RR
22 South Carolina RR
23 Georgia RR

West of the Confederacy. It was only finished on 22nd May 1864, but it saved the Confederate States from much earlier collapse because the Federals cut both the other routes. Owing to the rush to complete it, the Piedmont Railroad, as it was called, had many deficiencies. There were no stations or platforms, and even by the standard of railways in the South, sidings were inadequate. In addition there were no proper water stations, no supplies of wood fuel, and little rolling stock.[3]

Owing to the limited speed of the trains, travel was slow. The fastest train to North Carolina was the westbound mail. Leaving Goldsboro at 6.30 am it arrived at Raleigh, after running 48 miles, at 9.30 am, and at Hillsboro, after another 44 miles, at 12 noon. At 9.15 pm it reached Charlotte, having covered a total of 223 miles in $14\frac{3}{4}$ hours, or an average of about 15 mph, including 23 intermediate stops. On the South Carolina Railroad there was a rigid speed limit of 20 mph, 'unless greatly behind time, then not to exceed 25 mph.'

Freight trains, as would be expected, were even slower. The South Carolina Railroad limited them to 15 mph, and the running average was about 12 mph. On the Western & Atlantic Railroad a freight train was allowed 12 hours for the 138 miles between Chattanooga and Atlanta.

Trains in both North and South were not only slow, they were dangerous. Whereas at the outbreak of war, one railway passenger in 6,680,324 was killed in an accident in the United Kingdom, in the United States the accident rate was one in 188,000, or over 35 times as great![4]

Fremantle had some experience of train travel in the Confederacy. Of the Texan railways he wrote: 'There is only one class. The train from Allington consisted of two cars each holding about fifty persons. Their interior is like the aisle of a church, twelve seats on each side, each for two persons. The seats are comfortably stuffed. . . . Before starting the engine gives two preliminary snorts, which with a yell from the official of "all aboard", warn the passengers to hold on; for they are closely followed by a tremendous jerk which sets the cars in motion. . . . Richmond is on the Brazos River, which is crossed in a peculiar manner. A steep inclined plane leads to a low rickety trestle bridge, and a similar inclined plane is cut in the opposite bank. The engine cracks on all steam and gets sufficient impetus in going down the first incline to shoot across the bridge and up the second incline. But even in Texas, this method of crossing a river is considered dangerous.' There was worse to come. The next train in which he travelled started from Jackson, Mississippi, and the entry in his journal states: 'We then got into the cars at 6 pm for Meridian. This piece of railroad was in a most dangerous state, and enjoys the reputation of being the very worst of all the bad railroads in the South. It was completely worn out, and could not be repaired. . . . After we had proceeded

93

five miles, our engine ran off the track, which caused a stoppage of three hours. All male passengers had to get out to push along the cars.'[5]

Wood fuel on the Confederate railways was almost universal, and there were stacks of wood at intervals along all the lines. Wood was rated in cords—the cord being a cubic measure of 128 cubic feet—and the average engine ran about 50 or 60 miles per cord.

Signals were, on the whole, rudimentary. South of the Potomac telegraph communication along the railway was not yet common, and train movement was controlled principally by time-card and train-order.

In their effect on the war railways could probably be considered under the following headings: (a) Administrative movement of individuals and units; (b) Tactical movement of troops; (c) Strategical moves of units and formations from one theatre of operations to another; (d) Supply; and (d) As military objectives.

Administrative Movement

At the start of the war the concentration of the armies entailed a great deal of movement by rail, and much bureaucracy and muddle was encountered in the initial use of such a comparative newcomer to the march tables. Resentment by railway officials at having their normal authority over-ridden and the incompetent exercise of military 'red tape' combined to frustrate Colonel E. B. Harvey when he was ordered to take his new regiment, the 7th Pennsylvania Reserve Corps Infantry, from Harrisburg, Pennsylvania, to Washington, after the Battle of Bull Run. He relates his experiences as follows: 'Our orders at Harrisburg were to report to the commandant at Baltimore, General Dix. Our journey towards Baltimore, during daylight, was one constant scene of cheering. . . . When we reached the State line, we concluded to prepare for any emergency. We felt that we were hovering between two authorities—passing from Pennsylvania State authority to the United States authority; and during this transit I concluded I would be the authority and the regiment cheerfully accepted it. We ordered the train to stop and the men, out. Ammunition was distributed and the men loaded their pieces. We then moved on the train to within four miles of the city, and there stopped till daylight. We next moved into the city and stopped at the Bolton Station. The men got out of the cars and formed a line on the side of the street, where we remained for five hours awaiting orders. Immediately on our arrival in the city we reported by telegraph to General Dix at Fort McHenry our presence. At about ten o'clock am a despatch was received from that officer directing us to procure something to eat and then proceed to Washington as soon as we could obtain transportation. The mayor or provost marshal, attentive to our wants, sent Mr S. Robinson of that city with a police force to conduct us to some grove to take refreshment. We formed, and under the pilotage of a policeman, started, as we supposed, for the grove aforementioned. After half an hour's march through the city, the head of our line halted at the Camden Depot! I inquired if this was where we were to get our breakfast and the three last meals not yet had. I was met by the policeman, who informed me that he had been ordered to conduct us to that depot, that we might be moved on to Washington at once. Just then some of the managers of the railroad came up and insisted on us going ahead as the train was already in waiting. I informed them that we should not leave Baltimore until the men had one full meal. We had bounded for two days and nights on one meal. . . . I then marched the regiment back to the Bolton Depot. The Quartermaster, Judge Lane, and Mr E. Robinson had just returned, and the men enjoyed one good meal. I next authorized Mr Robinson to make arrangements and contracts for the transportation of my regiment—nine hundred men, baggage, horses, and equipments, to Washington;—and to move precisely at 9 pm. Mr Robinson soon returned, having made the arrangements. At seven o'clock we moved the regiment once more from the Bolton Station to the Camden Station, and were there informed that the cars placed on the track were for us and were ready. We loaded up. There were twelve cars. We filled them full leaving four companies still on the platform! The superintendent, managers, &c., came along blustering and scolding us for not getting ahead. I remonstrated with them about the accommodations provided, but only received in return threats that if we did not load up in the twelve cars they would move the trains and leave us behind. In addition to this, they refused to take the cars containing our horses, surplus arms and ammunition. Our contract called for nine-o'clock as the moving hour; it was then eight o'clock. I at length went to the head of the train, detached the locomotive, and placed Captain John Jameson on the platform with three companies to prevent the re-attachment of the locomotive or the moving of the train with part of my command until I should give the proper order. . . . I next repaired to the railroad office, when I met some eight smooth gentlemen who talked pompously and indulged in a few threats. . . . I only replied that that train would not move before nine o'clock, and that then it would take none of my regiment unless it took all. . . . I then returned to the locomotive, found my orders strictly enforced. . . . I was followed by a stranger and asked to return to the railroad office. I sought Mr Robinson, who made the contract, and we returned to the office together. When I got back a Mr White, clerk of the road, and a man calling himself president of the road, were present, who informed me that they had just received a despatch from Honorable Simon Cameron, ordering me forward at once, and that we were to proceed in twelve cars, leaving the horses and baggage behind. He next presented me with a certificate which professed to show that the company had furnished transportation to me for my regiment. I thereupon demanded a certified copy of the Washington despatch. They refused to give it to me saying that I had no business with it. . . . Just at this moment stepped in a man who, in a loud voice, proclaimed himself assistant-quartermaster of the United States, and demanded information as to who was interfering with and preventing transportation! I . . . replied it was myself. He responded that he would not have country colonels interfering with his business. . . . I thereupon said to this blustering major that I had possession of the locomotive and cars. . . . I then wrote a despatch to General Cameron, Secretary of War, stating our condition. . . . They soon presented us with a reply, purporting to be from Secretary Cameron, ordering us forward. I ordered a certified copy of it which they refused. I then left the office and returned to the cars, and waited till nearly nine o'clock, still refusing to move, when the aforementioned United States major, or quartermaster, came to me and said they would furnish three more cars, that we might leave at nine o'clock. This was done, and we finally took our departure for Washington, where we arrived about one o'clock next morning.'[6] (Harvey had been Captain of the Wyoming Bank Infantry of Luzerne county, one of the companies which combined to form the Seventh Regiment, and he, in accordance with the custom of the time, had been elected Colonel of the Regiment. He was subsequently promoted Brigadier-General. Precautions were necessary in Baltimore because there had been rioting in this Maryland town by Confederate sympathisers against troops passing through it.)

On the Confederate side, the concentration at Corinth before the Battle of Shiloh was perhaps that which entailed the biggest movements by rail. The Mobile & Ohio Railroad carried a number of infantry brigades northward, mostly from Pensacola in western Florida. The New Orleans, Jackson, & Great Northern, and the Mississippi Central Railroads brought nine infantry regiments and four batteries of artillery from New Orleans. The Memphis & Charleston and the Mobile & Ohio transported units located in various parts of Tennessee.[7]

After the Confederate defeat at Shiloh there was a rapid concentration at Corinth, and from Memphis the Memphis & Charleston brought four brigades in four days. Later Corinth was evacuated and the railways were fully used in transporting troops to the south. Most were carried by the Mobile & Ohio, but many trains travelled westwards on the Memphis & Charleston to Grand Junction, where this line joined that of the Mississippi Central. Six train loads of military stores and supplies were ordered to take this route, but they were held too long in Corinth and so were unable to reach Grand junction before a Confederate demolition detachment had destroyed the Tuscumbia Bridge on this route. The trains, therefore, had to be burnt to save them from falling into the hands of the Federals.[8] Sherman comments on this episode from the Federal angle: 'That night, viz, May 29th, we heard unusual sounds in Corinth, the constant whistling of locomotives, and soon after daylight occurred a series of explosions followed by a dense smoke rising high over the town.' The Federal forces entered Corinth and a few days later Sherman was ordered to Chewalla with instructions, 'to rescue the wrecked trains there, to reconnoitre westward and estimate the amount of damage to the railroad as far as Grand Junction, about fifty miles. . . . I found six locomotives and about sixty cars thrown off the track, parts of the machinery detached and hidden in the surrounding swamps, and all damaged as much by fire as possible. It seems that these trains were inside of Corinth during the night of evacuation, loading up with all sorts of commissary stores, etc., and about daylight were starting west; but the cavalry picket stationed at the Tuscumbia Bridge had, by mistake or panic, burned the bridge before the trains got to them. The trains, therefore, were caught, and the engineers and guards hastily scattered the stores into the swamp and disabled the trains as far as they could, before our cavalry had discovered their critical situation. The weather was hot, and the swamps fairly stunk with the putrid flour and fermenting sugar and molasses.'[9]

Tactical Movement

The first tactical move of troops by rail took place very early in the war. General J. E. Johnston used the Manassas Gap Railroad to move his infantry from their position facing the army of the Federal General Patterson in the Shenandoah Valley, to reinforce General Beauregard's army at Bull Run, in time to ensure victory in the first major battle of the conflict. Jackson's Brigade marched from its camp at noon on 18th July and bivouacked, after a 17-mile march, at Paris. The other three brigades (Bee's, Bartow's, and Elzey's) followed and marched about 13 miles. On 19th Jackson's Brigade marched six miles to Piedmont station (34 miles from Manassas), and at 8 am they started entraining. The first train left two hours later and by 1 pm the whole brigade, 2,500 strong, had detrained at Manassas. The other brigades arrived at Piedmont in the afternoon; but the railway could only send forward on that day two more regiments, the 7th and 8th Georgia of Bartow's Brigade. The trouble was that the railway company had only one shift of staff, and these men refused to work longer than their normal hours. The cavalry and artillery marched by road. On 20th July Johnston himself entrained, together with the 4th Alabama, 2nd Mississippi, and two companies of the 11th Mississippi.

97

These were the last troops from the Valley to arrive in time for the opening of the battle. Four more regiments, however, arrived at Manassas at noon on 21st and hurried to the battlefield in time to change defeat into victory. The remainder of Johnston's infantry did not get there till the day after the battle.[10]

Some complex tactical moves took place before the campaign of the Seven Days in the Peninsula. Lee decided to reinforce Jackson sufficiently for him to drive back the enemy, so that he could disengage from the Shenandoah Valley and join the main army about Richmond for an offensive against McClellan. As reinforcements he selected a brigade newly arrived from Georgia under Alexander Lawton, and the brigades of Hood and Law which were withdrawn on 11th June from the troops facing McClellan's army and despatched under the command of General W. H. C. Whiting. Lawton's Brigade was got ready for despatch by rail from Petersburg, whilst Whiting's Division marched through the streets of Richmond to the station of the 5ft gauge Danville Railroad. Departure from both places was delayed by either administrative muddle or deliberate deception. All the available cars on both the Southside and Danville Railroads had been sent to Lynchburg, from whence they were returning in trains carrying Federal prisoners for exchange. It has been suggested that it was intended that the repatriated prisoners should see these regiments departing for the Valley in order to deceive the authorities at Washington as to Lee's intentions. Rolling stock for the move was eventually borrowed from the Norfolk & Petersburg Railroad. (All these railroads were of 5ft gauge.) At Lynchburg the troops had to change trains to continue their journey on the 4ft 8½in gauge Orange & Alexandria Railroad. On 15th June the trains were entering Charlottesville, junction for the Staunton line of the Virginia Central Railroad; and here they were reversed and pulled through the Blue Ridge by Virginia Central locomotives. On 17th all troops of Jackson's command began the move towards Richmond. The railway was only of limited assistance because the Virginia Central had been cut beyond Frederickshall (50 miles from Richmond) by raiding Federal cavalry and only 200 cars could be collected on the western side of the cut. Whiting's and Lawton's troops were moved by rail to Gordonsville. Between this town and Frederickshall infantry marched parallel to the track and trains shuttled back and forth, taking up rear brigades in succession and transporting them to Frederickshall.[11]

After the Confederate victory at Chickamauga in September 1863, Longstreet's Corps was sent to recapture Knoxville and free the East Tennessee and Virginia Railroad. It was decided to move the Corps by rail from Chattanooga to Sweetwater, Tennessee, within 40 miles of

Knoxville. The artillery and McLaws's Division were marched to Tyner's Station on 4th November, and Hood's Division to the tunnel through the Missionary Ridge on the night of 5th. But it was not till 12th November that trains carrying the last of these troops left for Sweetwater. The men and guns of Alexander's artillery battalion were transported in a train of flat cars on 10th November, the train taking over twelve hours to cover the 60 miles. The gunners had to pump water for the engine and cut up fence rails along the route for fuel. The horses were driven along the roads.[12]

In the previous chapter Sherman's signal to General Corse to go to Allatoona was recounted. Corse was at Rome which was at the end of a branch from the railway between Chattanooga to Atlanta. Corse telegraphed to Kingston, which was about 15 miles away at the junction of the branch with the main line, and asked for a train. A locomotive hauling 30 empty cars was despatched as quickly as possible, but 10 of these ran off the appalling track and caused delay. At 7 pm the remaining 20 cars arrived at Rome and Corse loaded on Colonel Rowett's Brigade and part of the 12th Illinois infantry. The train left Rome at 8 pm and reached Allatoona, 35 miles away, at 1 am. It was then sent back by Corse for more men. The garrison at Allatoona consisted of 890 men under the command of Colonel Tourtellotte, and Corse's first train load was 1,054.

The Confederate force which arrived to attack Allatoona was French's Division, variously reported as being between 4,000 and 5,000 strong. By 8 am the Confederates had surrounded Allatoona, and the following exchange of notes took place under a flag of truce:

Around Allatoona, October 5, 1864
Commanding Officer, United States Forces, Allatoona:
I have placed the forces under my command in such positions that you are surrounded, and to avoid a needless effusion of blood I call on you to surrender your forces at once, and unconditionally.

Five minutes will be allowed you to decide. Should you accede to this, you will be treated in the most honorable manner as prisoners of war.

I have the honor to be, very respectively yours,
S. G. French
Major-General commanding forces Confederate States

General Corse replied immediately:

Headquarters Fourth Division, Fifteenth Corps
Allatoona, Georgia, 8.30 am, October 5, 1864
Major-General S. G. French, Confederate States, etc.:
Your communication demanding surrender of my command I acknowledge receipt

of, and respectfully reply that we are prepared for the "needless effusion of blood" whenever it is agreeable to you.

I am, very respectfully, your obedient servant,
John M. Corse
Brigadier-General commanding forces United States

Sherman says that the following day his aide, Colonel Dayton, received the following 'characteristic despatch': 'I am short a cheek-bone and an ear, but am able to whip all hell yet! My losses are very heavy. A force moving from Stilesboro' to Kingston gives me some anxiety. Tell me where Sherman is. John M. Corse, Brigadier-General.'

On the railway the Confederates burnt every sleeper and bent all the rails for eight miles; but 10,000 men were put on to repairing the track and in about a week trains were running again.[13]

Strategical Troop Movement

The largest single Confederate strategical movement of troops took place in the Western theatre in the summer of 1862. General Braxton Bragg had relieved Beauregard in command of the Confederate Army of the Mississippi, which was grouped about Tupelo. The Federal Army of the Ohio was marching towards the immensely important strategic centre of Chattanooga, and Bragg decided that he must switch the greater part of his army there to forestall the Federals under General Buell. However, to get to Chattanooga was no easy matter because the Federals held a large part of the Memphis & Charleston Railroad.

A move to Chattanooga by rail was so long and complicated, that Bragg decided to try it out first with only one division. The route was southward by the Mobile & Ohio Railroad to Mobile, then across Mobile Bay by ferry, and then by five different railways, entailing two changes of gauge, through Montgomery and Atlanta. The total distance of this journey was 776 miles.

The movement order for the division was issued on 27th June, and on 3rd July the first trains steamed into Chattanooga. Following this success, the bulk of the army, some 31,000 all ranks, was ordered to follow; though horse-drawn vehicles were to march by road, a much shorter distance of about 200 miles. The whole operation was very well organised with movement control staff officers at all junction points. The first train left Tupelo on 23rd July and was followed by a continuous succession of other trains for about a week.[14] This move excited Sherman's admiration, for he wrote: 'General Bragg had reorganised the army of Beauregard at Tupelo, carried it rapidly and skilfully towards Chattanooga, whence he boldly assumed the offensive, moving straight for Nashville and

Louisville, and compelling General Buell to fall back to the Ohio River at Louisville.'[15]

The other principal Confederate strategical rail movement was that of Longstreet's Corps from the Eastern to the Western theatre of war in September 1863 to reinforce Bragg's Army at Chattanooga. The route through Knoxville by the East Tennessee & Virginia Railroad was severed by the Federal occupation of that town, and the line between Greensboro and Danville had not, of course, been completed. There was therefore available only the railway running south from Richmond through Petersburg and Weldon; though from Hickston Junction in Virginia trains, instead of continuing on the direct line to Wilmington, could be alternatively routed via Raleigh and Greensboro to Charlotte (all in North Carolina), where there was a change from the 4ft 8½in gauge to the 5ft. This route continued through Columbia, South Carolina, to Kingsville Junction, where it rejoined the route through Wilmington. All trains then had to follow the same tracks through Augusta, Atlanta, and Dalton to Catoosa and other detraining points south of Chattanooga.

From 9th September there was a constant succession of trains carrying Longstreet's troops, the infantry being given priority. The first trains arrived at Catoosa station on 18th September. The Battle of Chickamauga was fought on 19th and 20th September, by which time only five of Longstreet's nine infantry brigades had arrived, but this was enough to ensure a Confederate victory.

Alexander's artillery battalion marched to Petersburg and about 4 pm on 17th September boarded its several trains (which were despatched in a batch). At 2 am on Sunday 20th the leading train steamed into Wilmington, having covered 225 miles in 58 hours (an overall average of just under 4 mph). Here the battalion crossed the river by ferry and were loaded on to trains on the 5ft gauge. After a run of 28 hours duration they arrived at Kingsville Junction, 192 miles from Wilmington (6.8 mph). The battalion had to change trains at the junction, and this, with all their guns, vehicles, and horses, took six hours. Augusta, 140 miles from Kingsville, was reached at 2 pm on 22nd. The trains left again at 7 pm and arrived at Atlanta, 140 miles, at 2 pm on 23rd (19 hours and an average speed of 7 mph). Leaving Atlanta at 4 am on 24th the trains arrived at Ringgold station, 12 miles from the battlefield and 115 miles from Atlanta, at 2 am on 25th (5 mph). The whole journey of 843 miles had thus taken about 7½ days. Although scarcely fast, Alexander considered it very creditable under the circumstances, and his account was written after many years of senior railway experience. He says: 'We found ourselves restricted to the use of one long roundabout line of single-track road of light construction, much of it of the "stringer track" of those days, a 16-pound rail on stringers, with very moderate equipment and of different gauges, for the entire service at the time of a great battle of the principal armies of the Confederacy. The task would have taxed a double-tracked road with modern equipment.'[16]

On the Federal side, the best examples of large strategic movement were, firstly, the transfer of the XI and XII Corps (23,000 men) under Hooker from the Eastern theatre to the Western before the Battle of Chattanooga, a journey of 1,192 miles which took seven days; and secondly, the move of the Army of Ohio under Schofield (15,000 men) from the Tennessee Valley to Washington in January 1865, for onward passage by sea to North Carolina, a rail journey of 1,400 miles taking eleven days.[17]

Supply by Rail

In a letter to General Grant on 20th October 1863, Halleck (then General-in Chief) wrote: 'A single-track railroad can supply an army of sixty or seventy thousand men with the usual number of cavalry and artillery; but beyond that number, or with a large mounted force, the difficulty of supply is very great.[18]

Without a nearby rail head, prolonged supply to an army in the field was not practicable (unless it was based on the sea or a major waterway). For instance, the Confederate Army of Northern Virginia could not have stayed long in Maryland at the time of the Sharpsburg campaign because there was no rail communication to the South; and in fact no force large enough to encounter the Army of the Potomac with success could be supported and supplied for long by wagon trains, when this entailed journeys from the nearest rail head at Staunton, 150 miles away.[19] Therefore a Confederate victory would have had to have been followed by rapid contact with the Orange & Alexandria Railroad.

Grant was faced with perhaps his greatest railway problem in the relief of the Federal army beleagured in Chattanooga after its defeat at Chickamauga. The Nashville & Chattanooga Railroad was in bad condition, was poorly operated, and accidents to its trains were frequent. Grant told the new superintendent of military railroads at Nashville that an absolute minimum of thirty freight wagons of rations must be despatched to Bridgeport every day. The Nashville & Chattanooga was, of course, single track, and to supply the full requirements of the army two tracks were needed. The Nashville & Chattanooga joined the Memphis & Charleston at Stevenson; 70 miles further west, at Decatur, the 100-mile-long Nashville & Decatur also joined the Memphis & Charleston Railroad. By using these railways to form a one-way circuit (Nashville–Stevenson–Decatur–Nashville) the equivalent of a double track railway could be provided; but the southern half of the Nashville & Decatur had been very thoroughly wrecked by the Confederate cavalry, with eighteen bridges destroyed, much of the track torn up, and the greater part of the rolling stock put out of action or removed. However, Grant allotted a complete infantry division to the task of restoring this railway to working order, and he instructed McPherson, commanding at Vicksburg, to collect all the locomotives and freight cars in his area and, with the exception of two locomotives and ten cars for his own use, to send them all north to the Memphis & Charleston. Rails and sleepers were obtained by tearing up branch lines all over Tennessee and Kentucky.[20]

By these methods a railway system of sorts was provided for the Battle of Chattanooga. But after the successful issue of the battle, the Nashville & Chattanooga needed much more work to make it suitable as a link in the main artery of supply to sustain any further advance by the Federal Army. One officer reported the line as 'a rickety, stringer-tie, dilapidated affair, never worth much before the rebellion', and added that, 'the whole line of the road was a vast cemetery of rolling stock'. Grant got the War Department's Superintendent of Military Railroads sent to take personal charge, and by 14th January 1864 there was a reliable train service from Nashville into Chattanooga, operated by locomotives and cars obtained from various sources.[21]

When Grant became General-in-Chief, Sherman took over command in the West and his Atlanta campaign depended absolutely on the lines Louisville–Nashville (185 miles), Nashville–Chattanooga (151 miles), and, as he advanced, Chattanooga–Atlanta (137 miles); all of them being single track. The chief supply depot was at Nashville, and this needed to be strongly guarded because it was in country which was partially hostile. Between Louisville and Nashville the track was liable to attack, and from Nashville forward to Chattanooga it was so vulnerable to Confederate cavalry raids that the whole line had to be closely protected by military posts and patrols.

In spite of the improvements which had been effected, the capacity of all the above railways was still far too low, mainly because of the acute shortage of locomotives and freight cars. The daily needs of the army could barely be met, and it was impossible to establish the forward dumps which would be necessary before the army could advance. The available cars were not even being put to the most economical use, because many of them were loaded every day with men returning from leave and others with cattle and horses. In addition, the carriage by rail of food for local inhabitants had been authorised because of the desolation of the country-side.

On 6th April Sherman issued an order limiting the use of railway cars to the transport of essential food, ammunition, and equipment for the army, and prohibiting all civilian traffic. Commanders of posts within 30 miles of Nashville were to haul their own supplies in wagons, all troops destined for the front were to march, and all beef cattle were to be driven on their own legs.

These measures freed a substantial number of cars to build up stocks; but it was not yet enough. In conjunction with his staff Sherman worked out the requirements of an army of 100,000 men with 35,000 saddle and draught horses, for an advance into Georgia. To be certain of these requirements being met, 130 cars of 10 tons each would have to reach Chattanooga daily. This only allowed 5lb of oats or corn per day for each animal and no hay, and all troops would have to march and cattle be driven. In addition, extra cars would be needed to allow a reasonable percentage destruction from Confederate raids and train accidents. Even with these restrictions on transport, there were only 60 serviceable locomotives and about 600 cars for the task which was not nearly enough. Sherman accordingly issued instructions that all trains arriving at Nashville from Louisville were to be held, and none allowed to return until sufficient locomotives and cars had been obtained; the number needed having been estimated as at least 100 locomotives and 1,000 cars.

Guthrie, President of the Louisville & Nashville Railroad, protested to Sherman, saying that with his diminished stock, he would not be able to bring forward the necessary stores from Louisville to Nashville. Sherman appealed to his patriotism and advised him to hold all trains coming into Jeffersonville, Indiana; Guthrie did so, and he and General Allen, Quartermaster-General at Louisville, arranged a ferry to transfer trains across the Ohio River from Jeffersonville to Louisville. 'In a short time,' writes Sherman, 'we had cars and locomotives from almost every road in the North; months afterwards I was amused to see, away down in Georgia, cars marked "Pittsburg & Fort Wayne", "Delaware & Lackawanna", "Baltimore & Ohio", and indeed with the names of almost every railroad north of the Ohio River. How these railroad companies ever recovered their property, or settled their transportation accounts, I have never heard, but to this fact, as much as to any other single fact, I attribute the perfect success which afterward attended our campaigns; and I have always felt grateful to Mr Guthrie, of Louisville, who had sense enough and patriotism enough to subordinate the interests of his railroad company to the cause of his country.'[22]

After the war General J. E. Johnston told Sherman that the Federals' feats of bridge building and repair of railways had excited his admiration. He instanced the occasion at Kenesaw in June 1864, when an officer of Wheeler's cavalry had reported to him in person that he had come from

General Wheeler who had made a bad break in the railway about Tilton station, which he said would take at least a fortnight to repair. While they were talking a train was seen coming down the line which had passed that very break![23]

The strategy of the Army of the Potomac was governed largely by problems of railway lines of communication. A force advancing from Washington against Richmond, and at the same time covering the former, was dependent on one of two railways; the Orange & Alexandria or the Richmond, Fredericksburg, and Potomac. During the various campaigns in Virginia, Pope and Meade tried the former, and Burnside and Hooker the latter. Both had disadvantages. The Orange & Alexandria ran through Charlottesville to Lynchburg, and was some 60 miles west of Richmond at its nearest point. A force following its route covered Washington well, but encountered difficult offensive country beyond the Rapidan. The Richmond, Fredericksburg & Potomac Railroad ran due south to Richmond and offered an easier line of advance, but an army using this route left Washington exposed, and a threat against the Union capital was sufficient to make a Federal army side-step towards the Orange & Alexandria.[24]

The Army of Northern Virginia's acute shortage of rations and clothing was due largely to inability of the single-track railways of the south, with their shortage of rolling stock, to meet demands. Complaints of shortages to the Commissary-General were met with the standard reply: 'Stop running passenger trains, and I can run more freight trains and supply you.'[25]

Railways as Military Objectives

It will be apparent from what has been said above that railways were extremely important military objectives; whether to deprive the enemy of the means of movement and supply, or to secure them for the use of one's own forces. The loss of the line connecting Richmond through Knoxville, to Chattanooga and the Mississippi was a severe blow to the Confederates, because it denied them the rapid use of their interior lines in switching troops and opened large areas to the Federals. The ex-Secretary of War, Walker, telegraphed Lee early in the war that: 'The railroad line from Memphis to Richmond must be defended at all hazards'. Earlier he had said that the 'Memphis and Charleston Road is the vertebrae of the Confederacy.'[26]

Sherman always expected to have a desperate fight to gain possession of the Macon & Western Railroad, because it was finally the only railway link left to supply the vital city of Atlanta. And General A. A. Humphreys, in his *The Virginia Campaigns of '64 and '65* (1883), says that Grant's reason for crossing the James River was, 'to carry out the plan with which the Army of the Potomac began the campaign, that is, to destroy the lines of supply to the Confederate depot, Richmond, on the south side of the James as close to that city as practicable after those on the north side had been rendered useless.'[27] It was not, in other words, necessary to destroy Lee's army if the railway lines which supplied it could be cut.

Rolling stock was nearly as important as track. Early in the war Jackson captured five locomotives of the Baltimore & Ohio Railroad and dragged them south down the Valley Pike behind teams of horses to Strasburg, where they were re-railed. It was said at the time that these engines were worth at least an infantry division to the Confederates.[28]

In the spring of 1862, when the Confederate Army withdrew from its positions beyond Manassas, most of the railway equipment was evacuated to the south. The single track Orange & Alexandria became completely congested as a result, and some trains took 36 hours to cover the 51 miles from Manassas Junction to Gordonsville.[29] But every locomotive and every passenger and freight car was vital to the Confederacy in its struggle to keep its armies in the field.

Notes

1   R. C. Black, *The Railroads of the Confederacy*, 1952
2   Nicholas Wood, *A Practical Treatise on Rail-Roads*, 1838, Third Edition.
3   Black, op. cit.
4   ibid.
5   Lieutenant-Colonel A. J. L. Fremantle, *The Fremantle Diary*; ed. Walter Lord, 1956
6   J. R. Sypher, *History of the Pennsylvania Reserve Corps*, 1865
7   Black, op. cit.
8   ibid.
9   General W. T. Sherman, *Memoirs*, 1875
10 General E. P. Alexander, *Military Memoirs of a Confederate*, 1907
11 Black, op. cit.
    Colonel G. F. R. Henderson, *Stonewall Jackson*, 1898
    William Swinton, *Campaigns of the Army of the Potomac*, 1866
    Clifford Dowdey, *Lee*, 1970
12 Alexander, op. cit.
13 Sherman, op. cit.
14 Black, op. cit.
15 Sherman, op. cit.
16 Alexander, op. cit.
    Black, op. cit.
17 Sherman, op. cit.
18 ibid.
19 Alexander, op. cit.
20 Bruce Catton, *Grant Takes Command*, 1968

21 ibid.
22 Sherman, op. cit.
23 ibid.
24 Swinton, op. cit.
25 Alexander, op. cit.
26 Black, op. cit.
27 Quoted by Catton, op. cit.
28 Black, op. cit.
29 ibid.

CHAPTER SEVEN

Supply and Transport

SUPPLY AND TRANSPORT HAVE been dealt with to a certain extent in the previous chapter on railways. This chapter, however, is concerned more with the supplies themselves and with their carriage and movement in the road wagon trains; and the term 'supply' is used in its widest sense, to include ammunition, clothing, food, forage, and all the various other requirements of an army in the field.

On the whole, with the vast resources of the Union behind it, the Federal Army was adequately supplied with all its needs—or rather, its base depots were—and the problems in this sphere were mainly concerned with the transport of these needs to the troops: a matter of vehicles, roads, march tables, and supply dumps.

In the Confederate Army, on the other hand, not only was practically everything short of requirements, but, owing to the inadequate railway system, even all that was available could not be moved forward to the army's rail heads. The Confederates, therefore, depended for many things largely on local procurement and captures from the enemy. Of these latter, Wolseley wrote: 'It was amusing to see "US" marked upon every wagon and upon almost all ambulance-carts which we passed. The North have not only clothed and equipped the millions of men whom they boast of having had at various times enrolled, but they have also similarly supplied the Southern armies. Into whatever camp you go, you are sure to see tents, carts, horses, and guns all marked with the "US". Officers have declared to me, that they have seen whole regiments go into action with smooth-bore muskets and without greatcoats, and known them in the evening to be well provided with everything—having changed their old muskets for rifles!'[1]

Supply in both armies came under three departments, the Quartermaster, the Commissary, and the Ordnance. The Quartermaster Department was responsible for such items as clothing, tents, bridging equipment, wagons, horses, and mules. It either built or purchased the wagons and supplied the teamsters who drove them. In the field there was a Quartermaster on each echelon of command. At army headquarters he was a colonel and at corps headquarters a lieutenant-colonel, and at both these he was styled a Chief Quartermaster. At divisional, brigade, and regimental headquarters there were a major, a captain, and a lieutenant, respectively, all of whom were styled Quartermaster. Each of these officers had a staff appropriate to his responsibilities.[2]

The Commissary Department was concerned with food and forage. These were allocated in bulk by the Commissary-General to the Commissaries of armies, who distributed them to corps, where they were broken down for issue through divisions to brigades and regiments and to corps troops. The rations most usually issued to the soldiers consisted of ham, bacon, beef (either salted or on the hoof), beans, flour, salt, sugar, coffee, biscuits, and sometimes fresh bread from the bakeries. Salt in large quantities was a most important commodity, because without it there could be no meat issue unless an army was accompanied by live cattle. Confederate soldiers, however, often got none of these things; whilst Federal troops, in the later stages of the war, often had the luxury of mobile bakeries.[3]

An additional source of food supply was provided by the sutler; a civilian who operated a mobile canteen. In the Federal Army one was allowed to each regiment, and he was appointed either by the governor of the State from which the regiment came or by the regimental or brigade officers.[4]

The Ordnance Bureau was charged with supplying ammunition for artillery and small arms, and also for artillery equipment and personal weapons. There was an ordnance officer or sergeant in every regiment who was responsible for furnishing weekly returns to the Chief Ordnance Officer of the army, showing the state of arms and the ammunition held in hand, in cartridge boxes, and in the regimental wagons.

In the Confederate Army reserve storehouses were established at rail heads, and reserve wagon trains ran between these and the formations in the field. For emergency use the Chief Ordnance Officer had under his control a train of ammunition and battery wagons equipped with tools and manned by expert mechanics, to undertake any repair from a broken main spring to a spiked field piece.[5]

Roads

The appalling roads constituted one of the principle obstacles to military movement. Practically all the roads in the Confederacy were unmetalled earth tracks which dissolved into mud after a shower of rain. According to Wolseley, 'The road down the Shenandoah Valley is macadamised, being, I believe, the only regularly metalled road in the State.'[6] A Confederate newspaper reporter said of the roads in Virginia in 1861: 'Much work was entailed in keeping open the roads in country where, after a light shower of rain, a team and wagon could easily become mired six to ten inches deep.'[7]

Alexander had personal experience of how bad roads could be during the Confederate withdrawal from Yorktown in the Peninsula in May 1862. He writes: 'I recall that night's march as particularly disagreeable. The whole soil of that section seemed to have no bottom and no supporting power. The roads were but long strings of guns, wagons, and ambulances, mixed in with infantry, artillery, and cavalry, splashing and bogging through the darkness in a river of mud, with frequent long halts when some stalled vehicle blocked the road. Then men from the nearest ranks would swarm in to help the jaded horses pull the vehicle out. Meanwhile everything in the rear must halt and wait, and so it went on all night—a march of one or two minutes, and halt for no one could guess how long. The average time made by the column was under a mile an hour.' In Jackson's move against the Federal General Milroy in the same month, he took, 'three days in moving his guns and trains through 12 miles of mud to reach a metalled road.'[8]

But perhaps the roads of Virginia showed at their worst on the occasion of the notorious 'mud march' of the Army of the Potomac in January 1863. Burnside, the then army commander, decided to move from Fredericksburg and cross the Rappahannock about six miles further upstream. The move started on 19th January and during 20th preparations were made for the crossing; but during that night there was a terrible storm, the effect of which on the clay roads and fields was appalling. According to Swinton, 'The nature of the upper geologic deposits of this region affords unequalled elements for bad roads, for it is a soil out of which, when it rains, the bottom drops, and yet it is so tenacious that extrication from its clutch is next to impossible.' There was more rain and storm on the following day, and 'An indescribable chaos of pontoons, vehicles, and artillery encumbered all the roads—supply wagons upset by the road-side, guns stalled in the mud, ammunition trains mired by the way, and hundreds of horses and mules buried in the liquid muck. The army, in fact, was embargoed: it was no longer a question of how to go forward—it was a question of how to get back. The three-days' rations brought on the persons of the men were exhausted, and the supply trains could not be moved up. To aid the return all the available force was put to work to corduroy the rotten roads.'[9] (A corduroy road was made by laying logs lengthways, putting another layer of logs crossways on top of them, and covering the lot with soil to make a reasonably smooth surface.)

Sherman had much trouble with roads during his march through the Carolinas. The distance from Savannah to Goldsboro was 425 miles and five large navigable rivers had to be crossed. 'The country generally was in a state of nature, with innumerable swamps, with simple mud roads, nearly every mile of which had to be corduroyed.'[10]

Perhaps the worst road ever to be used for supply columns during the war was that to which the Federals were restricted when the Army of the Cumberland was bottled up in Chattanooga. It was so bad that over the seventy or so miles of circuitous route, which connected the rail head at Bridgeport with Chattanooga, a loaded wagon train took eight days. The first ten miles as far as the village of Jasper were fairly easy. The road then ran north-east for over twenty miles up the valley of the Sequatchie River. This was not too bad in dry weather, but after a long period of heavy rain the draught mules could sink up to their bellies in mud and the fords became unusable. But it was the last and longest stretch that was the worst; for the road now turned south-east to cross the craggy and formidable Walden's Ridge, and it degenerated into a track which frequently clung to the hillside with the aid of logs on the projecting ledges. Wagons had often to be lightened by throwing away part of their loads before the struggling teams could pull them on. Even then there might be sixteen mules on one wagon with soldiers pushing behind. Those wagons that got through with rations for the army had often discarded the forage for their own teams; so the mules got weaker and the loads they could pull got lighter and some 10,000 of the unfortunate animals died on this dreadful road.

After proper communications had been re-established the Chief Quartermaster of the Army reported to the War Department that the animals would need three months rest before they would be of any use for further service, and recommended that they should all be sent back to Louisville to be got back into condition. As a result, any idea of advancing before the following spring had to be discarded.[11]

Wagons and Wagon Trains

The standard US wagon was 10 feet long in the body and had a canvas top on which was usually painted the corps badge, the number or name of the formation or unit to which it was attached, and a description of the contents. The wagon was drawn by a six-mule team, managed by a single driver who rode on the near-wheeler and guided the near lead mule with a single rein. Connected to the collar of the near-leader there was an iron rod which was attached at its other end to the bit of the off-leader. A steady pull on the rein steered the team to the left and short jerks steered it to the right. Some teams would respond to voice directions only; such as 'haw' for a turn to the left, 'gee' meaning turn right, and 'yay' for straight on.[12]

However, every conceivable kind of vehicle was taken into service to meet the insatiable demands of the armies. Grant's supply train at Vicksburg, for instance, was an extraordinary assembly of private carriages, farm wagons, long coupled wagons fitted with racks to carry bales of cotton, and any other vehicles which could be collected from the plantations. Some were drawn by mules and some by oxen, and every description of orthodox and improvised harness was used.[13]

The standard wagon of the Federal Army, described above, would carry 3,000lb net, which was adequate to accommodate the food for an infantry regiment at full establishment for one day; or for two days if the beef ration was driven separately on the hoof. For his Atlanta campaign Sherman insisted on there being 20 days supplies on hand at any one time; and these were normally in the wagon trains belonging to each corps, the distribution of which was controlled, under the general direction of corps headquarters, by quartermasters and commissaries. The strength of the seven army corps under Sherman varied between 15,000 and 20,000 men, except for the strong XVI Corps, which had 32,000. The average corps needed 300 wagons to carry these supplies, that is, 15 wagons for each day. To lift forage, clothing, ammunition, and other stores, a corps needed another 300 wagons, making a total of 600. The total number of wagons in the train was thus not far short of 5,000. In addition, each regiment was allowed one wagon for distributing rations down to companies, and each company might be allotted two pack mules for the carriage of rations, so that the men might be certain of having a meal on reaching camp without awaiting the arrival of the trains.[14]

To make his troops as mobile as possible, Sherman issued orders that each officer and soldier was to carry on his horse or person food and clothing sufficient for five days. Each regiment had a wagon for baggage and an ambulance, and the officers of a company were allowed a pack horse or mule between them. Tents were forbidden except for a few to accommodate sick and wounded, and one for each headquarters for use as an office.[15]

For his march through Georgia from Atlanta to the sea, Sherman made special arrangements, because he was cutting loose from his line of communications and relying on local subsistence. The army was organised into two wings, each consisting of two corps, and marched wherever practicable by four roads as nearly parallel as possible. Each corps had a train of about 800 wagons and ambulances, which occupied about five

Battery A, 2nd U.S. Artillery, and Batteries C and G, 3rd U.S. Artillery; Regular units of the Federal Army, equipped and organised as Horse Artillery. The photograph was taken just before the Battle of Fair Oaks in the Peninsula campaign of 1862. [Photo No. 235-CM-431 in the U.S. National Archives]

Guns at the Federal Fort Totten, near Washington D.C. Note the implements used by the gunners to traverse the guns. [Photo No. 235-CM-268 in the U.S. National Archives]

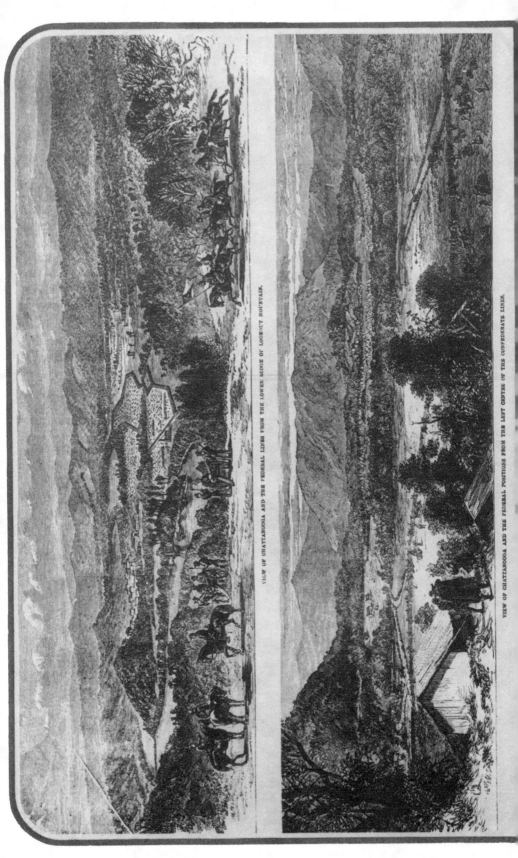

VIEW OF CHATTANOOGA AND THE FEDERAL LINES FROM THE LOWER RIDGE OF LOOKOUT MOUNTAIN.

VIEW OF CHATTANOOGA AND THE FEDERAL POSITIONS FROM THE LEFT CENTRE OF THE CONFEDERATE LINES.

A Federal wooden pontoon boat on its wagon, 1864. [U.S. War Dept. General Staff photo No. 165-SB-58 in the National Archives]

Confederate shell-proof 'dug-outs' in front of Petersburg, Virginia [Cook Collection, Valentine Musuem, Richmond, Virginia]

LEFT: *Federal 20-pr. Parrot rifled muzzle-loading guns near Richmond, Virginia. These are the pieces which had such an unfortunate reputation for bursting.* [Photo No. 235-CM-443 in the U.S. National Archives. BELOW LEFT: *The Confederate Palmetto Battery, Charleston, South Carolina. In this obviously posed photograph the charge is being rammed down the muzzle of each of the two guns. The two limbers can be seen in the rear. Note the comparatively immaculate appearance of the Confederate Artillery.* [The Museum of the Confederacy, Richmond, Virginia]

OPPOSITE PAGE: *A Confederate battery in action, by Frank Vizetelly. The charge is being rammed home and the 'ventsman' has his thumb on vent ('serving the vent') to prevent a rush of air which, if the previous sponging had left any burning fragments, might cause a premature explosion of the charge.* [Illustrated London News]

ILLUSTRATIONS OF THE WAR IN AMERICA, BY OUR SPECIAL ARTIST: HOWLETT'S BATTERY, ON THE JAMES RIVER, ENGAGING THE FEDERAL MONITORS.

A typical 4-4-0 locomotive of the Civil War period. The engine has been damaged, apparently by a shell-burst. [U.S. Signal Corps photo No. 111-B-6328 (Brady Collection) in the National Archives]

A Federal field hospital at City Point, Virginia in 1864. Note the 4-4-0 locomotives in the background, doubtless used to haul the hospital trains evacuating wounded from the Petersburg area. The right-hand locomotive has the initials USMRR (U.S. Military Railroads) on its tender. At City Point the more seriously wounded would have been embarked in hospital ships lying in the James River. [U.S. Signal Corps photo No. 111-B-462 (Brady Collection) in the National Archives]

LEFT: *An ambulance unit of the 57th New York Volunteers ('National Guard Rifles') of the Army of the Potomac. (One vehicle has 'Ambulance 57th N.Y.V.' painted on its cover.) The photograph shows wounded being loaded on to the ambulances. Note the two-wheeled and four-wheeled vehicles; the former only having one horse between the shafts. The regiment itself appears to be drawn up on parade in the background.*[U.S. Signal Corps photo III-B-50 (Brady Collection) in the National Archives.]

BELOW LEFT: *Major-General George G. Meade and the staff of the Army of the Potomac. Note the generally meticulous 'turn-out' of the officers. Meade is seated in the center facing the camera.* [U.S. Signal Corps photo No. III-B-27 (Brady Colletion) in the National Archives.]

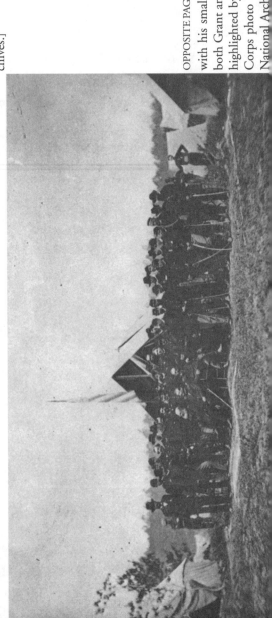

OPPOSITE PAGE: Lieutenant-General Ulysses S. Grant with his small staff in Virginia 1864. The dress of both Grant and his officers is somewhat haphazard, highlighted by the hat on the ground! [U.S. Signal Corps photo No. III-B-2 (Brady Colletion) in the National Archives]

THE WAR IN AMERICA: CAMP OF FEDERAL PRISONERS ON BELLE ISLE, RICHMOND.—FROM A SKETCH BY OUR SPECIAL ARTIST.

OPPOSITE PAGE: *The prisoner-of-war camp at Richmond, Virginia, by Frank Vizetelly; published in the Illustrated London News on 9th April 1864.* [Illustrated London News]

ABOVE LEFT: *The famous Confederate warship 'Alabama', by Frank Vizetelly. This sketch was published in the Illustrated London News on 15th November 1862.* [Illustrated London News]. LEFT: *The blockade-runner 'Lilian', with Frank Vizetelly on board, on his way back to the Confederate States after a visit to England. Published by the Illustrated London News on 16th July 1864. Note the Confederate flag flown by the ship.* [Illustrated London News]

A panoramic view of Petersburg, by Frank Vizetelly. [Illustrated London News] Of this sketch (which it published on 3rd September 1864) the Illustrated London News said: 'Our Special Artist in the camp of General Lee has sent us his sketch of a panoromic view of the town of Petersburg and adjacent country including the camp of General Grant. The Engraving of this view extends twice across two pages of our Paper, the lower half being intended to join the upper half, to end. . . In our present Illustration, though it been impossible to show the lines of the two conting armies, their relative positions can partly be n out by starting from the tents of the Federal sola which are shown upon a rising ground at the ext left of the upper half of our Engraving, and follo from left to right the indications of earthworks

fiepits until they are concealed by the foliage of the ...ood. At the extreme right-hand corner of the second ...rtion of the view we come upon General Lee, with ...s staff officers, partly sheltered behind a clump of ...ees, and watching the enemy's movements through a ...ld-glass. Our correspondent, writing on the 18th of ...ly, says that the shell-firing from the Federal side has ...n entirely bestowed upon the women and children, who still remained in the town, and that it had not done the slightest injury to the Confederate troops, who were lying snug enough in their trenches beyond the belt of wood which surrounds Petersburg. The men of the advanced posts on both sides would sometimes leave off shooting at each other, come forward, and have a friendly talk.

General Beauregard's headquarters at Fairfax Courthouse after the First Battle of Bull Run, 1861, Drawn by Frank Vizetelly, and published in the Illustrated London News, November 1861. [Illustrated London News]

THE BATTLE OF FREDERICKSBURG: ASSAULT OF THE FEDERALS ON MARYE'S HILL AND THE BATTERY OF THE WASHINGTON ARTILLERY.—FROM A SKETCH BY OUR SPECIAL ARTIST.—1863.

Although this illustration is entitled the Battle of Fredericksburg, it actually portrays the fight at Fredericksburg by Early's division during the Battle of Chancellorsville, as described in Chapter 11. Frank Vizetelly shows the heavy *Federal columns attacking Marye's Hill defended by the thin lines of the 18th and 21st Mississippi Regiments. This must be one of the most dramatic of battle pictures by a war correspondent and artist.* [Illustrated London News]

General R. E. Lee and his staff. Reading clockwise from the top, the staff officers are: Brigadier-General M. H. Stevens, Chief Engineer; Lieutenant-Colonel Charles Marshall, A.D.C.; Lieutenant-Colonel J. L. Corley, Chief Quartermaster; Lieutenant-Colonel B. G. Baldwin, Chief of Ordnance; Surgeon Lafayette Guild, Medical Director; Major H. E. Young, A.A.G.; Brigadier-General W. N. Pendleton, Chief of Artillery; Lieutenant-Colonel H. E. Peyton, A.A.G.; Major G. B. Cooke, A.A.G.; Lieutenant-Colonel W. H. Taylor, A.A.G.; Lieutenant-Colonel R. G. Cole, Chief Commissary; Lieutenant-Colonel C. S. Venable, A.D.C. Checking by the ranks of the officers and the dates of appointment, the photograph was apparently prepared in November 1864. (Lee nearly always wore the badges of rank of a Colonel.) [The Museum of the Confederacy, Richmond, Virginia]

miles of road. Normally trains were split up so that an appropriate proportion of ammunition wagons, provision wagons and ambulances followed each brigade; but if a strong enemy attack was expected, corps commanders changed their orders of march, so that the leading and rear brigades were unencumbered by wheels. For mobility, wagon loads were limited to 2,500lb and each wagon carried the forage for its own team. (A wagon was pulled by six mules and an ambulance by two horses.) Ammunition wagons each carried enough cartridges to make up about 200 rounds per man and enough assorted ammunition to provide 200 rounds per gun.[16]

Though having a much easier logistical problem, the Army of the Potomac had just as many wagons as Sherman's Military Division of the Mississippi; but in this magnificently equipped army there was some specialisation. Immediately behind the infantry came the 'fighting wagons', or first echelon of unit transport, and after them followed the second echelon, which included the 'spring wagons' with the officers' personal baggage. Well behind these marched the heavy wagons of the train and the herd of cattle.[17]

These immense trains of animal-drawn vehicles were a tremendous handicap to mobility. But much as Grant would have liked to have reduced them in the Army of the Potomac, he was unable to accomplish much. In Virginia no dependence could be placed on local procurement, for during the years in which the armies had swayed back and forth across it, the countryside had been bereft of most of its food supplies. The area over which the army could manoeuvre was therefore largely circumscribed by the rations that could be carried on the soldiers and in the wagons. This was never more than sufficient for sixteen days, so that reduction of the number of wagons would also reduce the radius of action.[18] It is true, of course, that the Army of the Potomac was fed on a much more lavish scale than the Confederate Army of Northern Virginia, but to increase mobility for a particular operation by reducing the scale of rations would probably have raised a political storm.

The Confederates often moved with a wagon train as large as the Federal, but this was often for collecting rations, rather than carrying them—for there was often little to carry. Fremantle says that when Lee's army entered Maryland, prior to the Gettysburg campaign, the wagon train was 42 miles long. On Sherman's figures of five miles of road space for 800 vehicles, this would infer a train of about 6,500 vehicles. Fremantle adds that on the retreat from Gettysburg the train was much longer due to the wagons and carts requisitioned in Pennsylvania.[19]

In his General Orders No 74 of 4th July 1863, Lee gives the following directions for the movement of the train:

'The trains which accompany the army will habitually move between the leading and the rear corps, each under the charge of their respective chief quartermasters. Lieutenant-Colonel Corley, chief quartermaster of the army, will regulate the order in which they shall move. Corps commanders will see that the officers remain with their trains, and that they move steadily and quietly, and that the animals are properly cared for.'[20]

The Confederate transport position deteriorated steadily due to shortage of both animals and vehicles, and by February 1865 it would no longer have been possible, for instance, for Lee's army to join Johnston's for an attack on Sherman because there was no longer the transport to make such a move practicable.[21]

Supply

The problem of supply governed the movements of the armies of both sides almost more than anything else. Confederate shortages were, as stated in the last chapter, due primarily to the inability of the railways to carry sufficient to meet demands; but another factor was the failure to stockpile in the early days of the war. Heros von Borcke, who served in the Confederate Army, says in his *Memoirs of the Confederate War of Independence* that this early maladministration was responsible for the terrible privations to which man and animal were subjected in the last two years of the war. In *A Belle of the Fifties* Mrs Clay writes that in May 1862, 'We had sugar in abundance, and pyramids of the richest butter.' And in March of the following year: 'The contrast between the comfort in this pretty city (Macon) of lower Georgia, a city of beautiful homes and plentiful tables, and our poverty-stricken capital and meagre starving camps, was terrible to picture.' She wrote to her husband: 'Why does not the President or some proper authority order on from here and other wealthy towns . . . the thousands of provisions that fill the land? Monopolists and misers hold enough meat and grain in their clutches to feed our army and Lincoln's!'[22]

An additional factor was the method of procuring supplies in the CSA. In a statement to Swinton after the war, General J. E. Johnston said that they, 'instead of being honestly raised, were impressed by a band of commissaries and quartermasters, who only paid one half the market value. As might have been expected, this was enough to prevent their getting anything. These (supplies that they obtained) they took by force, and did it with the greatest injustice. You can imagine what disorganisation of labor and what discontent this produced.'[23]

Worry about supplies appears constantly in Lee's reports. He wrote to Jefferson Davis from Hagerstown, Maryland, on 12th September 1862, 'We have found in this city about fifteen hundred barrels of flour, and I am led to hope that a supply can be gathered from the mills in the country, though I fear we shall have to haul from the Valley of Virginia. The supply of beef has been very small, and we have been able to procure no bacon. A thousand pairs of shoes and some clothing were obtained in Frederickstown, two hundred and fifty pairs in Williamsport, and about four hundred pairs in this city. They will not be sufficient to cover the bare feet of the army.'[24]

The strength of the Confederate Army of Northern Virginia at this time did not exceed 45,000 men. This low strength was not due so much to casualties in battle as to losses from long and rapid marches with insufficient food and without shoes. According to Long, 'It frequently happened that the only food of the soldiers was the green corn and fruit gathered from the fields and orchards adjacent to the line of march, and often the bravest men were seen with lacerated feet painfully striving to keep pace with their comrades, until, worn out with pain and fatigue, they were obliged to yield and wait to be taken up by the ambulances or wagons, to be carried where their wants could be supplied.'[25] When he was asked, after the war, why he had crossed the Potomac before the Sharpsburg campaign, Lee replied, 'Because my men had nothing to eat, I went to Maryland to feed my army.'[26]

Initially, at any rate, the Confederate soldiers in the West seem to have fared better. In April 1863 newspaper reporters wrote favourably in general of conditions in Bragg's army. The rations were adequate but monotonous; 'corn bread and fat bacon, day after day', which resulted in much diarrhoea. The troops were well clothed. In January of the previous year, however, a reporter in the Western theatre stated that there was no straw for man or beast, and that as a result of a shortage of hay, horses and mules suffered from colic and gnawed anything they could get their teeth into. Many of the wagon bodies were almost eaten up and mules could not be secured with rope halters as they chewed themselves loose.[27]

But apparently the lines of communication were inadequate to meet demands after the Battle of Chickamauga. Longstreet's Corps, which had reinforced Bragg, suffered badly on the march to Knoxville. The food supplied to the men, says Alexander, was 'frequently not even the reduced rations issued to the whole army. Corn, unground, was often the only ration.' Footwear was again a problem and Alexander saw the bloody stains left on the frozen road where the infantry had passed. In his own artillery battalion: 'We took the shoes from the feet of the drivers to give to the cannoneers who had to march.' Horse-shoes were so scarce that the shoes and nails were removed from the hooves of all dead horses, and all wounded and broken-down animals were killed and their shoes salvaged.[28]

The difficulties of supplying the Army of the Potomac in an advance on Richmond by the direct route via Fredericksburg are shown in a memorandum submitted to President Lincoln by Generals W. B. Franklin and W. F. Smith. The first paragraph of this is as follows:

'The distance from this point (Fredericksburg) to Richmond is sixty-one miles.

'It will be necessary to keep open our communications with Aquia Creek Landing from all points of this route. To effect this, the presence of large bodies of troops on the road will be necessary at many points. The result of making these detachments would be, that the enemy will attack them, interrupt the communications, and the army will be obliged to return to drive him away.

'If the railroad be rebuilt as the army marches, it will be destroyed at important points by the enemy.

'If we do not depend upon the railroad, but upon wagon transportation, the trains will be so enormous that a great deal of the strength of the army will be required to guard them, and the troops will be so separated by the trains, and the roads so blocked by them, that the advance and rear of the army could not be within supporting distance of each other.'[29]

This is, of course, a rather defeatist argument and not one which would ever have been submitted by Sherman.

In his second crossing of the Potomac, before the Gettysburg campaign, Lee again depended largely on local supplies for the subsistence of his army. He had intended that his powerful cavalry force, in addition to providing him with information as to the enemy's movements, would have been able to collect all the supplies he needed from the fertile Cumberland Valley, which he knew had stocks of provisions sufficient for an army of any size. Unfortunately, Stuart's misunderstanding of his orders deprived Lee of both information and supplies. As regards the latter, he managed to obtain a certain amount by despatching infantry detachments mounted on artillery and wagon horses to farms and hamlets in the vicinity of the line of march.[30] When Lee withdrew across the Potomac after the Battle of Gettysburg, he retired up the Shenandoah Valley. But Meade did not consider he could follow him owing to the difficulty of supplying an army as large as the one he commanded on this route. He therefore compromised by marching up the Loudon Valley, keeping as close to the Blue Ridge as possible.[31]

Supply presented the major Federal difficulty in prosecuting the campaign against Vicksburg, as narrated in Chapter One; and the whole of Grant's strategy, when he crossed the Mississippi south of Vicksburg, was based on taking a risk over supply. His line of communications for food and ammunition ran north up the Mississippi, and he gambled on cutting loose from this and capturing Vicksburg before his supplies were exhausted. He directed Sherman to organise a supply train and load it with 100,000 rations from the transports. This would give five days' rations for Sherman's Corps and two days each for McPherson's and McClernand's which had gone on ahead with three days' rations carried by each man. Sherman had reminded him that 'this road will be jammed as sure as life if you attempt to supply 50,000 men by one single road'. To this Grant replied that he did not intend to do so but to 'get up what rations of hard bread, coffee, and salt we can, and make the country furnish the balance'. This completely deceived the Confederate commander Pemberton, who intended to force Grant to withdraw by attacking his line of communications—but there was no such line to attack.[32]

In the previous chapter it is told how Sherman stopped all the civilian traffic on the railway before the start of his Atlanta campaign. This resulted in a public outcry and political pressure by appeals to the President. Lincoln urged Sherman to relax his prohibition, but Sherman, refusing to jeopardise his army's success for political reasons, replied that the railway could not supply army and people, adding, 'I will not change my order, and I beg of you to be satisfied that the clamour is partly humbug . . . and to test it, I advise you to tell the bearers of the appeal to hurry into Kentucky and make up a caravan . . .to relieve their suffering friends by foot, as they needed to do before the railroad was built.[33]

For the Confederate armies, ordnance and ammunition supply was, perhaps surprisingly, more plentiful than provisions and clothing; and indeed no action was fought in which adequate ammunition was not available to the commander of the force concerned. In a country with a primarily agricultural community this is the reverse of what one might expect.

Richmond, the capital, was an important, perhaps the most important, centre for the manufacture of ordnance and ammunition; Atlanta probably came next in importance, with a large number of foundries and machine shops, and there were new ordnance works at Selma, Alabama. The various Confederate arsenals soon began the manufacture of rifled ordnance, but this always presented a difficulty due to the lack of men skilled in its construction and the shortage of the copper and brass required. The Ordnance Bureau at Richmond was responsible for arranging the supply of the enormous quantity of ordnance and ammunition required during the war, and Alexander says no government department deserved more credit.[34]

Percussion caps, which were needed for all small arms (except the flintlocks, which were in fairly wide use at the start of the war) required nitric acid, mercury, and copper for their manufacture. The Nitric Acid and Mining Bureau learned to make saltpetre from caves and from the earth under old barns and smokehouses, and from all kinds of nitrogenous waste material; and from the saltpetre the chemists could make nitric acid. Mercury came from Mexico, but after the fall of Vicksburg and the consequent Federal capture of the whole line of the Mississippi, supplies were cut off; and at about the same time the supply of sheet copper was exhausted. The chemists discovered that a mixture of chlorate of potash and sulphuret of antimony could be used instead of fulminate of mercury; and all the turpentine and apple brandy stills in the country were collected and sent to Richmond to be cut up and re-rolled into copper strips. From this copper and the products of the chemists all the percussion caps used during the last year of the war were made; but at its close the copper stills were exhausted and Alexander did not know what they could have done if the surrender at Appomattox had not occurred when it did.[35]

Perhaps none of the generals on either side gave so much attention to logistics as Sherman. In reference to his supplies during his advance to Atlanta, he wrote to his wife, '. . . . for one hundred days not a man or horse has been without ample food or a musket or gun without adequate ammunition. I esteem this a triumph greater than any success that has attended me in battle or strategy, but it has not been the result of blind chance. At this moment I have abundant supplies for twenty days, and I keep a construction party in Chattanooga that can in ten days repair any breach that can be made to my rear. I keep a large depot of supplies at Chattanooga and at Allatoona, two mountain fastnesses which no cavalry force of the enemy can reach, and in our wagons generally manage to have from ten to twenty days supplies.'[36] Even Sherman, though, was short of clothing for his troops by the time his army reached Goldsboro, towards the end of his great march through the Carolinas. A large number of his soldiers had been trudging along barefooted, whilst thousands had their clothing in rags and their boots split.[37] But then of course Sherman had discarded his line of communications and there were no local sources from which he could obtain footwear.

In early June 1864, when Lee had withdrawn to the neighbourhood of Richmond, newspaper correspondents with his army reported that the food was more abundant and satisfying than it had been for a long time. One of them wrote on 11th June that the soldiers were being issued with full rations of salt meat, bread, coffee, and sugar, together with a fair amount of onions and greens.[38] But this temporary alleviation of hardship did not last. At the end of the year a Federal General, A. A. Humphreys (at that time chief-of-staff of the Army of the Potomac) noted the deteriorating conditions in the Confederate Army. In his book *Virginia Campaign* he writes:

'The winter of '64–65 was one of unusual severity, making the picket duty in front of the entrenchments very severe. It was especially so to the Confederate troops with their threadbare, insufficient clothing and meagre food. Meat they had but little of, and their Subsistence Department was actually importing it from abroad. Of coffee or tea or sugar, they had none except in the hospitals.

'It is stated that in a secret session of the Confederate Congress the condition of the Confederacy as to subsistence was declared to be:

That there was not meat enough in the Confederacy for the armies in the field. That there was not in Va. either meat or bread enough for the armies within her limits.

That the supply of bread for those armies to be obtained from other places depended absolutely upon keeping open the railroad connections of the South.

That the meat must be obtained from abroad through a seaport.

That the transportation was not now adequate, from whatever cause, to meet the necessary demands of the service.

'The condition of the deserters who constantly came into our lines during the winter appeared to prove that there was no exaggeration in this statement.'[39]

Notes

1 Lieutenant-Colonel Garnet Wolseley, *A Month's Visit to the Confederate Head-quarters,* Blackwood's Magazine, January 1863
2 Jack Coggins, *Arms and Equipment of the Civil War,* 1962
3 ibid.
4 ibid.
5 General E. P. Alexander, *Military Memoirs of a Confederate,* 1907
6 Wolseley, op. cit.
7 J. Cutler Andrews, *The South Reports the Civil War,* 1970
8 Alexander, op. cit.
9 William Swinton, *Campaigns of the Army of the Potomac,* 1866
10 General W. T. Sherman, *Memoirs,* 1875
11 Major-General J. F. C. Fuller, *Grant and Lee,* 1933
    Bruce Catton, *Grant Takes Command,* 1968
12 Coggins, op. cit.
13 Major-General J. F. C. Fuller, *The Decisive Battles of the Western World,* Vol. III, 1957
14 Sherman, op. cit.
15 ibid.
16 ibid.
17 Clifford Dowdey, *Lee,* 1970

18 Swinton, op. cit.
19 Lieutenant-Colonel A. J. L. Fremantle, *The Fremantle Diary*; ed. Walter Lord, 1956
20 A. L. Long, *Memoirs of Robert E. Lee, 1887*
21 Alexander, op. cit.
22 Fuller, quoted in *Grant and Lee*
23 Swinton, op. cit.
24 Long, op. cit.
25 ibid.
26 Dowdey, op. cit.
27 J. Cutler Andrews, op. cit.
28 Alexander, op. cit.
29 Swinton, op. cit.
30 Long, op. cit.
31 Swinton, op. cit.
32 Fuller, *Decisive Battles*
    B. H. Liddell Hart, *Sherman*, 1929
33 ibid.
34 Alexander, op. cit.
35 ibid.
36 Liddell Hart, op. cit.
37 ibid.
38 Cutler Andrews, op. cit.
39 Alexander, quoted op. cit.

CHAPTER EIGHT

Medical

Casualties on both sides in the Civil War were heavy. In the Federal Army the total number of white officers and men who served during the war amounted to 2,494,592. Of these 359,528 lost their lives, but only 110,070, or less than one-third, were killed in action or mortally wounded. Of the remainder, 199,720 died of disease, 24,866 died as prisoners of war, 9,058 were killed in accidents, and 15,814 died from other causes.[1] The usual proportion of killed and mortally wounded to wounded was one to five, so that perhaps some 600,000 were wounded. This suggests considerable medical skill, because the proportion of those who were wounded and survived as compared with those who lost their lives was very much the same as it is to-day. There are no precise Confederate figures, but the proportionate losses seem to have been much the same. For instance, the losses in infantry and artillery on each side at the fiercely contested Battle of Chickamauga were as follows:

	KILLED	WOUNDED	MISSING	TOTAL	STRENGTH
Confederates	2,074	12,797	1,328	16,199	47,520
Federals	1,625	9,618	4,453	15,696	55,799[2]

(The Confederates attacked and won the battle.)

But the main trouble was sickness, and, remembering the conditions under which the war was fought, particularly on the side of the Confederacy, this is not surprising. At the very start of the war, Confederate reinforcements after the Battle of Bull Run were little more than enough to make good the losses from sickness in the summer of 1861; for the area was very malarial and the troops were very ignorant about sanitary measures. In addition, new regiments coming from country districts brought measles, which cut the effective strength of many units by half.[3] During the winter of that year infectious diseases (particularly measles, mumps, and typhoid) reduced the Confederate strength considerably, particularly amongst men coming from rural areas, who had little resistance to these mainly town complaints.[4] In May of the following year Beauregard, commanding the Confederates in the West, had over 18,000 men sick; and here the principal troubles were dysentry, pneumonia, and measles.[5] In January 1863 an epidemic of smallpox broke out in Vicksburg.

Apart from diseases, soldiers had to become hardened before they were immune to the many discomforts of soldiering. In the spring of 1862 Confederate soldiers in the low flat country about Yorktown had to occupy badly drained trenches which were frequently flooded due to the incessant rain. The Federal rifle pits were close and both artillery and sharpshooters with telescopic sights paid attention to any Confederate movement. At many points the crowded ranks in the trenches had to sit or crouch behind the parapet in water up to their knees, until darkness allowed them to stand up or even get out of the trench. At night there was only mud and water to sleep in, and although men were relieved in these particularly bad spots as often as possible, there was inevitably much sickness.[6]

The Federals suffered much in trenches after the Battle of Cold Harbor in June 1864. General A. A. Humphreys, in *Virginia Campaign*, writes: 'The men in the advance part of the lines, which were some miles in length, had to lie in close narrow trenches; with no water, except a little to drink, and that of the worst kind, being from surface drainage; they were exposed to great heat during the day; they had but little sleep; their cooking was of the rudest character. For over a month the army had no vegetables. . . . Dead mules and horses and offal were scattered all over the country, and between the lines were dead bodies of both parties lying unburied in a burning sun. The country was low and marshy in character. The exhausting effect of all this began to show itself, and sickness of malarial character increased largely.'[7]

Medical Organisation

The system for evacuating the wounded was very similar to that still used in most armies. The men either walked or were carried on stretchers to a forward dressing station, which was a regimental post. After being given first aid, those requiring further treatment were taken in ambulances to the divisional field hospital. Here urgent cases were operated on and all seriously wounded who could be moved were sent on to base or general hospitals.

In the Federal Army the divisional hospital train was a considerable affair, designed to cater for 7,000 to 8,000 wounded. There were 14 army wagons and 4 medical wagons; of which the former carried 22 hospital tents and the latter the surgical and medical supplies and equipment. In addition, one army wagon and one medical wagon were allotted to each brigade to equip forward dressing stations. There were 40 ambulances in the division under the command of a lieutenant. The standard Federal ambulance was the so-called 'rocker' type, which was a four-wheeled vehicle, pulled by two horses, and manned by a driver and two stretcher bearers. Under the driver's seat were stowed casks of drinking water, cans of beef stock, and bread, together with mess and cooking equipment. The Confederate wounded were carried, much more uncomfortably, in springless two-wheeled wagons hauled by two mules; though a large number of Federal ambulances had been captured and were used as far as possible.[8]

Railway hospital trains generally were made up of ordinary rolling stock; though the Federals had some special cars, each fitted with 30 stretchers suspended on rubber rings. Hospital ships were also used, both on the sea in the East and on the great rivers in the West. These were first operated on the Union side by the Quartermaster Corps, but were later taken over by the Medical Department. In addition, some of the States fitted out and ran hospital ships of their own.[9]

The treatment of the wounded inevitably came under criticism from the press. A Confederate correspondent reported on the medical handling of the large number of wounded men after the Battle of Sharpsburg. The wounds were dressed by the regimental surgeons, who, when necessary, set or amputated limbs before patients were sent to the rear. From Sharpsburg they were then sent across the Potomac to Shepherdstown and then on to Winchester and Staunton where base hospitals had been established. Although the proper general hospitals in Richmond and other places were good, those improvised in various towns were often poor and sometimes staffed by surgeons who had been sent to them because they were of little value in the proper hospitals. The correspondent thought that some surgeons were good, but that others were poor and sometimes incompetent. The majority of the field surgeons he considered conscientious. He was impressed, however, with the efficiency of the Georgia Relief and Hospital Association, which established itself in the town of Warrenton.[10]

Contrary to common opinion, chloroform was available as an anaesthetic, and even the Confederates seem to have had adequate quantities of this and also of morphia, opium, and quinine. 'Stonewall' Jackson was given chloroform when his arm was amputated after he was wounded at Chancellorsville.[11] But shortages of much more familiar substances led to discomfort. Lee reported on 19th January 1865 that there was great suffering in the army from a shortage of soap, adding that, 'The neglect of personal cleanliness has occasioned cutaneous diseases.'[12]

Sherman liked his wounded to stay with their regiments as far as possible. He thought that each regiment should have a surgeon and two assistants and that each brigade and division should have an experienced surgeon as medical director. He believed that the great majority of wounds and sickness should be treated by the regimental surgeon on the ground and under the eye of the colonel. As few as possible should be sent further back because he was sure that the men always received better care with their own regiments than with strangers. He noted, too, that wounds which in 1861 would have sent a man to hospital for months were in 1865 regarded as mere scratches—rather the subject for a joke than sorrow.[13]

Surgeon Lafayette Guild's Report

Something of medical problems in the field is conveyed by a report submitted by Surgeon Lafayette Guild, Medical Director Army of Northern Virginia, to Surgeon-General S. P. Moore at Richard after the Battle of Gettysburg. The following is an extract:

'Sir: At midnight July 3rd, after the fiercest and most sanguinary battle ever fought on this continent, the general commanding gave orders for our army to withdraw from Gettysburg and fall back to Hagerstown. . . . Every available means of transportation was called into requisition for removing the wounded from the field infirmaries, and on the evening of the 4th our ambulance trains took up their line of march by two routes, guarded as well as could be by our broken-down and inefficient cavalry. One train went by Cashtown, the other by Fairfax. The latter train was attacked by a body of the enemy's cavalry, who destroyed many wagons and paroled the wounded private soldiers, but taking with them all the officers who fell into their hands. The former train was more fortunate; however, it, too, was attacked by the enemy, and met with some loss in wagons and prisoners. The poor wounded suffered very much indeed in their rapid removal by day and night over rough roads, through mountain passes, and across streams toward the Potomac. Those who could be removed from the battlefield and infirmaries were concentrated at Williamsport and transferred to the Virginia bank of the river by rafts and ferryboats as rapidly as the swollen condition of the stream would permit. . . .

'On July 15th we encamped near Bunker Hill, twelve miles north of Winchester, and remained there until the 21st, refreshing the troops and removing to the rear our sick and wounded from Winchester and Jordan Springs, at which place I found about 4000 sick and wounded, steps for their removal to Staunton being immediately taken. All who could bear transportation were gotten off by the 22nd instant, less than 150 remaining at the two places. Mount Jackson and Harrisonburg have been used simply as wayside hospitals, where the sick and wounded were refreshed with food and wounds re-dressed, medical officers with supplies of all kinds being stationed at the two points.

'On the 22nd the army resumed its march, the First and Third corps taking different routes to Front Royal and Chester Gap, where they were convalesced and the march continued to this point (Culpeper Court House), where they encamped on the 25th, and are now resting after their arduous night-marches through great inclemency of weather. The Second army corps crossed the Blue Bridge at Thornton's Gap, south of Chester Gap, and will encamp in our vicinity to-day. Considerable sickness has been the consequence of their fatigues and exposure. Diarrhoea, dysentry, continued fever, and rheumatism preponderate. I have prohibited the establishment of a hospital at Culpeper Court-house, but organised a depot for the sick and wounded who cannot be treated in camp. Those who should go to general hospital are sent with all despatch to Gordonsville. It is or may be at any time exposed to cavalry raids, and the inhuman enemy invariably, when an opportunity offers, drag our sick and wounded officers (at the sacrifice of their lives) into their own lines.

'Mount Jackson and Harrisonburg, in the valley of the Shenandoah, should be abandoned as hospitals, as far as practicable, leaving only those patients whose lives would be endangered by transportation.

'I have ordered Surgeon Breckenridge, medical inspector of the army, to proceed to the hospitals near the army where our sick and wounded have been sent since the battle of Gettysburg, and to have all returned to their regiments who are fit for duty. . . .

'Complaints are very frequently made by medical officers and officers of the line that many of the sick and wounded who are sent to general hospitals are never heard from, the hospital surgeons failing to report deaths, discharges, furloughs, etc. I would again respectfully request that means be adopted for the correction of this neglect of duty on the part of medical officers in general hospital. . . .'[14]

Notes

1 Frederick H. Dyer, *A Compendium of the War of the Rebellion,* 1908
2 General E. P. Alexander, *Military Memoirs of a Confederate,* 1907
3 ibid.
4 J. Cutler Andrews, *The South Reports the Civil War,* 1970
5 ibid.
6 Alexander, op. cit.
7 Alexander, quoted op. cit.

8 Jack Coggins, *Arms and Equipment of the Civil War*, 1962
9 ibid.
10 Andrews, op. cit.
11 Coggins, op. cit.
    Colonel G. F. R. Henderson, *Stonewall Jackson*, 1898
12 A. L. Long, *Memoirs of Robert E. Lee,* 1887
13 General W. T. Sherman, *Memoirs,* 1875
14 Long, quoted, op. cit.

CHAPTER NINE

Command and Staff

Higher Organisation

T HE ORGANISATION OF THE units and formations of each of the fighting arms of the service is described in Chapters Two, Three, and Four. We are concerned here, in particular, with the organisation at army corps level and above, in so far as it has a bearing on the higher command. It is not proposed to describe this organisation in detail because, particularly on the Federal side, it was extremely complex. The whole area of the North, for instance, was divided geographically into military departments which differed considerably in their size and in the number of troops which they contained, and of which the boundaries and titles were liable to change. Some of them were so large and important that the name of the department was the same as that of an army based on it, whilst others contained little more than administrative troops and establishments.

Once the army corps organisation had been adopted, it became in many respects the basic formation, and divisions, instead of being numbered right through the Federal Army, became the 1st, 2nd, or 3rd of each corps. The numbers allotted to each army corps were, however, sometimes changed, and occasionally different armies had army corps of the same number. For instance, in June 1862, whilst the Army of the Potomac was still in the Peninsula, the Army of Virginia was formed under General Pope with corps numbered I, II, and III. Of these the I Corps was formed from troops in the Mountain Department (created in March 1862 from the Department of West Virginia), the II Corps had divisions belonging to the Department of the Shenandoah, and the III Corps came from the Department of the Rappahannock, the troops in which had formerly constituted the I Corps of the Army of the Potomac. In the Army of the Potomac, too, there were at this same time corps with the numbers II and III. In September 1862, after Pope's defeat, all these became merged into the Army of the Potomac. Pope's III Corps resumed its old designation of I, and his I and II became the XI and XII respectively. A year later these latter two were transferred to the Army of the Cumberland and in 1864 they were amalgamated as the XX Corps.

The organisational traps which await the student of this war can perhaps best be illustrated by following the fortunes of the higher commands in the Western theatre, particularly those of the Department of the Cumberland. This department originated in a humble way with a small body of Kentucky volunteers assembling at Camp Joe Holt near Louisville, Kentucky, under the command of Colonel Lovell H. Rousseau (later a divisional commander in the Army of the Cumberland) in the spring of 1861. On 28th May 1861 that part of the State of Kentucky lying within 100 miles of the Ohio River was constituted the Department of Kentucky, and Brigadier-General Robert Anderson (who as Major Anderson surrendered Fort Sumter to the Confederates) was appointed to command it. On 15th August 1861 it blossomed out into the Department of the Cumberland, comprising the States of Kentucky and Tennessee. On 8th October Anderson went sick and was succeeded by his second-in-command, William Tecumseh Sherman. A month later, on 9th November 1861, the name was changed to the Department of the Ohio, and it now consisted of the States of Ohio, Michigan, Indiana, Tennessee, and that part of Kentucky east of the Cumberland River. At the same time Major-General D. C. Buell relieved Sherman in command.

Immediately west of the Department of the Ohio was the Department of Missouri, consisting of the States of Missouri, Iowa, Minnesota, Wisconsin, Arkansas, and Kentucky west of the Cumberland River. Its commander was Major-General H. W. Halleck. In March 1862 the Departments of Missouri and the Ohio were merged into a new Department of the Mississippi under Halleck's command, but the troops from the old Department of the Ohio retained their name of the Army of the Ohio. Buell still commanded this army but he was now subordinate to Halleck. The troops of Halleck's old Department of Missouri became the Army of West Tennessee, commanded by Major-General U. S. Grant.

On 29th September 1862 the Army of the Ohio was organised into the I, II, and III Army Corps. On 24th October 1862, Halleck having been appointed General-in-Chief of the Union Army, the Department of the Mississippi was divided again into its two previous components, but with different names and different boundaries. Instead of the Ohio there was the Department and Army of the Cumberland, and the former Missouri Department took the name of the existing Army and became the Department of the Tennessee. The Cumberland, now under the command of Major-General W. S. Rosecrans, comprised Tennessee east of the Tennessee River and such parts of Alabama and Georgia as might be

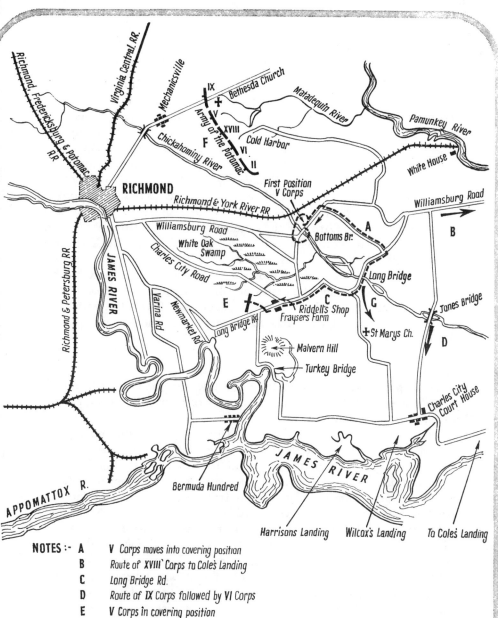

NOTES :-
A   V Corps moves into covering position
B   Route of XVIII Corps to Cole's Landing
C   Long Bridge Rd.
D   Route of IX Corps followed by VI Corps
E   V Corps in covering position
F   Battle of Cold Harbor
G   Route of II Corps

SCALE 0 1 2 3 4 5 6 7 MILES

FIG. 4   PLAN OF THE ARMY OF THE POTOMAC'S MOVE FROM COLD HARBOR TO THE RIGHT BANK OF THE JAMES - JUNE 1864

occupied by Federal troops. The Tennessee embraced Cairo, Fort Henry, Fort Donaldson, Northern Mississippi, and those parts of Kentucky and Tennessee west of the Tennessee River. Grant remained as its commander. The I, II, and III Corps of the Army of the Cumberland were amalgamated to form one XIV Corps, though this was divided into a Right Wing, a Centre, and a Left Wing, each with a varying number of divisions. The Army of the Tennessee initially consisted only of the XIII Corps; but on 18th December 1862 this was reconstituted into no less than four Corps, the XIII, XV, XVI, and XVII. Six months later, on 9th June 1863 the Army of the Cumberland was similarly reorganised; XIV Corps Centre became XIV Corps, the Right Wing became XX Corps, and the Left Wing XXI Corps.

Meanwhile on 19th August 1862 a new Department of the Ohio had been formed, to include the States of Ohio, Michigan, Indiana, Illinois, Wisconsin, and Kentucky east of the Tennessee River. On 27th April 1863 a new Army of the Ohio was created with the formation of the XXIII Corps.

Grant's great victory at Vicksburg was achieved with the XIII, XV, and XVII Corps of the Army of the Tennessee. On 7th August 1863 the XIII Corps was transferred to the Department of the Gulf, which comprised the coast of the Gulf of Mexico west of Pensacola Harbour and as much of the hinterland as was occupied.

After the defeat of the Army of the Cumberland at Chickamauga, the XX and XXI Corps were in October 1863 amalgamated into a new IV Corps (the IV Corps of the Army of the Potomac having been discontinued in August 1863). Also, as a result of the Chickamauga, the XI and XII Corps were transferred to it from the Army of the Potomac. (In April 1864 these last two were amalgamated to form a new XX Corps.)

On 18th October 1863 there was created the Military Division of the Mississippi, consisting of the Departments of the Tennessee, the Ohio, and the Cumberland, under the command of General Grant. Grant was subsequently appointed General-in-Chief and was relieved by Major-General W. T. Sherman on 18th March 1864.[1] In modern terminology this would have been called an army group because it consisted of three armies. It was with these three armies that Sherman carried out his Atlanta campaign, and they were organised as follows:

ARMY OF THE CUMBERLAND   IV Corps, XIV Corps, XX Corps, and a Cavalry Division
ARMY OF THE TENNESSEE   XV Corps, XVI Corps, and XVII Corps
ARMY OF THE OHIO   XXIII Corps and a Cavalry Corps.

Their strengths are interesting. The Army of the Cumberland had a total strength of over 170,000 men. Of those present, 10,000 were on special duty and 6,000 were sick. Of those absent, 20,000 were on detached service, 22,000 were on leave, 20,000 were sick, and 2,000 were absent without leave. (These figures are in round numbers.) About half the strength, therefore, were absent from the Colours, leaving about 90,000; but from these various detachments would have to be made guarding lines of communication, etc. The other armies, which were smaller, had similar proportions of their strengths away. Sherman decided on a compact field army of about 100,000 men, of which 50,000 would be provided by the Army of the Cumberland, 35,000 by the Army of the Tennessee, and 15,000 by the Army of the Ohio.[2]

After his capture of Atlanta, Sherman broke up the army organisation, and his march to the sea was carried out with four corps and a cavalry division, totalling about 60,000 men. The army advanced in two wings, each of two corps, the XV and XVII on the right (ex-Army of the Tennessee) and the XIV and XX Corps on the left (ex-Army of the Cumberland).[3]

Organisation and Functions of Command and Staff

The Staff organisation on each side was naturally very similar, because commanders naturally followed the system in which they had been trained in the old regular army. Staff categories in the various formations were therefore the same, though the number in each category differed according to the methods of command favoured by the general concerned. In the North the personal staff of a commander was governed by regulations. For instance, when Grant was made a Lieutenant-General, the Act which created this previously non-existing rank authorised a personal staff of a brigadier-general as chief-of-staff, four aides-de-camp with the rank of lieutenant-colonel, and two lieutenant-colonels as military secretaries. Earlier in the war when he had been made a Brigadier-General, Grant was allowed the naturally much more modest staff of a captain as assistant adjutant-general and two ADCs. For the former he selected Captain John Aaron Rawlins who had been the legal adviser to the family leather business. Rawlins remained as the chief officer of his staff until the end of the war; it was he who was promoted Brigadier-General on Grant's staff when the latter became General-in-Chief, and he finished the war as a Major-General.[4]

Grant's staff remained a modest affair, and the total when he took the field in 1864 amounted only to fourteen officers. In addition to the personal staff listed above, there were a lieutenant-colonel as assistant adjutant-general, two captains AAG, a lieutenant-colonel assistant inspector-general, a captain assistant quartermaster, and two additional junior officers as ADCs. But then, of course, his staff did not need to be big because he always established his headquarters close to those of Meade's headquarters of the Army of the Potomac.

Normally a higher formation staff included officers as assistant adjutant-generals, assistant inspector-generals, and quartermasters. The number of them and their ranks depended on the level of the headquarters. Between them these officers covered roughly the duties performed in the British Army by the adjutant-general, quartermaster-general, and general staffs. But there were important differences. The chief of staff for instance was officially adjutant and inspector-general, thus combining in himself these two staff functions. Many commanders, in fact, functioned as their own chiefs-of-staff, and most used their ADCs as general staff officers, despatching them with orders and expecting them to report on the situation in various parts of the field. What Grant required of these officers is recounted by one of them, General Horace Porter (then a Lieutenant-Colonel), as follows:

'I want you to discuss with me freely from time to time the details of the orders given for the conduct of a battle, and learn my views as fully as possible as to what course should be pursued in all the contingencies which may arise. I expect to send you to the critical points of the lines to keep me promptly advised of what is taking place, and in cases of great emergency, when new dispositions have to be made on the instant, or it becomes suddenly necessary to reinforce one command by sending to its aid troops from another, and there is not time to communicate with headquarters, I want you to explain my views to commanders and urge immediate action, looking to cooperation, without waiting for specific orders from me.' Grant added that he would locate his headquarters close to those of Meade's Army of the Potomac and communicate his instructions through Meade and through Burnside (whose corps was independent of Meade's command); but that emergencies might arise in which he himself would have to give immediate directions to troops when actually engaged in battle.[5]

In the field the ADCs were usually engaged in riding back and forth during the night between Grant's headquarters and the different commands, communicating instructions for the following day; and they had to fit in their sleep whenever they could.

If Grant had been commanding the Army of the Potomac one could not take exception to this method of working. But he was not, and it was unfair to Meade, the army commander, and difficult for his corps commanders, who received orders direct from both Grant and Meade. One cannot imagine Alexander by-passing Montgomery to issue orders direct to the corps commanders in the Eighth Army during the Battle of El Alamein! Meade, too, had succeeded where every other Union general, including Grant, failed—he had beaten Lee in battle, at Gettysburg.

The latitude in discussion that Grant allowed his staff was also surprising. Porter relates an animated argument amongst the staff, in front of Grant, about Meade's anomalous position and the embarrassments which were at times caused in the field through issuing orders through him instead of direct to corps commanders. They then urged on Grant that this wasted time and that there was a danger that orders might become changed in the process. They added that few responsibilities were given to Meade and yet he was charged with the duties of an army commander; that if he failed he could not be held responsible and if he succeeded he could not reap the full rewards; that, besides, he had an irascible temper and often irritated officers who came in contact with him. Grant, on the other hand, was even-tempered and succeeded in getting hearty co-operation from corps commanders when he dealt with them direct. At the close of the arguments Grant pointed out that he was commanding all the armies and could not neglect others by giving all his time to commanding the Army of the Potomac, which would entail performing all the detailed duties of an army commander.[6] This was a weak reply, because the obvious retort was that in that case he should let Meade command without interference in the same way as he did Sherman. He could not plead any failing in Meade because in a letter to the Secretary of War he wrote: 'General Meade has more than met my most sanguine expectations. He and Sherman are the fittest officers for large commands I have come in contact with.' Finally it seems an odd relaxation of discipline that permitted lieutenant-colonels to discuss in such terms an army commander.

Meade was one of the most loyal of men, even though he was irascible. He was also a strict disciplinarian and expected (in contrast to Grant and Sherman) a meticulous standard of turnout amongst his staff. Porter relates a story of an officer in the army who had formerly been a surgeon. One day he appeared at Meade's headquarters in a high state of indignation, complaining that some soldiers called out, 'Old Pills' after he had passed and requesting that this should be stopped. 'Meade just at that moment was not in the best possible frame of mind to be approached with such a complaint. He seized hold of the eye-glasses, conspicuously large in size, which he always wore, clapped them astride of his nose with both hands, glared through them at the officer and exclaimed: "Well, what of that? Why, I hear that, when I rode out the other day, some of the men called me a 'damned old goggle-eyed snapping turtle', and I can't even stop that".'[7]

When Grant became General-in-Chief, Meade's chief-of-staff was

General Andrew A. Humphreys, a very competent regular officer. After the war he wrote of the command set-up in Virginia that, 'There were two officers commanding the same army. Such a mixed command was not calculated to produce the best results that either singly was capable of bringing about. It naturally caused some vagueness and uncertainty as to the exact sphere of each, and sometimes took away from the positiveness, fullness and earnestness of the consideration of an intended operation or tactical movement that, had there been but one commander, would have had the most earnest attention and corresponding action.'[8]

Sherman had his own views on staff organisation. In his *Memoirs*, in dealing with the lessons of the war, he writes: 'I don't believe in a chief of staff at all, and any general commanding an army, corps, or division, that has a staff-officer who professes to know more than his chief is to be pitied. Each regiment should have a competent adjutant, quartermaster and commissary, with two or three medical officers. Each brigade commander should have the same staff, with the addition of a couple of young aides-de-camp, habitually selected from the brigade, who should be good riders, and intelligent enough to give and explain the orders of their general. The same staff will answer for a division. The general in command of a separate army, and of a *corps d'armée*, should have the same professional assistance, with two or more good engineers, and his adjutant-general should exercise all the functions usually ascribed to a chief of staff, viz., he should possess the ability to comprehend the scope of operations, and to make verbally and in writing all the orders and details necessary to carry into effect the views of his general, as well as to keep the returns and record of events for the information of the next higher authority and for history. A bulky staff implies a division of responsibility, slowness of action, and indecision, whereas a small staff implies activity and concentration of purpose.' And of the commander he wrote: 'No man can properly command an army from the rear, he must be "at the front"; and when a detachment is made, the commander thereof should be informed of the object to be accomplished, and left as free as possible to execute it in his own way; and when an army is divided up into several parts, the superior should always attend that one which he regards as most important. Some men think that modern armies may be so regulated that a general can sit in an office and play on his several columns as on the keys of a piano; this is a fearful mistake. The directing mind must be at the very head of the army—must be seen there, and the effect of his mind and personal energy must be felt by every officer and man present with it, to secure the best results. Every attempt to make war easy and safe will result in humiliation and disaster.'[9]

Sherman, when he took over command in the West, found he had a chief-of-staff in the person of Brigadier-General J. D. Webster. However, before the start of the Atlanta campaign he established a rear headquarters at Nashville, where he installed Webster, with a major and a captain AAGs, in charge of rear administration and with powers to issue orders in his name. The staff that remained with him in the field consisted of three ADCs (captains), a brigadier-general and two lieutenant-colonels as assistant inspector-generals, a brigadier-general as chief of artillery, a colonel as chief of engineers, a colonel as chief quartermaster, a colonel as chief commissary, a captain as chief of ordnance, and a surgeon as medical director. After the fall of Atlanta he acquired a major as judge advocate and another ADC.

Sherman's headquarters in the field consisted, apart from these officers, of half a dozen wagons, a company of Ohio sharpshooters as headquarter guard, and a company of Alabama irregular cavalry to provide orderlies and despatch riders. One of his ADCs acted as AAG, equipped with an order book, a letter book, and writing paper, all carried in a small chest. The only reports and returns called for were the ordinary tri-monthly returns of effective strengths, and as these were accumulated they were sent back to Nashville.[10]

One weakness in the Federal staff system was that the quartermaster, commissary, and ordnance departments were not under the control of the commanders in the field, but reported to their own departmental chiefs in Washington. Some, therefore, regarded themselves as independent, and justified in ignoring orders from the commander to whose staff they belonged, unless these orders were confirmed through their departmental channels. Grant insisted that a commander must have control, and took the matter up with the President. Lincoln said that he could not legally give the General-in-Chief authority over these departments, but added that only he could interfere with Grant's orders and he was not in the least likely to do so.[11]

On the Confederate side, Lee's opinions on staff were given in a letter to President Jefferson Davis, written on 21st March 1863. The following are extracts: 'The greatest difficulty I find is in causing orders and regulations to be obeyed. This arises not from a spirit of disobedience, but from ignorance. We therefore have need of a corps of officers to teach others their duty, see to the observance of orders, and to the regularity and precision of all movements. This is accomplished in the French service by their staff corps, educated, instructed, and practised for the purpose. The same circumstances that produced that corps exist in our own army. Can you not shape the staff of our army to produce equally good results? Although the staff of the French army is larger than that proposed by the Senate bill, I am in favor of keeping ours down, as it is so much easier to build up than to reduce if experience renders it necessary. I would therefore assign one general officer to a general commanding in the field, and give to his inspector-general, commissary-general, chief of ordnance, and medical director the provisional grade of colonel of cavalry. I would reduce his aides, and give to his chief of staff and inspector general assistants, as they will never be able to properly attend to their out-door and in-door work, which from the condition of our army, as heretofore stated, is very heavy. I would apply the same principles to the division and brigade staff, placing their chiefs on an equal footing, and giving each a complete organisation in itself, so that it can manoeuvre independently of the corps or division to which it is habitually attached, and be detached with promptness and facility when required. Each, therefore, in addition to its general staff, should have a surgeon, quartermaster, and commissary and ordnance officers. If you can then fill these positions with proper officers—not the relations and social friends of the commanders, who, however agreeable their company, are not always the most useful—you might hope to have the finest army in the world.'[12]

It will be noted that Lee favoured taking general staff duties away from ADCs and returning them to the inspectorate-general branch of the staff where they properly belonged. This should ensure that these duties were discharged by officers properly trained for the task. The Confederate Army suffered more than the Federal from poorly trained staffs, because it had a smaller proportion of the pre-war regular officers, and most of these were employed in command. Lee suffered badly in this respect, because as an army commander he liked, and rightly, to convey his orders verbally, but he lacked a staff trained to confirm these orders in writing and to see that they were received and understood by the headquarters of lower formations.

Lee's staff, after he took over command of the army in the Peninsula in 1862, included Colonel R. H. Chilton as Adjutant and Inspector-General (ie Chief-of-Staff), Colonel A. L. Long as Military Secretary, and as ADCs Major Walter H. Taylor, Major Charles Marshall, Major Charles Venable, and Captain T. A. R. Talcott. In selecting these ADCs Lee had to rely on his own judgment of personalities, because they were all completely lacking in staff training and experience. Chilton, who should on his paper qualifications have been invaluable, turned out to be a misfit in the field. He had been Paymaster-General in the old regular army, and had served subsequently in the office of the Adjutant-General in Richmond. He was intelligent, conscientious, and devoted, but he had been dealing with office administrative work for so long that the post of chief operational staff officer was quite beyond him. However, he dealt with the administrative side of Lee's staff until the beginning of 1864, when he returned to the Adjutant-General's office. Of the ADCs Taylor had been a business man, Marshall a lawyer, and Venable a professor of mathematics. Talcott was a young engineer officer, whose father, once in the Engineers of the old regular army, was a friend of Lee. All were expected to be able to deliver and receive verbal instructions, information, and reports accurately; in addition, each specialised in one aspect of staff duties. Venable carried out inspector-general duties, Taylor was responsible for office routine under Chilton, and Marshall took over some of the Military Secretary work from Long.[13]

By the time that Chilton left Lee's personal staff had been reduced to three; Venable, Marshall, and Taylor. Taylor was performing very ably the duties of assistant adjutant-general, but all three were used by Lee for transmitting orders, receiving reports, carrying out reconnaissances, and giving instructions for the movement of troops within the Commander-in-Chief's intention. All rose to the rank of colonel and remained with Lee till the end of the war. It was Marshall who accompanied Lee to the interview with Grant at Appomattox, where he surrendered his army; and Lee directed Marshall to draft his farewell order to his troops.

Taylor, in his book *Four Years with General Lee*, (1877), gives an interesting account of Lee's attitude to papers: 'He had,' he writes, 'a great dislike to reviewing army communications; this was so thoroughly appreciated by me that I would never present a paper for his action unless it was of decided importance and of a nature to demand his judgment and decision. On one occasion, when an audience had not been asked of him for several days, it became necessary to have one. The few papers requiring his action were submitted. He was not in a very pleasant humour; something irritated him, and he manifested his ill-humour by a little nervous twist or jerk of the neck and head peculiar to himself, accompanied by some harshness of manner. This was perceived by me, and I hastily concluded that my efforts to save him annoyance were not appreciated. In disposing of some cases of a vexatious character matters reached a climax; he became really worried, and, forgetting what was due to my superior, I petulantly threw the paper down at my side and gave evident signs of anger. Then in a perfectly calm and measured tone of voice, he said, "Colonel Taylor, when I lose my temper don't you let it make you angry".'[14]

Lee's objections to relations and friends as staff officers arose from the appalling inefficiency of the staffs of his subordinate commanders in the Peninsular campaign of 1862. Many of both divisional and brigade commanders had made up their staffs with relations and neighbours without any military experience, and with more capacity for hard drinking than hard work. After complete success in the Battles of the Seven Days had been forfeited by numerous and inexcusable staff failures, Lee tried to get commanders to improve both the quality and ability of their staffs.[15]

'Stonewall' Jackson, though one of the most able of Civil War generals, did not set a good example in his use of staff officers, and this led to one or two bad failures amidst his brilliant successes. He was very careful in his selection of officers, but he was so secretive that his staff often knew little or nothing of his plans, and were thus unable to pursue his intentions in his absence or to convey those intentions to lower commanders. One result of this was that Jackson's nervous exhaustion in the Seven Days' campaign resulted in the comparative failure of his headquarters to implement Lee's intentions.

There were some odd characters on Jackson's staff. Of them and of Jackson's methods, Henderson writes: 'For some months his chief of staff was a Presbyterian clergyman (Major the Reverend R. L. Dabney, DD), while his chief quartermaster was one of the hardest swearers in Virginia. The fact that the former could combine the duties of spiritual adviser with those of his official position made him a congenial comrade; but it was his energy and ability rather than this unusual qualification which attracted Jackson; and although the profanity of the quartermaster offended his susceptibilities, their relations were always cordial. . . . In all his campaigns, too, Jackson was practically his own chief of staff. He consulted no one. He never divulged his plans. He gave his orders, and his staff had only to see that these orders were obeyed. His topographical engineer, his medical director, his commissary, and his quartermaster, were selected, it is true, by reason of their special qualifications. Captain Hotchkiss, who filled the first position, was a young man of twenty-six, whose abilities as a surveyor were well known in the Valley. Major Harman, his chief quartermaster, was one of the proprietors of a line of stage coaches and a large farmer, and Major Hawks, his commissary, was the owner of a carriage manufactory. But the remainder of his assistants, with the exception of the chief of artillery, owed their appointments rather to their character than to their professional abilities.'[16]

Staff Work in the Field

Owing to the mainly inexperienced officers, staff work at the start of the war was very bad indeed; in the later stages it was on the whole good and sometimes very good. Most commanders preferred to rely on verbal orders, and, in the absence of trained staff officers to confirm these in writing, misunderstandings and mistakes inevitably occurred. Johnston's defeat at the Battle of Seven Pines in the Peninsula, for instance, was due to verbal orders, the inefficiency of his staff, and his own impatience with detail. Johnston's plan, says Alexander, was excellent and simple, but it was ruined through Longstreet's misunderstanding of his orders. Subsequent staff ineptitude led to the situation described by Alexander as follows: 'When one contemplates the fact that there was a commanding officer, hoping to win a great victory, then at his headquarters within two miles of this spot where nine brigades were thus passing and repassing each other, the whole performance seems incredible. And when it is further said that six of these brigades were lost, with their commander, and that the staff of the general was seeking them at that moment, high and low, miles away along the picket line, it is almost ludicrous.'[17]

Grant was something of an exception in that (probably because he had suffered so much from untrained staff officers early in the war) he wrote nearly all his orders and instructions with his own hand. And of these orders, General Meade, no mean judge, said: 'There is one striking feature . . . no matter how hurriedly he may write them in the field, no one ever has the slightest doubt as to their meaning, or ever has to read them over a second time to understand them.'[18]

Poor organisation and lack of a trained staff cost the Confederates their chance of a decisive victory at Chickamauga; a victory which might have made impossible Sherman's capture of Atlanta and subsequent march to the sea.[19]

Alexander considers that the inability of the Confederates to deliver a co-ordinated attack at Gettysburg on the third day of the battle was due to the lack of a proper staff; he says: 'I attribute it partially to the fact that our staff organisations were never sufficiently extensive and perfect to enable the Commanding General to be practically present everywhere and to thoroughly handle a large force on an extended field.'[20]

But staff ability on both sides in the latter stages of the war bore no relation to that of the earlier period. The manoeuvres in the period from the Wilderness to Cold Harbor could not have been executed without efficient staff officers in both the Confederate and Federal Armies; and the movement of the Army of the Potomac from Cold Harbor to the right bank of the James was a staff masterpiece. It involved withdrawing the army from close contact and executing a long march, including a major river crossing, without alerting the Confederates.

On 6th June Grant summoned two of his ADCs, Comstock and Porter, and told them that he was sending them on an important mission as a preliminary to a move of the Army of the Potomac. As a first step, he said, he was going to despatch Smith's XVIII Corps by a forced night march to Cole's Landing on the Chickahominy River, where it would be embarked and transferred to General Butler's position at Bermuda Hundred. The Corps would move without its transport or artillery, which would follow on later with the Army of the Potomac. The Army of the Potomac was to be ready to evacuate its existing position at short notice and to march rapidly to the James River and be prepared to cross. The two ADCs were to go to Bermuda Hundred, explain the whole operation to Butler, and see that this General (whose initials were appropriately 'B. F.') made the necessary preparations to make his position secure against an attack whilst the Army of the Potomac was on the move. They were then to select the best point on the James River for a crossing, bearing in mind the importance of choosing a place which would make the march of the Army of the Potomac as short as possible, whilst being far enough downstream to prevent any chance of Lee's army being able to attack it successfully during the crossing. The width of the river at the point of crossing and the type of country by which it would be approached were also to be taken into account.[21]

In accordance with Grant's instructions, the front at Cold Harbor was so entrenched as to establish a secure base. Warren's V Corps was then moved secretly to an area near to Bottom's Bridge over the Chickahominy. This move was intended to suggest to Lee, if he discovered it, that the Army of the Potomac was about to move either against Richmond via the road junction at Riddell's Shop or towards Turkey Bridge near the James, which was the direct route to Bermuda Hundred.

Porter and Comstock had selected Wilcox's Landing (some 15 miles downstream from Bermuda Hundred) as the best place to cross the James, and here was constructed a 13-foot wide pontoon bridge, supported by 92 boats and braced by three schooners, anchored in 85 feet of water, near the centre. The Army of the Potomac engineers built the bridge in ten hours, finishing it at midnight.

The withdrawal started at nightfall on 12th June. Warren's Corps marched further upstream and crossed the Chickahominy at Long Bridge, and then Burnside's IX Corps crossed the same river still further upstream at Jones Bridge. The movement of these Corps was covered by Hancock's II and Wright's VI Corps, manning the Cold Harbor position. The II Corps then followed the V across Long Bridge and the VI followed the IX over Jones Bridge; their withdrawal being covered by Wilson's Cavalry Division. The V Corps, after crossing the Chickahominy, marched west and took up a position south of the White Oak Swamp to cover the march to Charles City Court House of the other three corps. As soon as they were clear it followed the II Corps. The Army's wagon trains had been about White House, and from there they marched to Cole's Landing.

The II Corps reached Wilcox's Landing and started crossing the new bridge on the afternoon of 13th June, whilst the VI and IX Corps arrived at Charles City Court House the same day. By midnight on 16th over half the infantry, 4,000 cavalry, a train of wagons and artillery 35 miles long, and 3,500 beef cattle were on the south side of the James River.

Of this operation General Fuller writes: 'As far as staff duties are concerned, this is surely one of the finest operations of war ever carried out.'[22] The overall plan was Grant's; but the detailed planning must have been carried out by General Meade and his staff, headed by General Humphreys—a triumph of staff planning for which they have been given inadequate credit.

Personnel

A less publicised worry of commanders related to the discipline and morale of the troops under their command. The most brilliant plan, the most able staff work, are of no avail if the weapon on which they depend is ineffective. Something of these matters has been mentioned in earlier chapters, and it has been shown that high morale was often offset by poor discipline. Perhaps the factor which militated most against discipline was the lack of trained regimental officers. In the spring of 1862 Dabney, Jackson's chief-of-staff, wrote: 'The lack of competent and energetic officers was at this time the bane of the service. In many there was neither an intelligent comprehension of their duties nor zeal in their performance. Appointed by the votes of their neighbours and friends, they would neither exercise that rigidity in governing, nor that detailed care in providing for the wants of their men, which are necessary to keep soldiers efficient. . . . It was seldom that these officers were guilty of cowardice upon the field of battle, but they were often in the wrong place, fighting as common soldiers when they should have been directing others. Above all was their inefficiency marked in their inability to keep their men in the ranks. Absenteeism grew under them to a monstrous evil, and every poltroon and laggard found a way of escape. Hence the frequent phenomenon that regiments, which on the books of the commissary appeared as consumers of 500 or 1,000 rations, were reported as carrying into action 250 or 300 bayonets.'[23] The absentees were sometimes greater than this. In a letter to President Jefferson Davis on 21st September 1862, Lee wrote: 'A great many men belonging to the army never entered Maryland at all; many returned after getting there, while others who crossed the river kept aloof. The stream has not lessened since crossing the Potomac, though the cavalry has been constantly employed in endeavoring to arrest it. . . . Some immediate legislation, in my opinion, is required, and the most summary punishment should be authorized. It ought to be construed as desertion in face of the enemy. . . . To give you an idea of its extent, in some brigades, I will mention that on the morning after the battle on the 17th, Gen. Evans reported to me on the field, where he was holding the front position, that he had but 120 of his brigade present, and that the next brigade to his, that of Gen. Garnett, consisted of but 100 men. Gen. Pendleton reported that the brigades of Gens. Lawton and Armistead, left to guard the ford at Sheperdstown, together contained but 600 men. This is a woeful condition of affairs.'[24] This must surely rank as one of the great understatements of military history!

The election of officers, which had taken place in the Confederate Army at the beginning of the war, was staged all over again in the spring of 1862. Of that occasion, Alexander, then with the army about York-town, wrote: 'During our stay here a reorganisation of the army took place. The majority of our troops had enlisted for a year in the spring of 1861. It was now necessary to re-enlist them for the war. Congress had enacted that re-enlistment furloughs should be given to a few men at a time, and that a re-election of officers should take place in each regiment. This feature was very detrimental to the standard of good discipline.'[25] Few soldiers would disagree with Alexander's statement. Indeed, that the officers of a regiment in close contact with the enemy should be liable to be replaced by the votes of men under their command is incredible.

The Federal Army suffered similar troubles from poor regimental officers. Desertions from the Army of the Potomac after the Battle of Fredericksburg averaged over 200 a day, and the official rolls, at the time when Burnside was relieved of his command of that army, showed that over 80,000 men were 'absent from causes unknown'.[26]

After the first inevitable panics by untrained officers and men at the start of the war, morale remained generally good and, as these pages have recorded, it was often outstanding. Indeed, having regard to their privations, never in the history of war has a higher morale been displayed than in the ranks of the infantry of the Confederate Army of Northern Virginia. During the latter part of the war there was a deterioration of morale in some units and formations, generally due to the poor quality of men drafted into the ranks to replace casualties and the departure of time-expired men. Lyman has some comments on deterioration in fighting ability in the Army of the Potomac. In the Battle of the Wilderness Mott's Division behaved badly, and yet this was Hooker's old fighting division with a record at one time second to none in the Federal Army. It had had two poor commanders and there had been some trouble over re-enlist-ments. 'Most of this once crack division,' he says, 'has conducted itself most discreditably in this new campaign.' And again at Spotsylvania, 'Mott's behaved shamefully'. Of another division Lyman writes, 'General Rickett's division of the 6th Corps, composed of troops from Winchester, known as "Milroy's weary boys", never has done well. They ran in the

Mine Run campaign, and they have run ever since.' And again, 'General Robinson's division behaved badly.'[27] On 25th August 1864 Hancock put in an attack on the Weldon Railroad, south of Petersburg, and reported that Gibbon's Division of his Corps had fought poorly. This had been one of the best divisions in the Army of the Potomac, and its bad showing was due to the presence in its ranks of a large proportion of indifferent recruits; the veteran soldiers had fought as well as ever. The II Corps had an unusually large number of partially trained and very poor reinforcements; and it was apparent that it could not be used again in offensive operations for some time.

The II Corps does not appear to have been the worst, for of the IX Corps, in the summer of 1864 Swinton writes: 'The old Ninth, than which there never was a better, had been reduced by long and varied service to a mere nucleus, with which had been agglomerated (not *fused*) a mass of new, heterogeneous, and inferior material. The first division was largely made up of foot-artillerists and dismounted cavalry, and the fourth division was composed exclusively of Blacks. To such an extent had the morale of the Ninth Corps become impaired, that its inspecting officers a short time before the assault (at Petersburg) declared the three White divisions to be in so bad a condition that the division of Blacks was to be preferred for the duty.'[28] There is no doubt, too, that the heavy casualties incurred in Grant's three successive battles of the Wilderness, Spotsylvania, and Cold Harbor, had blunted the offensive spirit of army. As Swinton says: 'The Army of the Potomac . . . shaken in its structure, its valor quenched in blood, and thousands of its ablest officers killed and wounded, was the Army of the Potomac no more.'[29]

The poor quality of the men reaching the Army of the Potomac was due partly to civil inefficiency in the way the men were raised, and partly to military inefficiency in sending useless soldiers to field formations. The source of the excellent volunteer soldiers of the earlier part of the war had dried up; there remained the 'draft' and 'substitute' volunteers. When the President issued a call for more men, each Congressional District had to raise its own quota by one of these two means. If the quota could be met by volunteers nobody was conscripted. The substitute brokers (who undertook to find substitutes for men who had been drafted and who were willing to pay their fees) found a lucrative employment in taking advantage of the enormous bounty of $1,000 for each volunteer. But the 'volunteers' they produced were the worst possible type of recruits who had no intention of fighting and every intention of deserting at the first opportunity and of selling their services again. In addition there were movements in several States to organise collective resistance to the draft.[30] Fremantle, when he got to New York, found great resistance to the draft. He has the following amusing story of being appealed to by Irishmen (and the American-Irish of New York have never been noted for pro-British enthusiasm). At his hotel: 'At breakfast this morning two Irish waiters, seeing I was a Britisher, came up to me one after another, and whispered at intervals in hoarse Hibernian accents—"It's disgraceful, sir, I've been drafted sir. I'm a Briton. I love my country. I love the Union Jack, sir".'[31]

From the Army of the Potomac a large force was despatched to New York to enforce the draft because of the riots in the city against the attempts to execute it. But the unreliable recruits which Meade's army got as a result can hardly have been worth the trouble entailed.

Another Federal command problem lay in the second rate units composed of men who had been enlisted for only 100 days. In August 1864 the term of service of a number of these expired, and the task they had performed in guarding railway lines, supply dumps, and other vulnerable points had to be taken over by fighting units. The 100-day units had been notoriously unreliable; two Ohio regiments, for instance, which had been posted to guard 500,000 rations at Meadow Bridge, Virginia, were, according to Swinton, 'stampeded by a contemptible handful of guerillas and, after burning about half the stores, carried off the remainder.'[32]

The loss of experienced officers to discipline the new recruits was another factor militating against efficiency, and one which had exercised commanders for some time. During the siege of Vicksburg Sherman, in a letter to his wife, wrote that an order had just been received from Washington to consolidate the old regiments. Regiments below 500 in strength were to be reduced to battalions; and instead of keeping the regiments and filling them up to strength with new privates, half the officers and NCOs, being surplus to establishment were to be discharged. 'If the worst enemy of the United States were to devise a plan to break down our army a better one could not be attempted. Two years have been spent in educating colonels, captains, sergeants, and corporals, and now they are to be driven out of the service in order that governors may have a due proportion of officers for the drafted men.'[33] (ie by raising new regiments).

To be fair, it was not always the fault of the State Governors that existing regiments were not kept up to establishment, as the experiences of the Pennsylvania Reserve Corps (admittedly a special case) show. The circumstances are shown in the following letter from General Meade to General Franklin commanding the Left Grand Division (I and VI Corps) of the Army of the Potomac on the eve of the former's departure to command the V Corps:

144

GENERAL: *I submit for your consideration a statement showing the present condition of the thirteen regiments of infantry constituting the Pennsylvania Reserve Corps, and forming, together with two new regiments, the One Hundred and Twenty-first and One Hundred and Forty-second Pennsylvania volunteers, the Third division, First army corps. You will perceive there are present for duty one hundred and ninety-five officers and four thousand two hundred and forty-nine enlisted men. Absent, by authority, one hundred and fifty-nine officers and three thousand seven hundred and forty men. I have to observe, however, of the number reported as absent, a very large proportion are the wounded, most of whom are so maimed and disabled that no expectation need be formed of their returning to active duty. I should therefore say, as an estimate, that to re-organize the command there would be required the appointment of over two hundred officers, and the enlistment of over seven thousand men. This paper is forwarded to you on the eve of my giving up the command of the division, to call your attention to the necessity of some measure being immediately adopted to increase the efficiency of this command.*

'*The plan of sending officers into the State to recruit has been on three separate occasions attempted, and proved in each case a signal failure. There remains, then, two courses to adopt. One is to consolidate the existing force with a number of regiments equal to the number of officers and men for duty. The objection to this plan is that it destroys the organization and the prestige which the good conduct of the Corps has acquired for it. Another plan would be to withdraw the command temporarily from the field, say for a period of two or three months, and return them to Pennsylvania, where it is believed from the great reputation the Corps has acquired, the pride the State takes in it, and the enthusiasm its return would create, that in a short time its ranks would be filled, after pruning them of all useless members. Soon after the battle of Antietam, his Excellency, the Governor of Pennsylvania, proposed to the general commanding the Army of the Potomac, to receive and re-organize the Corps; and it is believed the proposition was favorably received by the commanding general, but the exigencies of the movement prevented its execution.*

'*The further reduction of the Corps in the recent battle (Fredericksburg), where it lost over one thousand seven hundred officers and men, and the probability that its services might, at this moment be spared, together with the earnest desire I have that the organization which has contributed so largely to its success may be preserved, are the considerations which induce me to suggest this plan to you and recommend its adoption.*'[34]

However this proposal was turned down by the Secretary of War on the grounds that many similar applications had been submitted by other States, and all could not be approved without greatly reducing the strength of the Army. (The above letter is an interesting example of staff writing of the time, without a single numeral in the text.)

As a result of this decision, the Pennsylvania Reserve Corps maintained the remnants of its companies and regiments intact as far as possible, to preserve its esprit de corps.

Matters were no better arranged on the Confederate side. After the Seven Days campaign Jefferson Davis called for conscripts; but no great number were obtained because so many of those arriving at conscription age had already volunteered for the regiment of their choice. Those who were conscripted were distributed immediately amongst regiments to replace casualties, but this allowed no time for preliminary drill or training.[35] After the war General J. E. Johnston told Swinton that conscription was carried out centrally by the Confederate Government; instead of determining the number of troops wanted and then allotting a quota to each State for them to raise. A State had its own officers who knew every man in their particular areas, so that evasion would have been difficult. But the officers of the Confederate Government, charged with the duty, having no such knowledge, there was wholesale evasion and conscription broke down completely.[36] But State Governors were responsible for part of the blame. The Confederate conscription law applied to all men from the ages of 16 to 60; and of these, those of from 18 to 45 were liable to general military service and the remainder for service with the home guard. Many Governors, however, actually impeded the execution of the law by insisting, under their States rights, on all kinds of exemptions; and because States rights had been a primary reason for secession, the Confederate Government was in no position to override them. Initially, as in the North, a conscripted man could buy and supply a substitute; but the latter frequently deserted and hired himself again. So in December 1863 the substitute law was abolished, and reluctant conscripts searched for other means of evading service. The result of their efforts was that in 1864, though 150,000 men were called up, the Conscript Bureau only succeeded in despatching 13,000 to units. Not that these few were very much welcomed, for the volunteers loathed them and hated having them in the ranks.[37]

Towards the end of the war desertion became so widespread that the main armies of the Confederacy showed four men on their rolls to one in the ranks.[38] However, it is only fair to say that many of these desertions were caused by worry over their families during Sherman's march through Georgia and the Carolinas.

One source of reinforcement was discontinued in the last year of the war. Until then a prisoner of war had a good chance of being paroled or exchanged. If he was paroled after capture, he signed a document agreeing not to fight again until 'regularly exchanged', and he was then allowed to go to his home. As soon as an exchange had been effected he received written notification that he was released from parole.

146

For the exchange of prisoners there was a scale of equivalents agreed by the two sides on 22nd July 1862. The unit of exchange was the private soldier, and the rank equivalents in numbers of private soldiers were as follows: NCO 2, lieutenant 4, captain 6, major 8, lieutenant-colonel 10, colonel 15, brigadier-general 20, and major-general 40. All exchange of prisoners was stopped by Grant in April 1864 to deprive the Confederates of trained manpower.[39]

Stopping prisoner exchange had tragic results. The Confederate prisoner of war camp at Andersonville achieved notoriety on account of the bad conditions under which the prisoners lived and the number of deaths. The camp commandant, indeed, was hanged by the Federals after the war as a criminal. In fact, Federal prisoners in Andersonville received the same inadequate rations and medical supplies as the Confederate soldiers, and there was a very high mortality amongst the Confederate sick in the last year of the war. However, in condemning the South for its treatment of prisoners, the North conveniently forgot its own record. There was plenty of food and supplies of everything in the North, yet the figures released by the Federal War Department showed that 13% of Confederate prisoners in the Northern camps died as compared with 8% of Federal prisoners in the Southern camps. In the Elmira camp, New York, in the freezing winter, soldiers from the Lower South of the Confederacy were given only one blanket for sleeping on the ground in tents, and men contracted diseases of the chest from which they never regained their health. All of which perhaps shows that there are never war criminals on the winning side.[40]

Notes

1   Frederick H. Dyer, *A Compendium of the War of the Rebellion*, 1908
2   General William T. Sherman, *Memoirs*, 1875
3   ibid.
4   General Sir James Marshall-Cornwall, *Grant as Military Commander*, 1970
5   General Horace Porter, *Campaigning with Grant*, 1897
6   ibid.
7   ibid.
8   Bruce Catton, *Grant Takes Command*, 1968
9   Sherman, op. cit.
10 ibid.
11 Catton, op. cit.
12 A. L. Long, quoted in *Memoirs of Robert E. Lee*, 1887
13 Clifford Dowdey, *Lee*, 1965
14 A. L. Long, *Memoirs of Robert E. Lee*, 1887
15 Dowdey, op. cit.
16 Colonel G. F. R. Henderson, *Stonewall Jackson*, 1898

17 General E. P. Alexander, *Military Memoirs of a Confederate*, 1907
18 Porter, op. cit.
19 Alexander, op. cit.
20 ibid.
21 Porter, op. cit.
22 Major-General J. F. C. Fuller, *The Generalship of Ulysses S. Grant*, 1929
23 Henderson, op. cit.
24 Alexander, op. cit.
25 ibid.
26 William Swinton, *Campaigns of the Army of the Potomac*, 1866, quoting the *Report on the Conduct of the War*, second series, Vol. i, 112
27 Colonel Theodore Lyman, *Meade's Headquarters 1863–1865*; Letters, Massachusetts Historical Society, 1922
28 William Swinton, *Campaigns of the Army of the Potomac*, 1866
29 ibid.
30 Catton, op. cit.
31 Lieutenant-Colonel A. J. L. Fremantle, *The Fremantle Diary*; ed. Walter Lord, 1956
32 Swinton, op. cit.
33 B. H. Liddell Hart, *Sherman*, 1929
34 J. R. Sypher, *History of the Pennsylvania Reserve Corps*, 1865
35 Alexander, op. cit.
36 Swinton, op. cit.
37 Fremantle, op. cit.
38 Swinton, op. cit.
39 Fremantle, op. cit.
40 Dowdey, op. cit.

CHAPTER TEN

Naval Operations

BECAUSE THIS BOOK IS DEVOTED to a study of the opposing armies, it would be inappropriate to deal at length with naval affairs or with the detail of warships; subjects which would, indeed, need a full-length book to themselves. Nevertheless, because operations at sea and on the great rivers had a considerable influence on land operations, some aspects of naval affairs must be included. Broadly speaking, there were three ways in which naval operations affected the plans and actions of the armies: blockade, movement of troops and supplies, and support by gunboats on the great rivers.

The United States Navy had not possessed many ships before the war started, and most of what it did have had been neatly dispersed all over the world by the then Secretary of War, John B. Floyd. Floyd, later a Brigadier-General in the Confederate Army, had sent five ships to the East Indies, three to Brazil, seven to the Pacific, three to the Mediterranean, and seven to the coast of Africa. A Committee appointed by the House of Representatives on 21st February 1861 reported that the entire available naval force consisted of the 25-gun steamship *Brooklyn* and the steamship *Relief* with two guns, and that the latter was under orders for the African coast with stores for the African squadron. They added, since Charleston and Fort Sumter were looming large at this time, that the *Brooklyn* had too great a draft to enter Charleston harbour with safety except at spring tide. Apart from the ships in commission, there were 28 ships in home ports dismantled and unfit for service. No arrangements had been made for their repair, though plenty of money remained unexpended from the annual appropriation for naval repairs. Such was the umpromising situation that faced the new Secretary of the Navy, Gideon Welles.[1]

A start was made by the Federal Government buying or chartering any ship that was of any use, and by initiating the immediate repair of as many unserviceable ships as possible. (Ten of these had been burnt at Norfolk, Virginia, to prevent them falling into the hands of the Confederates.) In addition, eight new ships were ordered from Government shipyards and twenty-three gunboats from private yards. This was the start of a naval programme which, by the end of the war, produced a fleet of over 500 armed ships.

The types of ships built varied considerably; but typical was a wooden steam sloop, driven by screw and sail, and armed with 22 smooth-bore 9-in. guns on the broadside and with one rifled muzzle-loading 30-pr. gun on the forecastle and another on the poop. Almost every conceivable type of river craft were converted into gunboats, some fully armoured, others with varying degrees of armour protection, and a number with no armour at all. Some gunboats were, of course, especially built as such. The very useful Sacassus class of shallow-draft wooden paddle-steamers had no armour except on pilot houses and masthead lookouts; but they were double-enders with rudders at bow and stern and were extremely useful in narrow waters because they could steam equally well in either direction. A typical armament consisted of two 100-pr. RMLs and four 9-in. SB guns, and two or more 12-pr. or 24-pr. SB howitzers.[2]

The Confederacy started the war with no navy at all, and with practically no facilities for building anything but small craft. However, with the customary resource and ingenuity displayed in the South, difficulties were somehow surmounted, and by the end of the war 37 armoured warships had been built or were under construction. In addition, a number of warships were purchased from abroad. The most notable of these were the css *Florida* and the css *Alabama*, both built in England and handed over to the Confederate Navy in August 1862. The *Florida*, a steam corvette, did not have a long career as, in a breach of Brazilian neutrality, she was captured in Bahia Harbour by a Federal warship in October 1862. The *Alabama*, under her famous Captain Raphael Semmes, roamed the seas for very much longer, as she was finally sunk by the uss *Kearsage* off Cherbourg on 19th June 1864, after sinking one Federal warship and capturing 62 prizes.[3] Nevertheless, the Confederate Navy was never more than a fraction of the strength of its opponents and the depredations of these Confederate commerce raiders had little or no effect on the course of the war.

An additional disadvantage from which the South suffered was their lack of sea-faring population. The Navy never lacked recruits, but most of those volunteering had no knowledge of the sea, with the result that ships built abroad were generally manned by British crews, though the officers always held Confederate commissions.[4]

The Union had a small Marine Corps of about 4,000 all ranks, and all the larger ships had a detachment of marines who were included in any landing party and were generally responsible for manning some of the ship's guns.[5]

Blockade

It was in its blockade of the Southern ports that the Federal Navy exercised its most powerful influence on the course of the war. Its effect and the reason for it has been well described by Admiral A. T. Mahan, who himself served in the Federal Navy at the time. He writes:[6]

'Had the South had a people as numerous as it was warlike, and a navy commensurate to its other resources as a seapower, the great extent of its sea-coast and its numerous inlets would have been elements of great strength. The people of the United States and the Government of that day justly prided themselves on the effectiveness of the blockade of the whole Southern coast. It was a great feat, a very great feat; but it would have been an impossible feat had the Southerners been more numerous, and a nation of seamen. . . . Those who recall how the blockade was maintained, and the class of ships that blockaded during great parts of the war, know that the plan, correct under the circumstances, could not have been carried out in the face of a real navy. Scattered unsupported along the coast, the United States ships kept their places, singly or in small detachments, in face of an extensive network of inland water communications which favored secret concentration of the enemy. Behind the first line of water communications were long estuaries, and here and there strong fortresses, upon either of which the enemy's ships could always fall back to elude pursuit or to receive protection. Had there been a Southern navy to profit by such advantages, or by the scattered condition of the United States ships, the latter could not have been distributed as they were; and being forced to concentrate for mutual support, many small but useful approaches would have been left open to commerce. But as the Southern coast, from its extent and many inlets, might have been a source of strength, so, from those very characteristics, it became a fruitful source of injury. The great story of the opening of the Mississippi is but the most striking illustration of an action that was going on incessantly all over the South. At every branch of the sea frontier, war-ships were entering. The streams that had carried the wealth and supported the trade of the seceding States turned against them and admitted their enemies to their hearts. . . . Never did sea power play a greater or a more decisive part. . . .'

The blockade runners were much more important to the Confederate economy than were any of their warships. The great focal point of European trade with the Confederate States was Nassau in the Bahamas.

Here the ships from Great Britain and other European nations discharged their cargoes for Southern ports, receiving in exchange the Confederacy's cotton. From Nassau special ships built for blockade running carried the goods from Europe to Confederate ports. The most important of these was Wilmington, 570 miles from Nassau. The blockade-runners were fast little ships with a light draft. Painted grey and with a low silhouette, they were difficult to spot in the dark; they were faster than most of the Federal warships and could negotiate shallow waters off the Carolina coasts where the big ships could not follow. Most of them were British-built and British-owned, and it is said that some of them were commanded by officers of the Royal Navy on long leave.[7] After his capture of Savannah, Sherman says that: 'Admiral Dahlgren was extremely active, visited me repeatedly in the city while his fleet still watched Charleston, and all the avenues, for the blockade-runners that infested the coast, which were notoriously owned and managed by Englishmen, who used the island of New Providence (Nassau) as a sort of entrepot. One of these small blockade-runners came into Savannah after we were in full possession, and the master did not discover his mistake till he came ashore to visit the custom-house. Of course his vessel fell a prize to the navy.'[8]

Movement of Troops and Supplies

These pages have shown the extent to which the Federal Army benefited from the North's naval supremacy, both in the movement of troops and in the supply by sea of the armies in the field. It made possible the transfer of the Army of the Potomac, under McClellan, to the Peninsula and also its subsequent evacuation; and it was command of the sea that enabled Grant to switch his line of communications from land to sea and so made possible the flank move of the Army of the Potomac across the James River in the summer of 1864. Further, amphibious operations, such as the North Carolina coastal operations by General Burnside in 1862, and the threat of such operations entailed some dispersion of Confederate strength in guarding the coast. Immediately after the capture of Fort Sumter work was started on coastal defence, but many of the fortifications were badly located and built too hastily. A series of disasters followed as a result. On 27th November 1861 the Federals captured Port Royal, the best harbour in South Carolina; and later Burnside seized Roanoke Island and established himself on the coast of North Carolina.

In November 1861 Lee was appointed to the command of the Department of South Carolina, Georgia, and Florida. He arranged first for the securing of the most important points against immediate attack and then organised a proper system of coastal defence and directed the construction of heavy guns to arm the new batteries. By the end of 1861 many of these had already been completed. By the middle of March 1862 Lee had constructed a strong interior line of defence covering the major part of the Confederacy's Atlantic coast.[9]

The naval supremacy of the North trembled once. The Confederates in early 1862 had rebuilt the partially burnt out USS steam frigate *Merrimac*, which had been seized at the Norfolk Navy Yard, as an armoured ship. On 8th March 1862 the *Merrimac*, renamed the CSS *Virginia*, rammed and sank the USS *Cumberland* of 24 guns, and sank by gunfire the 50-gun USS *Congress*; whilst the 50-gun USS *Minnesota* was driven ashore. For a few hours it seemed that nothing could prevent the *Virginia* steaming up the Potomac and bombarding Washington, having sunk any Federal warship that attempted to bar her passage. But the following day a revolutionary armoured ship, the USS *Monitor*, arrived to redress the balance. The *Monitor* was a most extraordinary vessel with a very low freeboard and with two 11-in. SB guns mounted in a revolving turret. The two ships engaged in an indecisive action lasting four hours; but eventually the *Virginia* returned to Norfolk and the *Monitor* remained in control of Hampton Roads. Only then was it safe for McClellan to move his army to the Peninsula.

The River Gunboats

The most direct naval support for the Federal Army was that afforded by the river gunboats, and it was a support which could be very formidable indeed. In February 1862 five armoured gunboats under the command of Commodore Foote led the transports carrying Grant's force of 17,000 men up the Tennessee River. Together, these gunboats mounted 51 guns, consisting of SB 70-prs. RML 42-prs., SB 32-prs., and SB 12-pr. boat howitzers; an armament which was considerably greater than that installed in Fort Henry. After covering the disembarkation of the troops, Foote led his gunboats upstream without waiting for Grant. As soon as Fort Henry came in sight, one mile away the gunboats opened fire. The fort replied, but the gunboats' armour saved them from damage and, as they closed the range, they knocked out all the guns of the fort, so that it was forced to surrender.

After the fall of Fort Henry, Foote took his gunboats further upstream and destroyed the bridge carrying the railway linking the two wings of A. S. Johnston's Confederate army. He followed this exploit by taking his flotilla another 150 miles up the river to Florence, Alabama, spreading considerable alarm in the Confederate rear.

Against Fort Donelson, on the Cumberland River, the gunboats were less successful. Batteries of this fort were mounted at such a height that they were able to pierce the decks of the gunboats with plunging fire;

whilst the batteries were sighted too high above the river for the gunboats to use their main armament, and they could only reply with mortars.

No Federal general had more to do with gunboats than Sherman; and his cooperation with Admiral Porter provides a lesson in the conduct of joint operations. Porter and Sherman had a great mutual regard for each other. A remarkable example of this is provided by a reconnaissance ordered by Grant on 16th March 1863 to find a way through into the Yazoo River to operate against Vicksburg. Sherman issued orders for the military part of the expedition to move in boats and then embarked in a navy tug to overtake Admiral Porter. 'About sixty miles up Steele's Bayou,' he writes, 'we came to the gunboat Price, Lieutenant Woodworth, United States Navy, commanding, and then turned into Black Bayou, a narrow, crooked channel, obstructed by overchanging oaks, and filled with cypress and cotton-wood trees. The gunboats had forced their way through, pushing aside trees a foot in diameter. In about four miles we overtook the gunboat fleet just as it was emerging into Deer Creek, which was much wider and more free of trees. . . . Admiral Porter thought he had passed the worst. . . . He requested me to return and use all possible means to clear out Black Bayou. I returned to Hill's plantation. . . . The Diligent and Silver Wave then returned to Gwin's plantation and brought up Brigadier-General Giles A. Smith, with the Sixth Missouri, and part of the One Hundred and Sixteenth Illinois. Admiral Porter was then working up Deer Creek with his ironclads. . . . During the 19th I heard the heavy navy-guns booming more frequently than seemed consistent with mere guerrilla operations; and that night I got a message from Porter, written on tissue paper, brought me through the swamp by a negro, who had it concealed in a piece of tobacco.

'The Admiral stated that he had met a force of infantry and artillery which gave him great trouble by killing the men who had to expose themselves outside the iron armor to shove off the bows of the boats, which had so little headway they would not steer. He begged me to come to his rescue as soon as possible.' Sherman organised troops and boats and then drove ahead as rapidly as possible to Porter's aid. When he got near the spot 'a Major Kirby of the Eighth Missouri galloped down the road on a horse he had picked up the night before and met me. He explained the situation of affairs and offered me his horse. I got on *bareback*, and rode up the levee, the sailors coming out of their iron-clads and cheering most vociferously as I rode by, and as our men swept forward across the cotton-field in full view. I soon found Admiral Porter, who was on the deck of one of his iron-clads, with a shield made of the section of a smoke-stack, and I doubt if he was ever more glad to meet a friend than he was to see me.'[10]

Notes

1   J. R. Sypher, *History of the Pennsylvania Reserve Corps*, 1865
2   Jack Coggins, *Arms and Equipment of the Civil War*, 1962
3   R. E. Dupuy and T. N. Dupuy, *The Encyclopedia of Military History*, 1970
4   Coggins, op. cit.
5   ibid.
6   Captain A. T. Mahan, *The Influence of Sea Power upon History*, 1890
7   Coggins, op. cit.
8   General William T. Sherman, *Memoirs*, 1875
9   A. T. Long, *Memoirs of Robert E. Lee*, 1887
10 Sherman, op. cit.

CHAPTER ELEVEN

The Battle of Chancellorsville

P ROBABLY THE MOST SUITABLE way of summarising the
previous chapters is to give a description of one of the battles of the
American Civil War; and of these, perhaps the best for the purpose is
Chancellorsville—General R. E. Lee's most brilliant tactical performance,
and one of the most interesting and extraordinary battles in military
history. For it might be difficult to cite another instance where an army—
well-trained, well-equipped, well-disciplined, of high morale, and fighting
in a strong position of its own selection—was beaten by an opposing army
of less than half its strength and with inferior equipment. Chancellorsville,
then, is the obvious selection, because it includes those aspects of warfare
which have not so far received attention in these pages; the twin arts of
generalship and leadership.

After the Battle of Fredericksburg (as stated in Chapter Seven), Burnside, in January 1863, made an attempt to turn the Confederate positions
along the Rappahannock, but the movement became bogged down in
torrential rain and achieved military immortality as the 'Mud March'.
After this the two armies settled down in winter quarters facing each
other across the Rappahannock around Fredericksburg. News that a
large Federal expedition had sailed down the Potomac led the Confederate
high command to believe that an amphibious operation might be intended
against perhaps Richmond or Charleston. Accordingly Longstreet with
two divisions was detached from Lee's command and sent to Suffolk,
south of the lower reaches of the James River. This deprived Lee of
about one-quarter of his infantry.

Orders of Battle of the Opposing Armies
In April 1863 the orders of battle, the strengths, and the positions of
the Army of the Potomac and the Army of Northern Virginia were
as follows:

156

(a) Army of the Potomac

I Corps (Reynolds): Divisions of Wadsworth, Robinson, and Doubleday: strength 16,908.

II Corps (Couch): Divisions of Hancock, Gibbon, and French: strength 16,893

III Corps (Sickles): Divisions of Birney, Berry, and Whipple: strength 18,721

V Corps (Meade): Divisions of Griffin, Sykes, and Humphreys: strength 15,274

VI Corps (Sedgwick): Divisions of Brooks, Howe, Newton, and Burnham; strength 23,667

XI Corps (Howard): Divisions of Devens, Von Steinwehr, and Schurz: strength 12,977

XII Corps (Slocum): Divisions of Williams and Geary: strength 13,450

Cavalry Corps (Stoneman): Divisions of Pleasanton, Averill, and Gregg: strength 11,544

Total strength of the Army of the Potomac (including artillery reserve and provost guard), 133,711 men and 404 guns.

(b) Army of Northern Virginia

I Corps (Longstreet—absent with two divisions): Divisions of Anderson and McLaws: strength 17,649

II Corps (Jackson): Divisions of A. P. Hill, Rodes, Early, and Colston: strength 35,795

Cavalry Division (Stuart): strength 2,400

Total strength of the Army of Northern Virginia (including general reserve artillery) 56,444 men and 228 guns.

Jackson's corps was holding a line from Hamilton's crossing (about four miles below Fredericksburg) to Port Royal, a frontage of about twelve miles. Anderson's and McLaw's divisions occupied the key heights opposite Fredericksburg and watched Banks Ford. Westwards all the crossings of the Rappahannock were watched by the cavalry pickets of both sides. Lee's defence system was, however, very flexible. There were continuous lines of infantry parapets on the heights and battery emplacements had been sited to command all ground over which assaulting forces would have to move, but infantry and artillery units were so sited that a rapid concentration could be carried out to counter an enemy threat to any sector of the defence. The Confederate right flank was so positioned that it could not be turned; whilst on the left flank defence positions had been constructed as far upstream as United States Ford, so that it would be necessary to cross both the Rappahannock and Rapidan to turn them.

The Army of the Potomac lay along the Stafford Heights on the north side of the Rappahannock and opposite Fredericksburg. Hooker had spent the first three months of his command in restoring the confidence of the army and in intensive training, and it had now reached a high standard of efficiency in all arms; the somewhat bombastic Hooker, indeed, declared it to be 'the finest army on the planet'. Hooker, knowing that he had double Lee's strength in infantry, four times his strength in cavalry, and a great superiority in artillery, was determined to attack. A frontal attack (after the lesson of the battle of Fredericksburg) he regarded as impracticable, and it was clearly not possible to turn the Confederate right. He therefore decided to operate against Lee's left.

On 13th April 1863, as a preparatory move, Hooker ordered Stoneman with the Cavalry Corps to carry out a raid on the railway communications in Lee's rear. He hoped that a complete destruction of the railway would force Lee to retreat; he would then pursue the Confederates with the main body of his army whilst the cavalry harassed their withdrawal. Stoneman moved the next day, but in heavy rain which lasted 36 hours and made the Rappahannock impassable. The leading brigade had actually crossed, but then had to swim their horses back through the swollen river. This delayed matters for two weeks.

Hooker's Plan and Opening Moves

The plan on which Hooker ultimately decided was to send a strong column round the Confederate left, crossing the Rappahannock at Kelly's Ford, 27 miles above Fredericksburg, and then fording the Rapidan to take post in the area about Chancellorsville. This move was to be masked by a force crossing the Rappahannock in strength at Fredericksburg and threatening a frontal attack. At the same time the major part of the Cavalry Corps would resume their intended operation against the railways. (In fact, this cavalry raid, as so many in the war achieved little. Although the massive Federal force was opposed only by a small brigade under General W. H. F. Lee, the damage done to the railway was so quickly repaired that there was little delay to the movement of Lee's supply and ambulance trains.)

The Chancellorsville column consisted of the V, XI, and XII Corps. The march started on the morning of 27th April and the force reached the area around Kelly's Ford the following day. A pontoon bridge was constructed and the three corps crossed the river that night and the following morning, 29th. There was some slight opposition from a Confederate picket which was observing this ford. From the Rappahannock the three corps moved in two columns towards the Rapidan, the XI and XII Corps on the right to Germanna Ford and the V Corps on the left to Ely's Ford. These fords were deep and the water in some

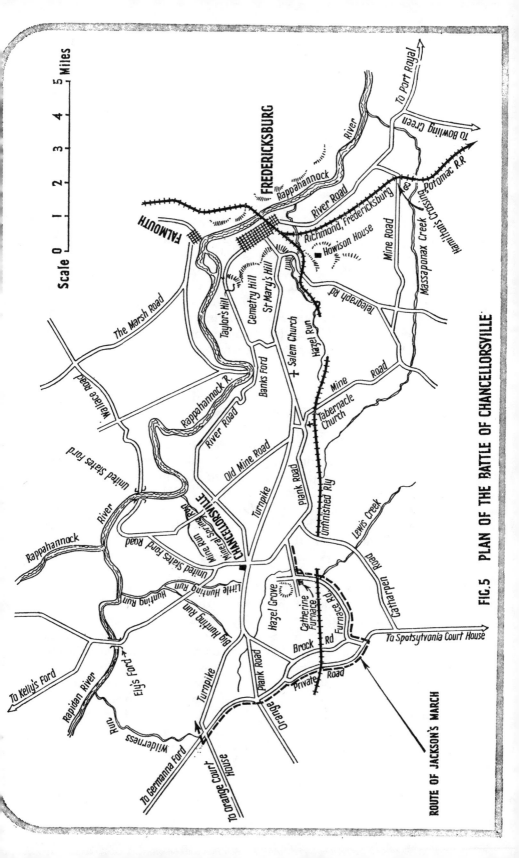

FIG.5   PLAN OF THE BATTLE OF CHANCELLORSVILLE

ROUTE OF JACKSON'S MARCH

parts came up to the men's armpits. Most of them carried their clothes and cartridge boxes aloft on their bayonets, but they were cheerful and there was much laughter. A cavalry picket was stationed downstream at each crossing to catch any men swept away by the current. The crossing continued during the night, illuminated by large bonfires. By the morning of 30th all the troops were over the Rapidan and that afternoon the three corps were concentrating about Chancellorsville.

Meanwhile the II Corps had moved upstream to United States Ford, with instructions to remain there until the troops from the turning column came down the south bank from the Chancellorsville area and uncovered the ford to allow a crossing. This was achieved on the afternoon of 30th, and the II Corps then built a pontoon bridge over the Rappahannock and marched to Chancellorsville. That night Hooker himself moved his headquarters to Chancellorsville, and issued the following order to his troops: 'It is with heartfelt satisfaction that the commanding general announces to his army that the operations of the last few days have determined that our enemy must either ingloriously fly or come out from behind his defences, and give battle on our own ground, where certain destruction awaits him.'[1]

The masking force, under the command of Sedgwick, consisted initially of the I, III, and VI Corps. As soon as the turning column was well on its way, preparations were made to cross the Rappahannock, and before dawn on 29th two pontoon bridges had been built over the river three miles below Fredericksburg. Two divisions were moved to the south bank and the Confederates opposite immediately began concentrating to meet an anticipated attack. By the night of 30th, this feint having served its purpose, the III Corps was directed to march to the Chancellorsville area. To his staff a triumphant Hooker was saying, 'The Confederate army is now the legitimate property of the Army of the Potomac. They may as well pack up their haversacks and make for Richmond, and I shall be after them.'[2]

So far Hooker had been brilliantly successful, and the whole operation testified to the excellence of the Army of the Potomac's staff planning. However, Hooker had made one serious mistake; he had sent off Stoneman with his entire cavalry force except for one brigade. A single brigade was quite insufficient to keep him informed of Confederate movements; though additional observation was provided by signal officers equipped with look-out posts, two balloons, and connection to headquarters by field telegraph. Even if Stoneman's raid had been worthwhile, little would have been lost by delaying him, because the height of the water prevented his troops from crossing the Rappahannock till the morning of 29th and he had still made little progress on 30th.

Lee's Reaction

By 30th April the character of Hooker's movement had become clear to Lee. He saw that the Fredericksburg move was only a feint and that quick action was needed. Swinton writes: 'Lee, with instant perception of the situation, now seized the masses of his force, and with the grasp of a Titan swung them into position as a giant might fling a mighty stone from a sling.'[3]

Lee left a force to hold the lines before Fredericksburg consisting of Early's division, Barksdale's brigade of McLaws's division, Pendleton's artillery reserve, and the Washington artillery; all under Early's command and totalling about 10,000 men and 54 guns. Early had a frontage of about six miles with, therefore, nine guns to the mile. Before midnight on 30th the remainder of the Army of Northern Virginia was on the march towards Chancellorsville. It included Jackson's II Corps, consisting of the divisions of A. P. Hill, Rodes, and Colston, and numbering about 25,000 men; Anderson's division of 8,000 men; McLaws's division (less Barksdale's brigade), about 6,000 strong; and Alexander's battalion of artillery. Thus Lee was on the march with about 40,000 men to attack Hooker who had 78,000 troops either at or approaching Chancellorsville.

Chancellorsville

Chancellorsville was not a village, or even a hamlet, but merely a sturdy brick farmhouse, with the usual outbuildings, which stood on the edge of a small field at a road junction, and about a mile inside a tract of country known as the Wilderness. There had once been a forest here but it had been cut down many years before when there was a flourishing charcoal industry in the area. In place of the forest there had now grown up dense thickets of secondary growth and scrub, making it a most difficult country for military movement, even by infantry. There were a few clearings, including one of considerable size west of the Chancellorsville house, and a few small creeks meandered through the jungle of black-jack oak and scrub-pines.

There were three roads between Chancellorsville and Fredericksburg: the Turnpike, which was the most direct; the Plank road, running to the south of the Turnpike, but joining it at about half the distance on the way to Fredericksburg at Tabernacle Church; and the River road, which followed fairly closely the south bank of the Rappahannock for most of the way. Towards Fredericksburg the country became open and rolling.

Hooker's Advance

Hooker established a strong defensive position, which from Chancellorsville ran about two miles to the north-east towards the Rappahannock, covering United States Ford, and to the west it extended some three miles, covering the Plank road. A breastwork of logs with abatis in front had been constructed.

Having completed his secure base, Hooker, at about 11 am on 1st May, pushed columns forward in the direction of Fredericksburg to seize the exits to the open country. Griffin's and Humphreys' divisions of V Corps advanced along the River road and Sykes's division of the same corps, supported by Hancock's division of II Corps, moved along the Turnpike. XII Corps marched along the Plank road. On the River road the Federals came in sight of Banks Ford without encountering any enemy troops. A series of ridges crossed the Turnpike, and on the first of these, about a mile east of Chancellorsville, the cavalry screen in front of Sykes's division bumped into Confederate troops and was driven back. Sykes deployed his division, moved forward at the double and drove back the Confederate advanced guard. On the Plank road Slocum advanced about the same distance as the other columns without encountering any enemy. The three columns now secured a ridge crossing all three roads, and on the edge of the open country.

Confederate Advance towards Chancellorsville

Meanwhile the Confederates had been advancing towards Chancellorsville. In the lead as advanced guard was Anderson's division, with the brigades of Wilcox and Mahone on the Turnpike and the brigades of Wright, Perry, and Posey on the Plank road. Following these, Alexander had one battery on the Turnpike and the remainder of his battalion on the Plank road. McLaws's division was on the Turnpike, behind Anderson's brigades, and the whole of Jackson's corps was following on the Plank road with Jackson riding at the head. There were no Confederate troops on the River road, and thus nothing to prevent the Federals seizing Banks Ford and shortening the distance between Chancellorsville and Fredericksburg by several miles.

As the Confederate skirmishers encountered the Federal cavalry, Lee rode up to join Jackson. It was the two brigades of Anderson's division on the Turnpike which encountered Sykes's division (two brigades of which were composed of regular troops), and Semmes's brigade of McLaws's division came up from behind on to Mahone's left. Sykes had only been ordered to advance to the ridge, so he held his position there against increasing Confederate pressure. On the Plank road the skirmishers of the Federal XII Corps were driven in by Wright's brigade, which was actually marching along an unfinished railway line from Fredericksburg which ran half a mile to a mile south of the Plank road.

At this juncture, to the dismay of the Federal corps commanders,

Hooker issued orders for the troops on all three roads to be withdrawn to Chancellorsville. Meade and Slocum, the commanders of V and XII Corps respectively, urged Hooker to reconsider his order, but in vain. He had decided that he wished to await attack on ground of his own choosing. Of this puzzling decision, Swinton writes: 'Having studied the case at the time when a spectator of these events, I have returned to its examination in the light of the whole body of evidence since developed, and the riddle still remains unsolved. Till he met the enemy Hooker showed a master-grasp of the elements of war, but the moment he confronted his antagonist, he seemed to suffer a collapse of all his powers. . . . It is probable that Hooker never expected that Lee would turn to meet him on that line, but that disconcerted by the suddenness of the primal stroke, he would beat a hasty retreat southward towards Richmond. When, on the contrary, he found his antagonist making a rapid change of front and hurrying forward to accept the gage of battle in the Wilderness, the general whose first stride had been that of a giant, shrunk to the proportions of a dwarf.'[4]

Hooker Consolidates

Hooker had received reports from the look-out stations and balloons of the march towards Chancellorsville of a Confederate force estimated at two corps. Rumours had also been brought by deserters that Hood's division from Suffolk had rejoined Lee (which was quite untrue). At 2 pm on 1st May he sent the following signal to his chief-of-staff, General Butterfield, at his main headquarters at Falmouth: 'From character of information have suspended attack. The enemy may attack me,—I will try it. Tell Sedgwick to keep a sharp lookout and attack if he can succeed.' Later he said to General Couch, commanding II Corps, 'It is all right, Couch, I have got Lee just where I want him. He must fight me on my own ground.'[5]

Hooker's position was strong, but there were weak points. It had been hurriedly prepared by tired troops who did not expect to fight there; there were several commanding positions which could be occupied by the enemy; the thicket was too dense for cavalry and artillery to be used effectively; and the right flank was in the air. Nevertheless, as Lee said in his report, 'The enemy had assumed a position of great natural strength, surrounded on all sides by a dense forest filled with tangled undergrowth, in the midst of which breastworks of logs had been constructed, with trees felled in front so as to form an almost impenetrable abatis. His artillery swept the few narrow roads by which his position could be approached from the front and commanded the adjacent woods. The left of his line extended from Chancellorsville toward the Rappahannock covering the Bark Mill (ie United States) Ford, where he communicated with the north bank of the river by a pontoon bridge. His right stretched westward along the Germanna Ford road more than two miles. Darkness was approaching before the strength and extent of his line could be ascertained, and as the nature of the country rendered it hazardous to attack at night, our troops were halted and formed a line of battle in front of Chancellorsville at right angles to the plank road, extending on the right to the (old) Mine road and to the left in the direction of the Catherine Furnace. Colonel Wickham, with the Fourth Virginia cavalry and Colonel Owen's regiment was stationed between the (old) Mine road and the Rappahannock. The rest of the cavalry was upon our left flank.'[6]

The withdrawal of the right and left Federal columns had been carried out without difficulty, though they were closely followed by the Confederates, but the centre column was closely pressed in front and in danger of envelopment. Hancock, however, moved up in support of Sykes and the two divisions managed to withdraw in good order. Once back in the Chancellorsville position, V Corps and one division of II Corps were posted on the left, XII Corps and one division of III Corps in the centre, and XI Corps on the right. V Corps and the remainder of II and III Corps were in reserve.

Hooker had succeeded in manoeuvring Lee out of his position without a battle, and the latter was now faced with the alternatives of attacking an army much stronger than his own and who were in a prepared position, or of retreating.

Lee Attacks the Federal Right

Although the Confederate lines were close to those of the Federals, the intervening brushwood thicket prevented the opposing troops from seeing each other. But patrols sent out by the Confederates discovered that the enemy position was protected by two strong lines of breastworks, one facing east and the other south. In front of these lines the brushwood had been cleared to a depth of 100 yards to give a field of fire for the infantry, and the road approaches were covered with artillery. Towards the north and west the position was open. It was clear that a frontal attack could not succeed.

Before dark in the evening of 1st May, Lee and Jackson were seated together in a small clearing by the Plank road, at its junction with a minor country road which ran west to the Catherine Furnace. Lee sent off Major Talcott, his staff engineer, and Captain Boswell, Jackson's chief engineer, on a reconnaissance of the Federal front. After they had gone, Stuart arrived and reported that General Fitzhugh Lee, commanding the cavalry brigade on the left, had discovered that the Federal right flank was in the air. At about 10 pm Talcott and Boswell returned with a detailed report of the strength of the enemy's position.

Lee bent over his maps and said, 'Now, how can I get at these people?' Jackson, knowing Lee's habits of speaking his thoughts when tackling a problem, replied to this rhetorical question, 'Show me what to do and we'll try to do it.'[7] It was apparent to Lee that only against the Federal right flank could an attack hope to succeed. But the risks were enormous. To carry out the necessary flank movement Lee, who had already divided his numerically much smaller army once, would have to divide it again, and that immediately in front of a much more powerful enemy. Three considerations underlined the danger of the movement: if the outflanking column were discovered during its march it would be unable to retreat; if the weakness of the force left to contain the Federals in front were found out, it could be swept away in a counter-attack; and if Sedgwick broke through Early's thin defences at Fredericksburg, the Confederates about Chancellorsville might be attacked in rear. In accepting the risks, Lee was no doubt influenced by his assessment of Hooker as a commander.

Having made his decision, Lee issued preliminary instructions to Jackson. He was to take an outflanking column, moving first south and then west to the Brock road, where he was to turn north to the Plank road, and, on reaching that, to turn east and strike the Federal flank. Jackson rose, saluted, and said, 'My troops will move at 4 o'clock.' He then went off to issue warning orders and to get some sleep. Lee was now joined by the Reverend B. K. Lacy, a chaplain in Jackson's corps, who had been sent by Stuart to give information about the area from his own personal knowledge. Lacy had been the pastor of a church not far from Chancellorsville and knew all the roads in this part of the Wilderness. He described a road by which the column could move which should be sufficiently remote from the Federal positions to escape observation. The distance to be marched would be about twelve miles.[8]

Before sunrise Lee, Jackson, Long, and Hotchkiss (Jackson's topographical engineer) were in discussion. In response to Lee's question, Jackson said that he proposed to take the three divisions of his corps which were with him, leaving only the divisions of Anderson and McLaws facing the Federal Chancellorsville position. Both of these were short of one of their brigades, for Wilcox's brigade of McLaws's division had been sent to hold Banks Ford. The risk was very great indeed! However, Lee's only comment to Jackson was, 'Well, go on.'[9]

Wilcox arrived at Banks Ford just in time, for some time after midnight Hooker had ordered Reynolds, with his I Corps, to leave Sedgwick and join the main body of the army at Chancellorsville. Reynolds started at sunrise on 2nd May and marched to Banks Ford, but, finding the Confederates in possession, he turned on to the road which took the much longer route via United States Ford.

While Jackson was starting his great march, the divisions of Anderson and McLaws were busy strengthening their entrenchments and making noisy demonstrations of threatened attack on the Federal position. The outflanking column was led by Fitzhugh Lee's cavalry brigade. The march of the column is described by Alexander, whose artillery battalion took part in it. The cavalry took some time to get clear and it was about 7 am when Lee standing by the roadside watched the head of the infantry pass. Rodes's division led, followed by Colston's, with A. P. Hill's bringing up the rear. The route led first to the crossroads near the Catherine Furnace; from there it went south for a mile, followed by two miles in a south-westerly direction, before turning due west to strike the Brock road within another mile. The column was closest to the Federal positions, and most exposed, at the Catherine Furnace cross-roads, and the 23rd Georgia Regiment of Colquitt's brigade in Rodes's division was left here as a flank guard while the troops passed.[10]

When the head of the column reached the Brock road it turned south for about a mile and then, almost doubling back on itself, took a track through the woods running slightly west of north, and nearly parallel to the Brock road, which it rejoined about three miles north of the point where the Brock road was first entered. The head of the column halted when it reached the crossing of the Brock and Plank roads, while Fitzhugh Lee took Jackson forward to a place from which he could see the Federal lines and the enemy troops, with their arms stacked, in bivouac behind their trenches. Jackson saw that by following the Brock road for another two miles, to where it met the Turnpike, he would be behind the Federal flank and could take it in rear. The march was then resumed, but Jackson left Paxton's brigade of Colston's division at the Plank and Brock cross-roads to act as a flank guard with the cavalry.[11]

During the march the pace at the head of the column was $2\frac{1}{2}$ miles per hour, but in the rear it was only $1\frac{1}{2}$, so that in spite of all efforts distance was lost. There were three halts of about twenty minutes each. The only vehicles taken were the gun carriages and limbers, the ammunition wagons, and the ambulances, and all these travelled behind the division to which they belonged. At the start of the march the column was ten miles long, of which the infantry took over six miles. It was about 4 pm before the leading infantry started to deploy astride the Turnpike.[12]

In spite of all the precautions taken, the Federals had spotted the march of Jackson's division, but, fortunately for Lee, they had misunderstood it. About a mile south-west of Chancellorsville was a cleared ridge on which stood the settlement of Hazel Grove. At about 8 am General Birney, whose

THE BATTLE OF CHANCELLORSVILLE

division of III Corps was holding Hazel Grove, saw a column of all arms passing across his front about a mile away (in fact, about the Catherine Furnace crossroads). He immediately brought up a battery which opened fire on a train of vehicles, throwing it into confusion and causing it to make a diversion. One of Jackson's batteries came rapidly into action to reply and to check any Federal infantry attack. Sickles, the corps commander, arrived quickly at Hazel Grove and sent a report to Hooker, with copies to Howard, XI Corps, and Slocum, XII Corps, inviting the co-operation of the latter two if Hooker ordered him to attack the Confederate column. Sickles watched the movement of the Confederates for three hours, and deduced that the march was directed either towards Orange Court House on the Orange and Alexandria Railroad or else Louisa Court House on the Virginia Central Railroad; and that the enemy was either withdrawing or mounting an operation against the Federal right flank—or perhaps both, for if the whole Confederate army was on the move a failure in the flank manoeuvre could be followed by a retreat along new lines of communication. Hooker, after leisurely consideration, decided that the Confederates were retreating, and at midday Sickles received orders to advance cautiously and attack the enemy columns. He immediately sent Birney's division forward and the 23rd Georgia Regiment was overwhelmed and captured. Archer, commanding the rearmost Confederate brigade, on his own responsibility (for it was quite impossible to communicate in time with Jackson at the head of the column) halted his own and Thomas's (the next ahead) brigades of A. P. Hill's division, together with one artillery battalion, and deployed to halt the Federal advance. Against this display of force Birney's division made no further movement, and after remaining in position for an hour, Archer reformed and followed after the remainder of the column; but it was dark before the two brigades caught it up. His march was delayed at the start because his rearguard had to fight off pursuing Federals; for Birney's division harried them for the first two miles.

It was nearly 6 pm before Jackson had eight brigades formed in two lines of battle and a ninth in a third line; and whilst this deployment was taking place Sickles was massing troops for an attack against what it was apparent must be a much weakened Confederate position. He brought up Whipple's division in support of Birney, and, having asked for reinforcements, he was sent Barlow's brigade, belonging to Von Steinwehr's division, which was on the right flank of XI Corps, and Williams's division from XII Corps, together with three regiments of cavalry and some horse artillery under Pleasanton.

The left flank of the two divisions remaining under Lee's immediate command was held by Posey's brigade of Anderson's division, and

Posey's skirmishers became hotly engaged with the left flank of Sickles advance. The Federals made several efforts to carry Posey's position but were repulsed each time. Sickles then prepared a plan to outflank and surround Posey's brigade, but by the time he was ready to launch his attack, Jackson had forestalled him and Sickles was ordered to withdraw. Hooker, up till this point, had been in an optimistic mood, and had sent off the following message to Sedgwick: 'We know the enemy is flying, trying to save his trains; two of Sickles's divisions are among them.'[13]

Besides Posey's, all the other five brigades facing the Federals at Chancellorsville were in action during the day. When the Federals attacked, that part of the Confederate line concerned remained in the trenches or behind breastworks and repulsed the attackers with a devastating fire. On the Confederate right, however, the Federal skirmish line under Colonel Miles was strongly posted and remained on the defensive. Here, therefore, it was desirable to threaten attack, and this Kershaw and Semmes, with their brigades of McLaws's division, did most successfully.

The right of the whole Federal line was held by Howard's XI Corps, and while the major part of the corps was drawn up along the Plank road facing south, the brigade on the extreme right was refused and faced west. At 6 pm Jackson ordered Rodes, commanding the first line of four brigades, to move forward to the attack. The signal was given by bugle and taken up and repeated by the bugles of all the brigades. The first the Federals knew of the attack was when long lines of Confederate infantry came into view on either side of the Turnpike, moving against their flank and rear. After an initial effort to stem the tide, Devens's division on the right of XI Corps dissolved into a mass of fugitives, and many of its batteries were overrun. The next XI Corps division was Schurz's, facing south along the Plank road. Schurz tried to change front to the west to meet the advancing Confederates, but most of his division was overwhelmed by Devens's fleeing soldiers and succumbed to the general panic, though one or two regiments managed to retire in good order. In the remaining division of XI Corps, Von Steinwehr's, there was only one brigade (the other having been lent to Sickles). If two of Jackson's brigades had not checked their advance through rumours of a cavalry threat to their flank, this brigade might have been captured. As it was, it formed into a defensive position and the Confederate advance came to a momentary halt. But one brigade could not halt the victorious Confederates for long and it was driven into retreat. Swinton writes: 'The open plain round Chancellorsville now presented such a spectacle as a simoom sweeping over the desert might make. Through the dusk of nightfall, a rushing whirlwind of men and artillery and wagons swept down the road, and past headquarters, and on towards the fords of the

Rappahannock; and it was in vain that the staff opposed their persons and drawn sabres to the panic-stricken refugees.'[14]

The odd thing was that, owing to what Alexander calls 'acoustic shadows', Sickles, who was only about 2½ miles away, heard nothing of the Confederate attack, and when he was informed of it he at first disbelieved the report. Hooker was sitting happily on the veranda of Chancellorsville house at 6.30 pm, confident that Lee's army was retreating with Sickles destroying its wagon trains. He and his staff could hear distant gunfire, but assumed it came from Sickles's artillery. One of his ADCs, happening to look down the Turnpike with his telescope, suddenly shouted, 'My God! Here they come!' There was a hurried mounting of horses as the fugitives of XI Corps streamed past.

The panic flight was checked by Pleasanton who, returning from his support of Sickles and hearing that the right wing was collapsing, swung his regiments into rapid mounted action, supported by the guns of his horse artillery. Hooker called for his old 'fighting division' (now Berry's and the reserve of III Corps), and other troops were rapidly collected, so that the Confederate advance was stemmed.

Darkness was in any case stopping the effectiveness of the Confederate pursuit, and a pause was necessary to re-organise and re-group. Jackson, with some of his staff and despatch riders, rode forward to reconnoitre. On the return of this party they were mistaken by a Confederate picket for Federal cavalry. The picket opened fire and Jackson fell mortally wounded. The command devolved on A. P. Hill, but he was himself soon wounded and he sent for Stuart to take over command of the II Corps. Stuart had started to attack the camps and trains of the Federals about Ely's Ford, but withdrew when the summons reached him and assumed command between 10 and 11 pm.

Stuart sent for Alexander, who was the senior surviving artillery officer in II Corps, and ordered him to reconnoitre positions for and to post before dawn as many guns as possible. Alexander could only find one outlet for the artillery, a ride through the forest 25 yards wide and 200 yards long, opening on to the cleared plateau of Hazel Grove which was held by the Federals. Near here he assembled several batteries.[15]

The three Confederate II Corps divisions were reformed astride the Plank road for a renewed attack on the following morning, 3rd May. All three divisions were deployed in line of brigades; A. P. Hill's in front, Colston's behind it in support, and Rodes's in reserve. The two right brigades of the six in Hill's division were echeloned to the rear so as to present a front to the right flank if necessary.[16]

Hooker, meanwhile, finding that the Confederate attack had halted, ordered Sickles to attack by the light of the moon with his III Corps from Hazel Grove. However, this attack lost direction and, after brushing against the right flank of Hill's division, Sickles's troops struck the right flank of Slocum's Federal XII Corps. A furious battle resulted, with XII Corps stories of the repulse of desperate Confederate attacks![17]

During the night Hooker ordered the construction of an interior defence line upon which the Army of the Potomac could fall back if Stuart forced his way through to a junction with Lee. A short line was quickly selected of great natural strength behind Hunting Run on the west and Mineral Spring Run on the east, with both flanks resting on the river and covering the Federal bridges. Alexander describes it as probably the strongest field entrenchment ever built in Virginia.[18] The army had lost XI Corps, which had ceased for the time being to exist as a fighting formation, but on the other hand Reynolds's I Corps had arrived during the night, after its diversion from Banks Ford and a consequent march of probably about 18 miles.

At 9 pm Hooker sent orders to Sedgwick, with his strong VI Corps, to cross the Rappahannock at Fredericksburg and march along the Chancellorsville road to join the main body of the army. He told him to leave all his trains behind except the pack trains of ammunition and to be in Hooker's vicinity by daylight. Gibbon's division of II Corps, which had been left with Sedgwick, was to take possession of Fredericksburg. Hooker added: 'You will probably fall upon the rear of the forces commanded by Gen. Lee, and between you and the major-general command ing, he expects to use him up.'[19] Sedgwick received this order at 11 pm.

The Fighting at Chancellorsville on 3rd May

At around dawn on 3rd May Hooker made the fatal mistake of withdrawing Sickles's III Corps from Hazel Grove. Sickles had been holding this position with two divisions and five batteries, but by the time the Confederate advance started there was nothing left on this ridge but a rearguard.

Soon after dawn Stuart gave the order to attack. Hazel Grove was soon captured, and Alexander's batteries, following close behind the assaulting infantry, came rapidly into action and opened a devastating fire on the Federal infantry and artillery positions. The Federal advanced line ran north and south across the Plank road for about 1¼ miles and was held by one division of XII Corps, one division of III Corps, and a brigade of II Corps. Behind in support were the two divisions from Hazel Grove. The total strength on this line was about 25,000 men and Stuart was attacking with approximately the same number. The remainder of XII Corps (one division) and Hancock's division of II Corps were facing Anderson's and McLaws's divisions, and covered the roads into Chancellorsville; and Hancock's division was extended to the left to guard United States Ford. Hooker's new interior line was already manned by I Corps, V Corps, II Corps (less one division and one brigade). Of this situation, Swinton writes: 'The corps-commanders saw that it was only a question of saving what they could of the army's honor, for the army was without a head'. To his new line in rear, 'Hooker had resolved to retire, and he seemed to be incapable of other resolve.'[20]

A. P. Hill's division drove the Federals rapidly from their first line defences and stormed on to attack the second line. However, a Federal counter-attack drove Hill's men back to the breastworks of the captured first line. Stuart ordered thirty more guns into position at Hazel Grove, and then attacked again, throwing both his second and third lines into the battle and keeping no reserves in hand. The fierce struggle which now ensued led inevitably to the three Confederate divisions becoming mixed up (and demonstrated, incidentally, the tactical weakness of putting divisions in line, one behind the other, instead of allotting them separate sectors). Finally, the massed Confederate guns at Hazel Grove had their effect and at about 9 am, with the Federal fire slackening from shortage of ammunition, a final attack by Stuart was successful. (Alexander says that Stuart had been conspicuous, 'everywhere encouraging the troops with his magnetic presence and bearing, and singing as he rode along the lines, "Old Joe Hooker, won't you come out of the Wilderness!" '[21] The Federal lines yielded and the guns at Hazel Grove moved forward across the valley and occupied the deserted Federal positions, making contact with Anderson's division which Lee had extended to the left to meet them. The Federals attempted to stand near the Chancellorsville house, but only briefly. Hooker, who was in the porch of the house, was knocked out for two or three hours by a piece of brick struck from a pillar by a round shot.

At about 10 am Lee, advancing with McLaws's division, met Stuart near the Chancellorsville house, which was now a smoking ruin. Colonel Charles Marshall described the scene as follows in an address at the Soldiers' Memorial Meeting in Baltimore:

'General Lee accompanied the troops in person, and as they emerged from the fierce combat they had waged in "the depths of that tangled wilderness", driving the superior forces of the enemy before them across the open ground, he rode into their midst. The scene is one that can never be effaced from the minds of those that witnessed it. The troops were pressing forward with all the ardour and enthusiasm of combat. The white smoke of musketry fringed the front of the line of battle, while the artillery on the hills in rear of the infantry shook the earth with its thunder and filled the air with the wild shrieks of the shells that plunged

THE CONFEDERATES AND FEDERALS AT WAR

into the masses of the retreating foe. To add greater horror and sublimity to the scene, the Chancellorsville house and the woods surrounding it were wrapped in flames. In the midst of this awful scene General Lee, mounted upon that horse we all remember so well, rode to the front of his advancing battalions. His presence was the signal for one of those uncontrollable outbursts of enthusiasm which none can appreciate who have not witnessed them.

'The fierce soldiers, with their faces blackened with the smoke of battle, the wounded, crawling with feeble limbs from the fury of the devouring flames, all seemed possessed with a common impulse. One long, unbroken cheer, in which the feeble cry of those who lay helpless on the earth blended with the strong voices of those who still fought, rose high above the roar of battle, and hailed the presence of the victorious chief. He sat in the full realization of all that soldiers dream of—triumph; and as I looked on him in the complete fruition of the success which his genius, courage, and confidence in his army had won, I thought that it must have been from such scene that men in ancient days ascended to the dignity of the gods.'[22]

Lee ordered infantry and artillery to replenish their ammunition in preparation for a renewal of the attack; but just at that time news arrived that Sedgwick had broke through at Fredericksburg and was moving up the Plank road.

Sedgwick's Attack

When Sedgwick received Hooker's order on the night of 2nd May, he was already on the south side of the river, but three miles below Fredericksburg. His previous orders had been to advance towards Richmond on the direct road via Bowling Green, and his troops were disposed accordingly. From where he was the distance to Chancellorsville by the Turnpike was about 12 miles. To carry out his new instructions he would have to re-deploy his corps, march to Fredericksburg, and then force the Confederate lines on Marye's Hill. He did not know the Confederate strength and Hooker had omitted to inform him that it was very low. However, it was apparent to Sedgwick that Hooker's expectation of seeing him at daylight was optimistic, to say the least!

Aided by a bright moon, Sedgwick was able to put his troops rapidly into motion in the new direction. He soon came into contact with the Confederate outposts, who fell back slowly before the Federal advance, and at some time before dawn on 3rd May Sedgwick's troops occupied Fredericksburg. Gibbon's division, which had been holding Falmouth, then crossed the river to join VI Corps.[23]

Early had under his command his own division of four brigades

(Gordòn, Hoke, Smith, and Hays) and Barksdale's brigade of McLaws's division. Barksdale and Hays were holding a line about three miles long from Taylor's Hill, by the Rappahannock, on the left to Howison House, south-east of Lee's Hill, on the right. The remainder of Early's division continued the line for about another four miles to Hamilton's Crossing, where the Richmond, Fredericksburg, & Potomac Railroad crossed Mine road. Barksdale's and Hays's brigades, to cover the long front, were stretched out in a single line, with many of the men yards apart from their neighbours and with wide intervals between regiments. On Marye's Hill, key to the Confederate position, the 18th and 21st Mississippi Regiments of Barksdale's brigade, with six guns of the Washington Artillery and two under Lieutenant Brown of Alexander's battalion, held half a mile of front from the Plank road to Hazel Creek.

At dawn on 3rd May Sedgwick sent two brigades to seize the Confederate works on Marye's Hill. Two attacks by these brigades were repulsed, and Sedgwick came to the conclusion that the Confederates were in considerably greater strength than they actually were. He then ordered Gibbon's division to attack the Confederate left, but the Federals were driven back here too. Soon after this, Wilcox's brigade of Anderson's division arrived to reinforce the Confederates. Wilcox had been observing Banks Ford, and at dawn on 3rd May he noticed that the enemy's pickets on the north side were wearing haversacks. He guessed, correctly, that they were about to leave for Chancellorsville; and he was about to march there himself when a despatch rider arrived with information of Gibbon's advance. Wilcox immediately marched to Taylor's Hill, leaving a picket to watch Banks Ford.

At about 10 am, after the failure of a probe against the Confederate right, Sedgwick decided to mount a heavy frontal attack against the enemy position. This attack went in at about 11 am. Two columns were formed from Newton's division—a right column of four regiments and a left column of two regiments—and to the left of this were another four regiments in line ('line of battle'). The columns moved along and to the right of the Plank road. The line of battle advanced to the left of the road, at the double, against a line of rifle pits along a stone wall at the base of Marye's Hill. This outpost line the Federals carried, and went straight on towards the crest of the hill. They were beaten back here after a fierce struggle and heavy casualties. A Federal officer now sent forward a flag of truce with a request to be allowed to remove the dead and wounded. Colonel Griffin of the 18th Mississippi, a gallant and able officer, most ill-advisedly received the flag without reference to his superior officer, granted the request, and thoughtlessly allowed his men to stand up while the wounded were handed over. The enemy saw how few were the defenders; with the advantage of this information a massive attack was made which broke through by sheer weight of numbers, taking a large part of the 18th Mississippi and part of the 21st Mississippi prisoners and capturing the guns of the Washington Artillery.

Early sent a message to Lee informing him of what had happened, and withdrew his whole division to form a new line of defence across the Telegraph road two miles in rear. This road ran south-west from Fredericksburg and away from the Plank road, but it was about the only way, having regard to the initial Confederate dispositions, that Early could re-group his division, and it now placed him on Sedgwick's flank. Under his immediate command here he had Gordon's, Hoke's, and Smith's brigades, and the remnants of Barksdale's. Hays's and Wilcox's brigades had withdrawn along the Plank road, but Early ordered Hays to rejoin the remainder of the division. This left Wilcox alone across the Plank road to delay Sedgwick's advance on Chancellorsville. Wilcox delayed this advance as much as possible, while he fell back slowly to Salem Church, where he had been informed that McLaws would meet him with reinforcements. He arrived there about 3 pm.

Lee, when he heard that Sedgwick had broken through Early's defence, ordered Mahone's brigade of Anderson's division and McLaws, with the three remaining brigades of his division (Kershaw, Wofford, and Semmes) to march to reinforce Wilcox, and sent an order to Early to place his division across Sedgwick's rear.

Sedgwick's advanced guard encountered the reinforced Confederates on Salem Heights at about 4 pm. Wilcox was around Salem Church whilst McLaws was deploying the other brigades to right and left of it. Wilcox had disposed his brigade with the 14th and 11th Alabama Regiments on the left of the Plank road and the 10th and 8th Alabama on the right of it; whilst the 9th Alabama was in reserve behind the 10th. He also put one company in Salem Church and another in a schoolhouse which was a short distance in front of it. His four guns were across the Plank road. The order of brigades, when they had deployed into line, was from right to left Wofford, Kershaw, Wilcox, Semmes, Mahone. There was a thick copse of young trees, about 200 yards in depth, stretching right across the Confederate front, and beyond the trees were open fields.

A Federal battery came into action 1,000 yards from Wilcox's brigade at about 4.30 pm. His own guns replied, but they were nearly out of ammunition and were withdrawn. The action which now followed is described by Alexander as one of the most brilliant and important minor affairs of the war.[24]

Sedgwick deployed two of his four divisions forward, both in two lines; Brooks's division was astride the Plank road and Newton's division was on its right. Of Brooks's division, Brown's brigade was on the right of the road, and so opposite the 14th and 11th Alabama, whilst Bartlett's on the left of the road faced the 10th and 8th Alabama. Bartlett's brigade (5th Maine, 16th New York, 27th New York, 121st New York, and 96th Pennsylvania Regiments) was, says Alexander, one of the best in the Federal Army, and it 'boasted that it had never been repulsed and had never failed to hold any position it was ordered to occupy'.[25] The Confederate position ran along the crest of a low ridge in rear of the copse and was hidden from view by thick undergrowth. The copse was held by skirmishers.

Bartlett's brigade pushed through the skirmishers and, reaching the church, drove out the company which was holding it and cut off the company in the schoolhouse. The 10th Alabama was taken in flank and driven back, but the 9th promptly charged and drove the Federals back, whilst the 8th attacked their left flank. Bartlett's brigade was routed; Wilcox's brigade followed up, and the two right regiments of Semmes's brigade joined in the counter-stroke. The whole Federal line was driven back with heavy casualties.

Confederate Victory

Anderson, with his three remaining brigades (Wright's, Perry's, and Posey's) had at 4 pm on 3rd May been despatched to watch the River road and to threaten Hooker's new position from that flank. Two hours after sunrise on 4th May Heth arrived, with three brigades of A. P. Hill's division to relieve Anderson, who was directed to march to Salem Church, six miles away, and report to McLaws. Anderson arrived at Salem about noon, by which time Lee had arrived to take over direct command of the operations against Sedgwick. That morning Sedgwick had learned of Early's threat to his rear, and he immediately deployed Howe's division to cover pontoon bridges over the Rappahannock which he had had built below Banks Ford the previous evening. His withdrawal had now become urgent because Early had re-occupied Marye's Hill, driving off a Federal picket, and VI Corps was in danger of being surrounded.

At 6 pm there was a general Confederate advance against Sedgwick's force, co-ordinated personally by Lee. But it was dark before an effective attack could be developed, and Sedgwick's troops retreated across the Rappahannock during the night.

The next morning, 5th May, Lee directed Early to remain in observation at Banks Ford and Fredericksburg, whilst the remainder of the army was ordered to return to Chancellorsville; for Lee intended to assault Hooker's position the following morning.

Hooker now had about 90,000 men to defend a strong fortified line about five miles long, and situated behind two streams covering about three-quarters of his front and with his flanks resting on the Rapidan and the Rappahannock. To attack this position, Lee had about 35,000 men. Alexander writes: 'It is the highest possible compliment to the army commended by Lee to say that there were two persons concerned who believed that, in spite of all the odds, it would have been victorious. These two persons were Gens. Lee and Hooker.'[26]

When the morning of 6th May dawned, Hooker's new lines were deserted. The Federals had gone.

Notes

1   Colonel G. F. R. Henderson, *Stonewall Jackson*, 1898
2   General E. P. Alexander, *Military Memoirs of a Confederate*, 1907
3   William Swinton, *Campaigns of the Army of the Potomac*, 1866
4   ibid.
5   Alexander, op. cit.
6   A. L. Long, *Memoirs of Robert E. Lee*, 1887
7   Clifford Dowdey, *Lee*, 1965
8   ibid.
    Long, op. cit.
9   Dowdey, op. cit.
10 Alexander, op. cit.
11 ibid.
12 ibid.
13 Swinton, op. cit.
14 ibid.
15 Alexander, op. cit.
16 ibid.
17 ibid.
18 ibid.
19 ibid.
20 Swinton, op. cit.
21 Alexander, op. cit.
22 Long, op. cit.
23 Swinton, op. cit.
24 Alexander, op. cit.
25 ibid.
26 ibid.

Frank Vizetelly — War Artist and Correspondent

by R. H. Smith

Born in London 1830
Killed in action in the Sudan 1883

FRANK VIZETELLY'S EARLY YEARS in journalism were spent as an illustrator and correspondent for various magazines. In 1859, during the war waged by Austria against Sardinia and France, he was given his first commission as a war correspondent and witnessed the bloody battle of Solferino. His brilliant recording of this and other lesser battles of the conflict brought him to the notice of the *Illustrated London News*. In 1860 the *Illustrated London News* sent him to Italy to join Garibaldi's expedition. His energetic and resourceful pursuit of a good story provided a wealth of action drawings.

During the spring of 1861 the now battle-hardened Vizetelly left England aboard the *Europa* en route to America to report the War of the Secession for the *Illustrated London News*. His first letter dated May 24, 1861, with a number of sketches, was despatched from New York. Many more sketches followed, recording the activities of the Federal Army, until the first battle of Bull Run. Dr. Russell's critical report of this affair in *The Times* and Vizetelly's sketches of the rout in the *Illustrated London News* put them out of favour with the Federal Government. They were refused permits to accompany forward troop movements. This was a severe blow to both correspondents. Disgusted with this treatment, but determined to see action of some kind, Vizetelly travelled several hundred miles to join the Federal Navy on the Mississippi and managed to get aboard one of the vessels in time for the attack and capture of Memphis in June 1862.

He returned to Washington to find a city bustling with final preparations for General McClellan's thrust towards the Confederate capital of Richmond. The Comte de Paris gave Vizetelly a permit allowing him 'to pass to any of the camps within the lines of the Army of the Potomac until further orders'. This was negatived by the Federal War Department.

Bitterly disappointed and frustrated by this turn of events and in dire need of battle action pictures, he resolved to join the 'enemy'. Following discreet enquiries he discovered the existence of an 'underground' route through the Federal lines to Richmond. He arrived there in the autumn of 1862 after an adventurous journey.

Vizetelly's first batch of sketches from the south created some surprise at the *Illustrated London News* which informed its readers that they were unaware of their Special Artist's decision to change sides, but that he was free to record events as he saw fit.

Unlike the Federal Government, the Southern headquarters greeted him with open arms and, as he later wrote, they gave him every possible facility to get close to the firing line—on some occasions too close for comfort. With this co-operation he was able to witness many exciting events of the Civil War.

During a lull in the fighting in the winter of 1863–64 Vizetelly ran the blockade to the outside world and returned to England without incident. His return to America was exciting. At Nassau he boarded the *Lilian*— new and Glasgow built—'one of the fleetest and most beautiful of the blockade running ships'. After a long chase by a Federal cruiser, and a hair-raising trip in darkness through the lines of anchored blockade vessels, she made Wilmington Harbour unharmed on 4th June 1864. Early in 1865 the Confederate cause was lost. President Jefferson Davis with his headquarters staff and some 1,500 troops endeavoured to escape to the Florida coast. Davis finally disbanded the remnants of his army and pressed on with a few loyal staff. Vizetelly remained with them until May 8th. Two days later Jefferson Davis, with a price of $100,000 on his head, was captured at Irwinville, Georgia.

Frank Vizetelly proved to be the only artist-correspondent in the South and so left to posterity a unique pictorial record of the outstanding fighting abilities of the Confederate Army and its famous Generals. The record of events in the *Illustrated London News* is not quite complete—to Vizetelly's disgust he discovered that several packets of sketches had failed to get through the Federal blockade. Some of the 'lost' sketches appeared in a New York newspaper.

In 1866 the *Illustrated London News* sent Vizetelly to Vienna en route to the short-lived conflict between Prussia and Austria, but once again he met with official procrastination and before he could obtain permits for the front line the war had finished. This was his last war-time commission for the *Illustrated London News*.

In 1873 a newspaper commissioned him to report the Carlist War in Spain. Ten years later he was employed by *The Graphic* as their special artist in the Sudan War. With other correspondents he set off with the

Egyptian army under Hicks Pasha (General William Hicks). At El Obeid Hicks's force was completely wiped out by the Mahdi's dervish hordes. Vizetelly was never seen again.

A tablet in St Paul's Cathedral commemorates the Special Correspondents who fell in the campaigns in the Sudan—1883, 1884, and 1885— Edmond O'Donovan, Frank Vizetelly, Frank Power, John Alexander Cameron, St Leger Algernon Herbert CMG, William Henry Gordon, and Frank J. L. Roberts.

Index

Absenteeism; 141–2
'Alabama', CSS; 140
Alexander, General E. P.,
 CSA; 44, artillery gallop at
 Gettysburg 77, 80, 85, 99,
 110, on roads 110, 115, 118,
 139, on staff failure at
 Gettysburg 139, 142, 161,
 166, 169, 170–1, 173–6
Ambulances; 123
Ammunition supply; 117
Anaesthetics; 123.
Anderson, General Richard H.,
 CSA; 25, 157, 161–2, 165–7,
 170–1, 173–5
Anderson, General Robert,
 USA; 128
Amtietam, battle of—see
 Sharpsburg
Appomattox Court House,
 surrender at; 25, 29, 118,
 137
Archer, General J. J., CSA;
 167
Armistead, General Lewis A,
 CSA; 142
Army formations and military
 departments, Federal;
 127–131
Army of the Cumberland,
 USA; 19, 24, 52, 111, 128–9
Army of the James, USA;
 21, 35
Army of Northern Virginia,
 CSA; 14, 20, 26–7, 29, 40,
 43, 52–3, 56, 66–7, 70, 102,
 105, 113, 115, 142, 157
Army of the Mississippi,
 CSA; 15, 16, 100
Army of the Ohio, USA; 15,
 19, 20, 100, 102, 128–9
Army of the Potomac, USA;
 11, 13–16, 18–22, 26, 29–31,

36, 42, 46, 52–3, 57, 59, 6
 70, 73, 75, 82, 84, 102,
 105–6, 110, 113, 116, 118,
 127, 130, 132, 139, 140,
 142–3, 145, 152, 157, 158,
 170
Army of the Tennessee, USA;
 15, 20, 128–9
Army of Virginia, USA; 14,
 15, 127.
Army, pre-war; 10
Artillery ammunition; 68–9,
 Confederate shortage of at
 Gettysburg 76–7, defective
 77
Artillery equipments; 66–8,
 71–2, 75, 77
Artillery indirect fire; 77
Artillery organisation; 69–71
Artillery, recoil of pieces; 77
Ashby, Colonel Turner, CSA;
 60
Atlanta, battle and capture of;
 22–4, 26, 35, 51, 131, 139
Averill, General W. W., USA;
 157
Ayres, General R. B., USA; 43

Balloon Corps, USA; 88
Balloons; 88, 160, 163
Banks, General N. P., USA;
 13–15, 22, 53
Barksdale, General W., CSA;
 161, 173–4
Barlow, General F. C., USA;
 45, 167
Barry, General W. F., USA;
 69, 70, 72
Bartlett, General W. F., USA;
 175
Bartow, Colonel F. S., CSA;
 97

Bayonets, use of in action;
 34–5
Beauregard, General P. G. T.,
 CSA; 12, 15, 21–2, 40, 85,
 97, 100, 122
Bee, General Barnard E.,
 CSA; 97
Bennett's House, surrender
 at; 25
Bentonville, battle of; 25
Berry, General H. G., USA;
 157, 169
Birney, General D. B., USA;
 45, 157, 169
Blockade; 151–2
Blunt, General James G.,
 USA; 24
Borcke, Major Heros von,
 CSA; 114
Boswell, Captain James K.,
 CSA; 164–5
Bragg, General Braxton, CSA;
 15–19, 25, 40–2, 100, 115
Breckenridge, General John J.,
 CSA; 21, 41
Brice's Cross Roads, battle of;
 22, 63–4
Brooks, General W. T. H.,
 USA; 167, 174–5
Brown, Colonel H. W., USA;
 175
Buell, General don Carlos,
 USA; 11, 12, 15–17, 100,
 128
Bull Run, first battle of; 11,
 14, 55, 67–71; 85, 94, 97, 121
Bull Run, second battle of; 15
Bullets, explosive; 34
Burnham, General H., USA;
 157
Burnside, General Ambrose E.,
 USA; 12, 16, 18–20, 105,
 110, 132, 140, 152, 156

181